POEMS OF ALLAN RAMSAY

VOL. II.

AMS PRESS

NEW YORK

THE

POEMS

OF

ALLAN RAMSAY.

WITH GLOSSARY, LIFE OF THE AUTHOR,

AND REMARKS ON HIS POEMS.

IN TWO VOLUMES.

VOL. II.

A NEW EDITION.

PAISLEY: ALEX. GARDNER.

1877.

Library of Congress Cataloging in Publication Data

Ramsay, Allan, 1685-1758.
　The poems of Allan Ramsay.

PR3657.A1　1973　　　821'.5　　　71-144498
ISBN 0-404-08584-9

Reprinted from the edition of 1877, Paisley
First AMS edition published in 1973
Manufactured in the United States of America

International Standard Book Number:
Complete Set:　0-404-08584-9
Volume II:　0-404-08586-5

AMS PRESS INC.
NEW YORK, N. Y.　10003

THE

POEMS

OF

ALLAN RAMSAY.

A NEW EDITION,

CORRECTED AND ENLARGED;

WITH A GLOSSARY.

TO WHICH ARE PREFIXED,

A LIFE OF THE AUTHOR,

FROM AUTHENTIC DOCUMENTS :

AND REMARKS ON HIS POEMS,

FROM A LARGE VIEW OF THEIR MERITS.

IN TWO VOLUMES.

VOL. II.

LONDON:

Printed by A. Strahan, Printers Street,

FOR T. CADELL JUN. AND W. DAVIES, STRAND.

1800.

CONTENTS OF THE SECOND VOLUME.

PASTORAL.

LYRIC.

EPISTOLARY.

FABLES AND TALES.

THE APPENDIX.

PASTORAL.

PASTORAL.

I.

RICHY AND SANDY.*

ON THE DEATH OF MR. ADDISON.

1721.

RICHY.

WHAT gars thee look sae dowf, dear Sandy, say?
Cheer up, dull fellow, take thy reed and play
" My apron deary, " or some wanton tune.
Be merry, lad, and keep thy heart aboon.

SANDY.

Na, na, it winna do; leave me to mane.
This aught days twice o'er tell'd I'll whistle nane.

RICHY.

Wow, man, that's unco' sad!—Is't that ye'r jo
Has ta'en the strunt? Or has some bogle-bo,
Glowrin' frae 'mang auld waws, gi'en ye a fleg?
Or has some dauted wedder broke his leg?

SANDY.

Naithing like that, sic troubles eith were borne:
What's bogles, wedders, or what Mausy's scorn?

Our loss is meikle mair, and past remead:
Adie, that play'd and sang sae sweet, is dead.

RICHY.

Dead! say'st thou?—Oh, had up my heart, O Pan!
Ye gods, what laids ye lay on feckless man!
Alake therefore! I canna wyt ye'r wae;
I'll bear ye company for year and day.
A better lad ne'er lean'd out o'er a kent,
Or hounded coly o'er the mossy bent:
Blyth at the bught how aft ha' we three been,
Heartsome on hills, and gay upon the green.

SANDY.

That's true indeed; but now thae days are gane,
And, with him, a' that's pleasant on the plain.
A summer day I never thought it lang,
To hear him make a roundel or a sang.
How sweet he sung where vines and myrtles grow,
Of wimbling waters which in Latium flow.*
Titry the Mantuan herd, wha lang sinsyne,
Best sung on aeten reed the lover's pine,
Had he been to the fore now in our days,
Wi' Adie he had frankly dealt his bays.
As lang's the warld shall Amaryllis ken,
His Rosamond † shall echo thro' the glen:
While on burn banks the yellow gowan grows,
Or wand'ring lambs rin bleating after ewes,
His fame shall last: last shall his sang of weirs, ‡
While British bairns brag of their bauld forbeairs.
We'll meikle miss his blyth and witty jest,
At spaining time, or at our Lambmass feast.
O, Richy! but 'tis hard that death aye reaves
Away the best fowk, and the ill anes leaves.

---

* His poetic epistle from Italy to the Earl of Halifax.
† An opera wrote by him.   ‡ His Campaign, an heroic poem.

Hing down ye'r heads, ye hills, greet out ye springs,
Upon ye'r edge na mair the shepherd sings.

RICHY.

Then he had ay a good advice to gie,
And kend my thoughts amaist as well as me :
Had I been thowless, vext, or oughtlins sour,
He wad have made me blyth in haff an hour :
Had Rosie ta'en the dorts, or had the tod
Worry'd my lambs, or were my feet ill shod,
Kindly he'd laugh when sae he saw me dwine,
And tauk of happiness like a divine.
Of ilka thing he had an unco' skill ;
He kend be moon-light how tides ebb and fill ;
He kend (what kend he no ?) e'en to a hair
He'd tell or night gin neist day wad be fair.
Blind John,* ye mind, wha sang in kittle phrase,
How the ill sp'rit did the first mischief raise ;
Mony a time, beneath the auld birk-tree,
What's bonny in that sang he loot me see.
The lasses aft flung down their rakes and pails,
And held their tongues, O strange ! to hear his tales.

SANDY.

Sound be his sleep, and fast his wak'ning be ;
He's in a better case than thee or me :
He was o'er good for us ; the gods hae ta'en
Their ain but back—he was a borrow'd len' :
Let us be good, gin virtue be our drift,
Then we may yet forgether 'boon the lift.
But see the sheep are wysing to the cleugh ;
Thomas has loos'd his ousen frae the pleugh ;
Maggy by this has bewk the supper-scones ;
And muckle kye stand rowting in the loans :

---

* The famous Milton, the author of the excellent poem on " Paradise Lost," was
blind.

Come, Richy, let us truse and hame o'er bend,
And make the best of what we canna mend.

II.

ROBERT, RICHY, AND SANDY:

A PASTORAL ON THE DEATH OF MATTHEW PRIOR.

1728.

ROBERT the good, by a' the swains rever'd,
Wise are his words, like siller is his beard;
Near saxty shining simmers he has seen,
Tenting his hirsle on the moorland green;
Unshaken yet with mony a winter's wind,
Stout are his limbs, and youthfu' is his mind.
But now he droops, ane wad be wae to see
Him sae cast down; ye wadna trow 'tis he.
By break of day he seeks the dowy glen
That he may scowth to a' his mourning len;
Nane but the clinty craigs and scrogy briers
Were witness of a' his granes and tears.
Howder'd wi' hills a crystal burnie ran
Where twa young shepherds fand the good auld man.
Kind Richy Spec, a friend to a' distrest,
And Sandy, wha of shepherds sings the best,
With friendly looks they speer'd wherefore he mourn'd?
He rais'd his head, and sighing, thus return'd:

ROBERT.

O Matt! poor Matt!—my lads, e'en take a skair
Of a' my grief:—sweet-singing Matt's nae mair.
Ah heavens! did e'er this lyart head of mine
Think to have seen the cauldrife mools on thine.

RICHY.

My heart misga'e me when I came this way,
His dog its lane sat yowling on a brae;
I cry'd, "Isk! isk! poor Ringwood, fairy man:"
He wagg'd his tail, cour'd near, and lick'd my han':
I clapp'd his head, which eas'd a wee his pain;
But soon's I gade away, he yowl'd again.
Poor kindly beast!—Ah, sirs, how sic should be
Mair tender-hearted mony a time than we!

SANDY.

Last ouk I dream'd my tup that bears the bell,
And paths the snaw, out o'er a high craig fell,
And brak his leg.—I started frae my bed,
Awak'd, and leugh.—Ah! now my dream its red.
How dreigh's our cares! our joys how soon away,
Like sun-blinks on a cloudy winter's day!
Flow fast, ye tears, ye have free leave for me;
Dear sweet-tongu'd Matt! thousands shall greet for thee.

ROBERT.

Thanks to my friends, for ilka briny tear,
Ye shed for him; he to us a' was dear.
Sandy, I'm eas'd to see thee look sae wan;
Richy, thy sighs bespeak the kindly man.

RICHY.

But twice the summer's sun has thaw'd the snaw,
Since frae our heights Addie * was ta'en awa':
Fast Matt has follow'd.—Of sic twa bereft,
To smooth our sauls, alake! wha have we left?
Waes me! o'er short a tack of sic is given,
But wha may contradict the will of Heaven?

---

* Secretary Addison.

Yet mony a year he liv'd to hear the dale
Sing o'er his sangs, and tell his merry tale.
Last year I had a stately tall ash-tree,
Braid were its branches, a sweet shade to me ;
I thought it might have flourish'd on the brae,
Tho' past its prime, yet twenty years or sae :
But ae rough night the blatt'ring winds blew snell,
Torn frae its roots adown it souchan fell ;
Twin'd of its nourishment it lifeless lay,
Mixing its wither'd leaves amang the clay.
Sae flourish'd Matt ; but where's the tongue can tell
How fair he grew ? how much lamented fell ?

SANDY.

How snackly cou'd he gi'e a fool reproof,
E'en wi' a canty tale he'd tell aff loof ?
How did he warning to the dosen'd sing,
By auld Purganty, and the Dutchman's ring ?
And Lucky's siller ladle shaws how aft
Our greatest wishes are but vain and daft.
The wad-be wits, he bad them a' but pap
Their crazy heads into Tam Tinman's shap,
There they wad see a squirrel wi' his bells
Ay wrestling up, yet rising like themsells.
Thousands of things he wittily could say,
With fancy strang and saul as clear as day ;
Smart were his tales, but where's the tongue can tell
How blyth he was ? how much lamented fell ?

RICHY.

And as he blythsome was, sae was he wise,
Our laird himsell wa'd aft take his advice.
E'en cheek for chew he'd seat him 'mang them a',
And tauk his mind 'bout kittle points of law.
When clan Red-yards, * ye ken, wi' wicked feud,

---

* Louis XIV., King of France.

Had skail'd of ours, but mair of his ain blood ;
When I and mony mae that were right crouse,
Wad fain about his lugs have burnt his house ;
Yet Lady Anne, a woman meek and kind,
A foe to weirs, and of a peacefu' mind,
Since mony in the fray had got their dead,
To make the peace our friend was sent wi' speed.
The very faes had for him just regard,
Tho' sair he jib'd their formast singing bard.*
Careful was Matt, but where's the tongue can tell
How wise he was ? how much lamented fell ?

SANDY.

Wha cou'd like him, in a short sang, define
The bonny lass and her young lover's pine ?
I'll ne'er forget that ane he made on May,
Wha brang the poor blate Symie to his clay ;
To gratify the paughty wench's pride,
The silly shepherd " bow'd, obey'd, and dy'd."
Sic constant lasses, as the Nit-brown Maid,
Shall never want just praises duly paid ;
Sic claim'd his sang, and still it was his care,
With pleasing words to guide and reese the fair.
How sweet his voice when beauty was in view !
Smooth ran his lines, ay grac'd wi' something new ;
Nae word stood wrang ; but where's the tongue can tell
How saft he sung ? how much lamented fell ?

RICHY.

And when he had a mind to be mair grave,
A minister nae better cou'd behave.
Far out of sight of sic he aften flew,
When he of haly wonders took a view.

---

* Boileau, whose ode on the taking of Namur by the French in 1692, he bur-
lesqued, on its being retaken by the English in 1695.

B

Well cou'd he praise the Power that made us a',
And bids us in return but tent his law ;
Wha guides us when we're waking or asleep,
With thousand times mair care than we our sheep.
While he of pleasure, power, and wisdom sang,
My heart lap high, my lugs wi' pleasure rang :
These to repeat braid spoken I wad spill,
Altho' I should employ my utmost skill.
He tow'r'd aboon ; but ah ! what tongue can tell
How high he flew ? how much lamented fell ?

ROBERT.

My benison, dear lads, light on ye baith,
Wha ha'e sae true a feeling of our skaith.
O Sandy ! draw his likeness in smooth verse,
As well ye can ; then shepherds shall rehearse
His merit, while the sun metes out the day,
While ewes shall bleat, and little lambkins mae.
I've been a fauter, now three days are past,
While I for grief have hardly broke my fast.
Come to my shiel, there let's forget our care,
I dinna want a routh of country fare ;
Sic as it is, ye're welcome to a skair.
Besides, my lads, I have a browst of tip,
As good as ever wash'd a shepherd's lip ;
We'll take a scour o't to put aff our pain,
For a' our tears and sighs are but in vain.
Come, help me up ; yon sooty cloud shores rain.

III.

KEITHA : AN ELEGY ON THE DEATH OF MARY, THE COUNTESS OF WIGTON.

1721.

RINGAN.

O'ER ilka thing a gen'ral sadness hings :
The burds wi' melancholy droop their wings ;
My sheep and kye neglect to moup their food,
And seem to think as in a dumpish mood.
Hark ! how the winds scouch mournfu' thro' the broom,
The very lift puts on a heavy gloom.
My neighbour Colin, too, he bears a part,
His face speaks out the sairness of his heart.
Tell, tell me, Colin, for my boding thought,
A bang of fears into my breast has brought.

COLIN.

Where hast thou been, thou simpleton, wha speers
The cause of a' our sorrow and our tears ?
Wha unconcern'd can hear the common skaith
The warld receives by lovely Keitha's death ?
The bonniest sample of what's good and kind.
Fair was her make, and heav'nly was her mind :
But now this sweetest flower of a' our plain
Leaves us to sigh ; tho' a' our sighs are vaïn,
For never mair she'll grace the heartsome green ;
Ay heartsome, when she deign'd there to be seen.
Speak, flow'ry meadows, where she us'd to wauk ;
Speak, flocks and burds, wha've heard her sing or tauk ;
Did ever you sae meikle beauty bear ?
Or ye so mony heav'nly accents hear ?
Ye painted haughs, ye minstrels of the air,
Lament, for lovely Keitha is nae mair.

RINGAN.

Ye westlin winds, that gently us'd to play
On her white breast, and steal some sweets away,
Whilst her delicious breath perfum'd your breeze,
Which gratefu' Flora took to feed her bees ;
Bear on your wings round earth her spotless fame,
Worthy that noble race from whence she came.*
Resounding braes, where'er she us'd to lean,
And view the crystal burn glide o'er the green,
Return your echoes to our mournfu' sang,
And let the streams in murmurs bear't alang.
Ye unkend pow'rs wha water haunt or air,
Lament, for lovely Keitha is nae mair.

COLIN.

Ah ! wha cou'd tell the beauties of her face ?
Her mouth, that never op'd but wi' a grace ?
Her een, which did with heav'nly sparkles low ?
Her modest cheek, flush'd with a rosy glow ?
Her fair brent brow, smooth as th' unrunkled deep,
When a' the winds are in their caves asleep ?
Her presence like a simmer's morning ray
Lighten'd our hearts, and gart ilk place look gay.
Now twin'd of life, these charms look cauld and blae,
And what before gave joy now makes us wae.
Her goodness shin'd in ilka pious deed,—
A subject, Ringan, for a lofty reed.
A shepherd's sang maun sic high thoughts decline,
Lest rustic notes should darken what's divine.
Youth, beauty, graces, a' that's good and fair,
Lament ! for lovely Keitha is nae mair !

---

* She was daughter to the late Earl Marshal, the third of that honourable rank of
nobility.

RINGAN.

How tenderly she smooth'd our master's mind,
When round his manly waist her arms she twin'd,
And look'd a thousand saft things to his heart,
While native sweetness sought nae help frae art.
To him her merit still appear'd mair bright,
As, yielding, she own'd his superior right.
Baith saft and sound he slept within her arms,
Gay were his dreams, the influence of her charms.
Soon as the morning dawn'd he'd draw the screen,
And watch the op'ning of her fairer een,
Whence sweetest rays gusht out in sic a thrang,
Beyond expression in my rural sang.

COLIN.

O Clementina! sprouting fair remains
Of her wha was the glory of the plains ;
Dear innocence, with infant darkness blest,
Which hides the happiness that thou hast mist,
May a' thy mither's sweets thy portion be,
And a' thy mither's graces shine in thee.

RINGAN.

She loot us ne'er gae hungry to the hill,
And a' she ga'e, she gaed it wi' good will.
Fow mony, mony a ane will mind that day,
On which frae us she's tane sae soon away.
Baith hynds and herds whase cheeks bespake nae scant,
And thro' the howms could whistle, sing, and rant,
Will miss her sair till happily they find
Anither in her place sae good and kind.
The lasses wha did at her graces mint,
Hae by her death their bonniest pattern tint.
O ! ilka ane who did her bounty skair,
Lament ! for gen'rous Keitha is nae mair !

COLIN.

O Ringan, Ringan ! things gang sae unev'n,
I canna well take up the will of Heav'n.
Our crosses teughly last us mony a year,
But unco soon our blessings disappear.

RINGAN.

I'll tell thee, Colin, my last Sunday's note :
I tented well Mess Thomas' ilka jot.
The powers aboon are cautious as they're just,
And dinna like to gie o'er meikle trust
To this unconstant earth, with what's divine,
Lest in laigh damps they should their lustre tine.
Sae, let's leave aff our murmuring and tears,
And never value life by length of years ;
But as we can in goodness it employ,
Syne wha dies first, first gains eternal joy.
Come, Colin, dight your cheeks and banish care,
Our lady's happy, tho' with us nae mair.

IV.

AN ODE, WITH A PASTORAL RECITATIVE,

ON THE MARRIAGE OF JAMES EARL OF WEMYSS TO MISS JANET CHARTERIS.

RECITATIVE.

Last morn young Rosalind, with laughing een,
Met with the singing shepherd on the green,
Armyas height, wha us'd with tunefu' lay
To please the ear when he began to play :
Him with a smile the blooming lass addrest ;
Her cheerfu' look her inward joy confest.

ROSALIND.

Dear shepherd, now exert your wonted fire,
I'll tell you news that shall your thoughts inspire.

ARMYAS.

Out wi' them, bonny lass, and if they'll bear
But ceremony, you a sang shall hear.

ROSALIND.

They'll bear, and do invite the blythest strains;
The beauteous Charterissa of these plains,
Still to them dear, wha late made us sae wae,
When we heard tell she was far aff to gae,
And leave our heartsome fields, her native land,
Now's ta'en in time, and fix'd by Hymen's band.

ARMYAS.

To whom?—speak fast:—I hope ye dinna jeer.

ROSALIND.

No, no, my dear; 'tis true as we stand here.
The Thane of Fife, who lately wi' his flane,
And vizy leel, made the blyth bowl his ain;
He, the delight of baith the sma' and great,
Wha's bright beginning spae his sonsy fate,
Has gain'd her heart; and now their mutual flame
Retains the fair, and a' her wealth, at hame.

ARMYAS.

Now, Rosalind, may never sorrow twine
Sae near your heart as joys arise in mine.
Come kiss me, lassie, and you's hear me sing
A bridal sang that thro' the woods shall ring.

ROSALIND.

Ye're ay sae daft; come, take it and ha'e done;
Let a' the lines be saft, and sweet the tune.

ARMYAS *sings.*

Come, shepherds, a' your whistles join,
   And shaw your blythest faces.
The nymph that we were like to tine,
   At hame her pleasure places.
Lift up your notes both loud and gay,
   Yet sweet as Philomela's,
And yearly solemnize the day
   When this good luck befel us.

Hail to the Thane descended frae
   Macduff renown'd in story,
Wha Albion frae tyrannic sway
   Restor'd to ancient glory.
His early blossoms loud proclaim
   That frae this stem he rises,
Whase merits give him right to fame,
   And to the highest prizes.

His lovely countess sing, ye swains,
   Nae subject can be sweeter ;
The best of blood flows in her veins,
   Which makes ilk grace completer.
Bright are the beauties of her mind,
   Which frae her dawn of reason,
With a' the rays of wit hath shin'd,
   Which virtue still did season.

Straight as the plane, her features fair,
   And bonny to a wonder ;
Were Jove rampaging in the air,
   Her smiles might stap his thunder.
Rejoice in her, then, happy youth,
   Her innate worth's a treasure ;
Her sweetness a' your cares will soothe
   And furnish endless pleasure.

Lang may ye live t' enjoy her charms,
    And lang, lang may they blossom,
Securely screen'd within your arms,
    And lodged in your bosom.
Thrice happy parents, justly may
    Your breasts with joy be fir'd,
When you the darling pair survey,
    By a' the warld admir'd.

---

v.

A MASQUE *

PERFORMED AT CELEBRATING THE NUPTIALS OF JAMES DUKE OF HAMILTON AND LADY ANN COCHRAN.

CALLIOPE

(Playing upon a violincello) sings—

Joy to the bridegroom, prince of Clyde,
    Lang may his bliss and greatness blossom ;
Joy to his virtuous charming bride,
    Who gains this day his Grace's bosom.

---

* An unknown ingenious friend did me the honour of the following Introduction to the London edition of this "Masque ;" and being a poet, my vanity will be pardoned for inserting it here.

"The present poem being a revival of a good old form of poetry, in high repute with us, it may not be amiss to say something of a diversion once so agreeable, and so long interrupted or disused. The original of masques seems to be an imitation of the interludes of the ancients, presented on occasion of some ceremony performed in a great and noble family. The actors in this kind of half-dramatic poetry, have formerly been even kings, princes, and the first personages of the kingdom ; and in private families, the noblest and nearest branches. The machinery was of the greatest magnificence ; very showy, costly, and not uncommonly contrived by the ablest architects, as well as the best poets. Thus we see in Ben Jonson the name of Inigo Jones, and the same in Carew ; whether as the modeller only, or as poet in conjunction with them, seems to be doubtful, there being nothing of our English Vitruvius left (that I know of) which places him in the class

C

Appear, great Genius of his line,
    And bear a part in the rejoicing ;
Behold your ward, by pow'rs divine,
    Join'd with a mate of their ain choosing.

Forsake a while the Cyprian scene,
    Fair queen of smiles and saft embraces,
And hither come, with a' your train
    Of beauties, loves, and sports, and graces.

Come, Hymen, bless their nuptial vow,
    And them with mutual joys inspire :
Descend, Minerva, for 'tis you
    With virtue beats the haly fire.

(At the close of this sang, enters the GENIUS of the family, clad in a scarlet
robe, with a duke's coronet on his head, a shield on his left arm, with
the proper bearing of Hamilton.)

GENIUS.

Fair mistress of harmonious sounds, we hear
Thy invitation, gratefu' to the ear
Of a' the gods, who from th' Olympian height
Bow down their heads, and in thy notes delight :
Jove keeps this day in his imperial dome,
And I to lead th' invited guests am come.
(Enter VENUS attended by three GRACES, with MINERVA, and HYMEN; all
in their proper dresses.)

---

of writers. These shows we trace backwards as far as Henry VIII., from thence
to Queen Elizabeth and her successor King James, who was both a great encourager
and admirer of them. The last masque, and the best ever written, was that of
Milton, presented at Ludlow Castle, in the praise of which no words can be too
many ; and I remember to have heard the late excellent Mr. Addison agree with
me in that opinion. Coronations, princely nuptials, public feasts, the entertain-
ment of foreign quality, were the usual occasions of this performance, and the
best poet of the age was courted to be the author. MR. RAMSAY has made a noble
and successful attempt to revive this kind of poesy, on a late celebrated account.
And though he is often to be admired in all his writings, yet, I think, never more
than in his present composition. A particular friend gave it a second edition in
England ; which, I fancy, the public will agree that it deserved.''

CALLIOPE.

Welcome, ye bright divinities that guard
The brave and fair, and faithfu' love reward;
All hail! immortal progeny of Jove,
Who plaint, preserve, and prosper sacred love.

GENIUS.

Be still auspicious to th' united pair,
And let their purest pleasures be your care:
Your stores of genial blessings here employ,
To crown th' illustrious youth and fair ane's joy.

VENUS.

I'll breathe eternal sweets in ev'ry air;
He shall look always great, she ever fair;
Kind rays shall mix the sparkles of his eye,
Round her the loves in smiling crowds shall fly,
And bear frae ilka glance, on downy wings,
Into his ravish'd heart the saftest things.
And soon as Hymen has perform'd his rites,
I'll shower on them my hale Idalian sweets:
   They shall possess,
   In each caress,
   Delights shall tire
   The muse's fire,
  In highest numbers to express.

HYMEN.

I'll busk their bow'r, and lay them gently down,
Syne ilka langing wish with raptures crown;
The gloomy nights shall ne'er unwelcome prove,
That leads them to the silent scenes of love.
The sun at morn shall dart his kindest rays,
To cheer and animate each dear embrace.
Fond of the fair, he falds her in his arms;
She blushes secret, conscious of her charms.

Rejoice brave⁻youth,
In sic a fouth
Of joys the gods for thee provide ;
The rosy dawn,
The flow'ry lawn,
That spring has dress'd in a' its pride,
Claim no regard,
When⁻they're compar'd
With blooming beauties of thy bride.

MINERVA.

Fairest of a' the goddesses, and thou
That links the lovers to be ever true,
The gods and mortals own your mighty power,
But 'tis not you can make their sweets secure ;
That be my task, to make a friendship rise,
Shall raise their loves aboon the vulgar size.
Those near related to the brutal kind,
Ken naething of the wedlock of the mind ;
'Tis I can make a life a honey-moon,
And mould a love shall last like that aboon.
A' these sma' springs, whence cauld reserve and spleen
Take their first rise, and, favour'd, flow mair keen,
I shall discover in a proper view,
To keep their joys unmix'd, and ever new.
Nor jealousy, nor envious mouth,
Shall dare to blast their love ;
But wisdom, constancy, and truth,
Shall ev'ry bliss improve.

GENIUS.

Thrice happy chief, so much the care
Of a' the family of Jove,
A thousand blessings wait the fair,
Who is found worthy of his love.
Lang may the fair attractions of her mind
Make her still lovelier, him for ever kind.

MINERVA.

The ancestors of mightiest chiefs and kings,
Nae higher can derive than human springs ;
Yet frae the common soil each wond'rous root,
Aloft to heav'n their spreading branches shoot.
Bauld in my aid, these triumph'd over fate,
Fam'd for unbounded thought, or stern debate ;
Born high upon an undertaking mind,
Superior rise, and left the crowd behind.

GENIUS.

Frae these descending, laurell'd with renown,
My charge thro' ages draws his lineage down.
The paths of sic forbears lang may he trace,
And she be mother to as fam'd a race.
When blue diseases fill the drumly air,
And red-het bowts thro' flaughts of lightning rair,
Or mad'ning factions shake the sanguine sword,
With watchfu' eye I'll tent my darling lord
And his lov'd mate ; tho' furies should break loose,
Awake or sleeping, shall enjoy repose.

FIRST GRACE.

While gods keep halyday, and mortals smile,
Let nature with delights adorn the isle.
Be hush, bauld North, Favonius only blaw,
And cease, bleak clouds, to shed, or wet, or snaw ;
Shine bright thou radiant ruler of the year,
And gar the spring with earlier pride appear.

SECOND GRACE.

Thy mouth, great queen of goddesses, make gay,
Which gains new honours frae this marriage-day.
On Glotta's banks, ye healthfu' hynds, resort,
And with the landart lasses blythly sport.

THIRD GRACE.

Wear your best faces and your Sunday's weeds,
And rouse the dance with your maist tunefu' reeds;
Let tunefu' voices join the rural sound,
And wake responsive echo all around.

FIRST GRACE.

Sing your great master, Scotia's eldest son,
And the lov'd angel that his heart has won:
Come, sisters, let's frae art's hale stores collect
Whatever can her native beauties deck,
That in the day she may eclipse the light,
And ding the constellations of the night.

VENUS.

Cease, busy maids, your artfu' buskings raise
But small addition to her genuine rays;
Tho' ilka plain and ilka sea combine
To make her with their richest product shine;
Her lip, her bosom, and her sparkling een,
Excel the ruby, pearl, and diamond sheen.
These lesser ornaments, illustrious bride,
As bars to softer blessings, fling aside:
Steal frae them sweetly to your nuptial bed,
As frae its body slides the sainted shade,
Frae loath'd restraint to liberty above,
Where all is harmony and all is love.
Haste to these blessings, kiss the night away,
And make it ten times pleasanter than day.

HYMEN.

The whisper and caress shall shorten hours,
While, kindly as the beams on dewy flowers,
Thy sun, like him who the fresh bev'rage sips,
Shall feast upon the sweetness of thy lips.
My haly hand maun chastely now unloose
That zone which a' thy virgin charms inclose;

That zone should be less gratefu' to the fair,
Than easy bands of safter wedlock are ;
That lang unbuckled grows a hatefu' thing ;
The langer these are bound the mair of honour bring.

MINERVA.

Yes, happy pair, whate'er the gods inspire,
Pursue and gratify each just desire.
Enjoy your passions, with full transports mixt,
But still observe the bounds by virtue fixt.

Enter BACCHUS.

What brings Minerva here this rantin night ?
She's good for naething but to preach or fight.
Is this a time for either ?—Swith, away,
Or learn like us to be a thought mair gay.

MINERVA.

Peace, Theban roarer, while the milder pow'rs
Give entertainment, there's nae need of yours ;
The pure reflection of our calmer joys
Has mair of heaven than a' thy flashy noise.

BACCHUS.

Ye canna want it, faith ! you that appear
Anes at a bridal but in twenty year ;
A ferly 'tis your dortiship to see,
But where was ere a wedding without me ?
Blue een, remember, I'm baith hap and saul
To Venus there ; but me, she'd starve o' caul.

VENUS.

We awn the truth.   Minerva, cease to check
Our jolly brother with your disrespect ;
He's never absent at the treats of Jove,
And should be present at this feast of love.

GENIUS.

Maist welcome, Pow'r that cheers the vital streams,
When Pallas guards thee frae the wild extremes ;
Thy rosy visage at these solemn rites,
My generous charge with open smiling greets.

BACCHUS.

I'm nae great dab at speeches that maun clink,
But there's my paw, I shall fou tightly drink
A hearty health to thir same lovely twa,
That are sae meikle dauted by you a'.
Then with my juice a reaming bicker crown ;
I'll gi'e a toast, and see it fairly round.

Enter GANYMEDE

[With a flaggon in one hand, and a glass in the other.]

To you blyth beings, the benign director
Of gods and men, to keep your sauls in tift,
Has sent you here a present of his nectar,
As good as e'er was brew'n aboon the lift.

BACCHUS.

Ha ! Gany, come, my dainty boy,
  Skink't up, and let us prieve ;
Without it life wad be a toy :
  Here, gi'e me't in my nieve.

[Takes the glass.]

Good health to Hamilton, and his
  Lov'd mate !— O, father Jove ! we crave
Thou'lt grant them a lang tack of bliss,
  And rowth of bonny bairns and brave.
Pour on them, frae thy endless store,
  A' benisons that are divine,
With as good will as I waught o'er
  This flowing glass of heav'nly wine.

[Drinks, and causes all the company to drink round.]

Come, see't about ; and syne let's all advance,
Mortals and gods be pairs, and tak a dance.
Minerva mim, for a' your mortal stoor,
Ye shall with billy Bacchus fit the floor ;
Play up there, lassie, some blyth Scotish tune,
Syne a' be blyth, when wine and wit gae round.

[The health about, music and dancing begin.—The dancing over, before her Grace retires with the ladies to be undressed, CALLIOPE sings the]

EPITHALAMIUM.

Bright is the low of lawfu' love,
　　Which shining sauls impart,
It to perfection mounts above,
　　And glows about the heart.
It is the flame gives lasting worth,
To greatness, beauty, wealth, and birth.
On you, illustrious youthfu' pair,
Who are high heaven's delight and care,
　　The blissfu' beam darts warm and fair,
　　　　And shall improve the rest
　　Of a' these gifts baith great and rare
　　　　Of which ye are possest.
Bacchus, bear off your dinsome gang,
Hark ! frae yon howms the rural thrang
　　　　Invite you now away ;
　　　　　　While ilka hynd,
　　　　　　And maiden kind,
　　　　　　Dance in a ring,
　　　　　　While shepherds sing
　　　　In honour of the day.
　　　　　　Gae drink and dance
　　　　　　'Till morn advance,
　　　　And set the twinkling fires ;
　　　　　　While we prepare
　　　　　　To lead the fair
　　　　And brave to their desires.

D

Gae, Loves and Graces, take your place,
　　Around the nuptial bed abide;
Fair Venus heighten each embrace,
　　And smoothly make their minutes slide.
Gae, Hymen, put the couch in case;
　　Minerva, thither lead the Bride;
Neist, all attend his youthfu' Grace,
　　And lay him sweetly by her side.

VI.

A PASTORAL EPITHALAMIUM

UPON THE HAPPY MARRIAGE OF GEORGE LORD RAMSAY AND
LADY JEAN MAULE.

HAIL to the brave apparent chief,
　　Boast of the Ramsay's clanish name,
Whase ancestors stood the relief
　　Of Scotland, ages known to fame.

Hail to the lovely she, whose charms,
　　Complete in graces, meet his love;
Adorn'd with all that greatness warms,
　　And makes him grateful bow to Jove.

Both from the line of patriots rise,
　　Chiefs of Dalhousie and Panmure,
Whose loyal fames shall stains despise,
　　While ocean flows, and orbs endure.

The Ramsays! Caledonia's prop;
　　The Maules! struck still her foes with dread;
Now join'd, we from the union hope
　　A race of heroes shall succeed.

Let meaner souls transgress the rules,
   That's fix'd by honour, love, and truth ;
While little views proclaim them fools,
   Unworthy beauty, sense, and youth :

Whilst you, blest pair, belov'd by all
   The powers above, and blest below,
Shall have delights attend your call,
   And lasting pleasures on you flow.

What fate has fix'd, and love has done,
   The guardians of mankind approve.
Well may they finish what's begun,
   And from your joys all cares remove.

We wish'd—when straight a heavenly voice
   Inspir'd—we heard the blue-ey'd maid
Cry, "Who dare quarrel with the choice?
   The choice is mine, be mine their aid."

Be thine their aid, O wisest power !
   And soon again we hope to see
Their plains return, splendid their tower,
   And blossom broad the Edgewell tree.*

Whilst he with manly merits stor'd,
   Shall rise, the glory of his clan ;
She for celestial sweets ador'd,
   Shall ever charm the gracefu' man.

Soon may their royal bird † extend
   His sable plumes, and lordships claim,
Which to his valiant sires pertain'd,
   Ere earls in Albion were a name.

---

* See note, vol. i. p. 239.

† The spread eagle sable, or a field argent, in the arms of the Earl of Dalhousie.

Ye parents of the happy pair,
    With gen'rous smiles consenting, own
That they deserve your kindest care ;
    Thus, with the gods, their pleasure crown.

Haste, ev'ry Grace, each Love, and Smile,
    From fragrant Cyprus spread the wing ;
To deck their couch, exhaust your isle
    Of all the beauties of the spring.

On them attend with homage due,
    In him are Mars and Phœbus seen ;
And in the noble nymph you'll view
    The sage Minerva and your Queen.

VII.

BETTY AND KATE :

A PASTORAL FAREWELL TO MR. AIKMAN, WHEN HE WENT FOR LONDON.

BETTY.

Dear Katie, Willy's e'en away !
    Willy, of herds the wale,
To feed his flock, and make his hay
    Upon a distant dale.
Far to the southward of this height
    Where now we dowie stray,
Ay heartsome when he cheer'd our sight,
    And leugh with us a' day.

KATE.

O Willy ! can dale dainties please
    Thee mair than moorland ream ?
Does Isis flow with sweeter ease
    Than Fortha's gentle stream ?

Or takes thou rather mair delyt
 In the strae-hatted maid,
Than in the blooming red and whyt
 Of her that wears the plaid ?

BETTY.

Na, Kate, for that we needna mourn,
 He is not giv'n to change ;
But sauls of sic a shining turn,
 For honour like to range.
Our laird, and a' the gentry round,
 Wha mauna be said nay,
Sic pleasure in his art have found,
 They winna let him stay.
Blyth I have stood frae morn to een,
 To see how true and weel
He could delyt us on the green
 With a piece cawk and keel ;
On a slid stane, or smoother slate,
 He can the picture draw
Of you or me, or sheep or gait,
 The likest e'er ye saw.
Lass, think nae shame to ease your mind,
 I see ye 're like to greet ;
Let gae these tears, 'tis justly kind,
 For shepherd sae complete.

KATE.

Far, far, o'er far frae Spey and Clyde,
 Stands that great town of Lud,
To whilk our best lads rin and ride,
 That 's like to put us wood ;
For sindle times they e'er come back,
 Wha anes are heftit there ;
Sure, Bess, their hills are nae sae black,
 Nor yet their howms sae bare.

BETTY.

Our rigs are rich, and green our heights,
 And well our cares reward;
But yield, nae doubt, far less delights,
 In absence of our laird.
But we maun cawmly now submit,
 And our ill luck lament,
And leav't to his ain sense and wit,
 To find his heart's content.
A thousand gates he had to win
 The love of auld and young,
Did a' he did with little din,
 And in nae deed was dung.

KATE.

William and Mary never fail'd
 To welcome with a smile,
And hearten us, when aught we ail'd,
 Without designing guile.
Lang may she happily possess,
 Wha's in his breast infeft,
And may their bonny bairns increase,
 And a' with rowth be left.
O, William ! win your laurels fast,
 And syne we'll a' be fain
Soon as your wand'ring days are past,
 And you're returned again.

BETTY.

Revive her joys by your return,
 To whom you first gave pain ;
Judge how her passions for you burn,
 By these you bear your ain.
Sae may your kirn with fatness flow,
 And a' your kye be sleek,
And may your hearts with gladness glow
 In finding what ye seek.

THE GENTLE SHEPHERD:

A PASTORAL COMEDY.

1725.

DEDICATION

TO THE RIGHT HONOURABLE

SUSANNA, COUNTESS OF EGLINTOUN.

———

MADAM,

THE love of approbation, and a desire to please the best, have ever encouraged the Poets to finish their designs with cheerfulness. But, conscious of their own inability to oppose a storm of spleen and haughty ill-nature, it is generally an ingenious custom among them to choose some honourable shade.

Wherefore, I beg leave to put my Pastoral under your Ladyship's protection. If my Patroness says the shepherds speak as they ought, and that there are several natural flowers that beautify the rural wild, I shall have good reason to think myself safe from the awkward censure of some pretending judges that condemn before examination.

I am sure of vast numbers that will crowd into your Ladyship's opinion, and think it their honour to agree in their sentiments with the Countess of Eglintoun, whose penetration, superior wit, and sound judgment, shine with an uncommon lustre, while accompanied with the diviner charms of goodness and equality of mind.

If it were not for offending only your Ladyship, here, Madam, I might give the fullest liberty to my Muse to delineate the finest of women by drawing your Ladyship's character, and be in no hazard of being deemed a flatterer,—since flattery lies not in paying what is due to merit, but in praises misplaced.

Were I to begin with your Ladyship's honourable birth and alliance, the field is ample, and presents us with numberless great and good patriots that have dignified the names of Kennedy and Montgomery. Be that the care of the herald and historian. It is personal merit, and the heavenly sweetness of the fair, that inspire the tuneful lays. Here every Lesbia must be excepted whose tongues give liberty to the slaves

E

which their eyes have made captives. Such may be flattered, but your Ladyship justly claims our admiration and profoundest respect; for whilst you are possessed of every outward charm in the most perfect degree, the never-fading beauties of wisdom and piety, which adorn your Ladyship's mind command devotion.

"All this is very true," cries one of better sense than good-nature, "but what occasion have you to tell us the sun shines, when we have the use of our eyes and feel his influence?" Very true; but I have the liberty to use the poet's privilege, which is—"To speak what every body thinks." Indeed, there might be some strength in the reflection, if the Idalian registers were of as short duration as life; but the bard who fondly hopes for immortality has a certain praiseworthy pleasure in communicating to posterity the fame of distinguished characters. I write this last sentence with a hand that trembles between hope and fear; but if I shall prove so happy as to please your Ladyship in the following attempt, then all my doubts shall vanish like a morning vapour. I shall hope to be classed with Tasso and Guarini, and sing with Ovid—

> "If 'tis allow'd to poets to divine,
> One half of round eternity is mine."

MADAM,

    Your Ladyship's

        Most obedient and most devoted servant,

                ALLAN RAMSAY.

EDINBURGH, 25th June, 1725.

VIII.

TO THE COUNTESS OF EGLINTOUN,

WITH THE FOLLOWING PASTORAL.*

ACCEPT, O Eglintoun, the rural lays,
That, bound to thee, thy poet humbly pays.
The muse that oft has rais'd her tuneful strains,
A frequent guest on Scotia's blissful plains ;
That oft has sung, her list'ning youth to move,
The charms of beauty, and the force of love,
Once more resumes the still successful lay,
Delighted thro' the verdant meads to stray.
O ! come, invok'd, and pleas'd, with her repair
To breathe the balmy sweets of purer air ;
In the cool evening negligently laid,
Or near the stream, or in the rural shade,
Propitious hear, and as thou hear'st, approve
The " Gentle Shepherd's " tender tale of love.

Instructed from these scenes, what glowing fires
Inflame the breast that real love inspires !
The fair shall read of ardours, sighs, and tears,
All that a lover hopes, and all he fears.
Hence too, what passions in his bosom rise !
What dawning gladness sparkles in his eyes !
When first the fair one, piteous of his fate,
Cur'd of her scorn, and vanquish'd of her hate,
With willing mind is bounteous to relent,
And, blushing beauteous, smiles the kind consent.
Love's passion here in each extreme is shown,
In Charlotte's smile, or in Maria's frown.

---

* This address was written by William Hamilton of Bangour, an elegant and
original poet, and a most accomplished and amiable man.

With words like these, that fail'd not to engage,
Love courted beauty in a golden age ;
Pure and untaught, such nature first inspir'd,
Ere yet the fair affected phrase desir'd.
His secret thoughts were undisguis'd with art,
His words ne'er knew to differ from his heart ;
He speaks his love so artless and sincere,
As thy Eliza might be pleas'd to hear.

Heaven only to the rural state bestows
Conquest o'er life, and freedom from its woes ;
Secure alike from envy and from care,
Nor rais'd by hope, nor yet depress'd by fear ;
Nor want's lean hand its happiness constrains,
Nor riches torture with ill-gotten gains.
No secret guilt its stedfast peace destroys,
No wild ambition interrupts its joys ;
Blest still to spend the hours that heav'n has lent,
In humble goodness, and in calm content ;
Serenely gentle, as the thoughts that roll,
Sinless and pure, in fair Humeia's soul.

But now the rural state these joys has lost ;
Even swains no more that innocence can boast.
Love speaks no more what beauty may believe,
Prone to betray, and practis'd to deceive.
Now happiness forsakes her blest retreat,
The peaceful dwellings where she fix'd her seat ;
The pleasing fields she wont of old to grace,
Companion to an upright sober race,
When on the sunny hill or verdant plain,
Free and familiar with the sons of men,
To crown the pleasures of the blameless feast,
She uninvited came a welcome guest ;
Ere yet an age, grown rich in impious arts,
Brib'd from their innocence incautious hearts.
Then grudging hate, and sinful pride succeed,
Cruel revenge, and false unrighteous deed.

Then dow'rless beauty lost the power to move,
The rust of lucre stain'd the gold of love ;
Bounteous no more and hospitably good,
The genial hearth first blush'd with strangers' blood.
The friend no more upon the friend relies,
And semblant falsehood puts on truth's disguise ;
The peaceful household fill'd with dire alarms ;
The ravish'd virgin mourns her slighted charms ;
The voice of impious mirth is heard around,
In guilt they feast, in guilt the bowl is crown'd ;
Unpunish'd violence lords it o'er the plains,
And happiness forsakes the guilty swains.

O Happiness ! from human race retir'd,
Where art thou to be found, by all desir'd ?
Nun, sober and devout ! why art thou fled,
To hide in shades thy meek contented head ?
Virgin of aspect mild ! ah why, unkind,
Fly'st thou, displeas'd, the commerce of mankind ?
O ! teach our steps to find the secret cell,
Where, with thy sire Content, thou lov'st to dwell.
Or say, dost thou, a duteous handmaid, wait
Familiar at the chambers of the great ?
Dost thou pursue the voice of them that call
To noisy revel and to midnight ball ?
Or the full banquet, when we feast our soul,
Dost thou inspire the mirth, or mix the bowl ?
Or, with th' industrious planter dost thou talk,
Conversing freely in an evening walk ?
Say, does the miser e'er thy face behold,
Watchful and studious of the treasur'd gold ?
Seeks knowledge not in vain thy much lov'd pow'r,
Still musing silent at the morning hour ?
May we thy presence hope in war's alarms,
In Stair's wisdom, or in Erskine's charms ?

In vain our flatt'ring hopes our steps beguile,
The flying good eludes the searcher's toil ;

In vain we seek the city or the cell,
Alone with Virtue knows the power to dwell ;
Nor need mankind despair those joys to know,
The gift themselves may on themselves bestow.
Soon, soon we might the precious blessing boast,
But many passions must the blessing cost.
Infernal malice, inly pining hate,
And envy grieving at another's state ;
Revenge no more must in our hearts remain,
Or burning lust, or avarice of gain.
When these are in the human bosom nurst,
Can peace reside in dwellings so accurst ?
Unlike, O Eglintoun ! thy happy breast,
Calm and serene enjoys the heavenly guest ;
From the tumultuous rule of passions freed,
Pure in thy thought, and spotless in thy deed.
In virtues rich, in goodness unconfin'd,
Thou shin'st a fair example to thy kind ;
Sincere and equal to thy neighbour's name,
How swift to praise ! how guiltless to defame !
Bold in thy presence bashfulness appears,
And backward merit loses all its fears.
Supremely blest by heav'n, heav'n's richest grace
Confest is thine, an early blooming race,
Whose pleasing smiles shall guardian wisdom arm,
Divine instruction ! taught of thee to charm.
What transports shall they to thy soul impart,
(The conscious transports of a parent's heart,)
When thou behold'st them of each grace possest,
And sighing youths imploring to be blest :
After thy image form'd, with charms like thine,
Or in the visit or the dance to shine !
Thrice happy who succeed their mother's praise,
The lovely Eglintouns of other days.

Meanwhile, peruse the following tender scenes,
And listen to thy native poet's strains.

In ancient garb the home-bred muse appears,
The garb our muses wore in former years.
As in a glass reflected, here behold
How smiling goodness look'd in days of old :
Nor blush to read where beauty's praise is shewn,
Or virtuous love, the likeness of thy own ;
While 'midst the various gifts that gracious heaven
To thee, in whom it is well pleas'd, has given,
Let this, O Eglintoun ! delight thee most,
T' enjoy that innocence the world has lost.

W. H.

IX.

TO JOSIAH BURCHET, SECRETARY OF THE ADMIRALTY.

WITH THE FIRST SCENE OF "THE GENTLE SHEPHERD."*

THE nipping frosts and driving sna
Are o'er the hills and far awa ;
Bauld Boreas sleeps, the Zephyrs blaw,
　　And ilka thing
Sae dainty, youthfu', gay, and bra',
　　Invites to sing.

Then let's begin by creek of day,
Kind muse skiff to the bent away,
To try anes mair the landart lay,
　　With a' thy speed,
Since Burchet awns that thou can play
　　Upon the reed.

---

* The eclogue, intitled "Patie and Roger," which now forms the first scene of
the "Gentle Shepherd," was published several years before the author composed
the pastoral comedy of that name. It was from observing the talents displayed in
that eclogue, and a sequel to it, intitled "Jenny and Meggy," likewise separately
published, that his friends advised him to attempt a complete drama in the
pastoral style.

Anes, anes again beneath some tree,
Exert thy skill and nat'ral glee,
To him wha has sae courteously,
            To weaker sight,
Set these rude sonnets* sung by me
            In truest light.

In truest light may a' that's fine
In his fair character still shine,
Sma' need he has of sangs like mine
            To beet his name ;
For frae the north to southern line
            Wide gangs his fame.

His fame, which ever shall abide
Whilst hist'ries tell of tyrants' pride,
Wha vainly strave upon the tide
            T' invade these lands,
Where Britain's royal fleet doth ride,
            Which still commands

These doughty actions frae his pen ; †
Our age, and these to come, shall ken,
How stubborn navies did contend
            Upon the waves,
How free-born Britons fought like men,
            Their faes like slaves.

Sae far inscribing, Sir, to you
This country sang, my fancy flew,
Keen your just merit to pursue ?
            But ah ! I fear,
In giving praises that are due,
            I grate your ear.

---

* Having done me the honour of turning some of my pastoral poems into English, justly and elegantly.

† His valuable Naval History.

Yet, tent a poet's zealous prayer :
May powers aboon with kindly care
Grant you a lang and muckle skair
　　　　Of a' that's good,
'Till unto langest life and mair
　　　　　　You've healthfu' stood.

May never care your blessings sour,
And may the muses, ilka hour,
Improve your mind, and haunt your bow'r !
　　　　I'm but a callan ;
Yet, may I please you, while I'm your
　　　　　　Devoted ALLAN.

THE PERSONS.

SIR WILLIAM WORTHY.

PATIE, the Gentle Shepherd, in love with Peggy.

ROGER, a rich young Shepherd, in love with Jenny.

SYMON, ⎫
GLAUD, ⎭ two old Shepherds, tenants to Sir William.

BAULDY, a hynd, engaged with Neps.

PEGGY, thought to be Glaud's niece.

JENNY, Glaud's only daughter.

MAUSE, an old woman supposed to be a witch.

ELSPA, Symon's wife.

MADGE, Glaud's sister.

SCENE—A shepherd's village and fields some few miles from Edinburgh.

TIME OF ACTION—Within twenty-four hours.

> First Act begins at eight in the morning.
> Second Act begins at eleven in the forenoon.
> Third Act begins at four in the afternoon.
> Fourth Act begins at nine o'clock at night.
> Fifth Act begins by day-light next morning.

THE GENTLE SHEPHERD.

ACT I.

SCENE I.

PROLOGUE TO THE SCENE.

Beneath the south side of a craigy bield,
Where crystal springs the halesome waters yield,
Twa youthfu' shepherds on the gowans lay,
Tenting their flocks ae bonny morn of May.
Poor Roger granes, till hollow echoes ring;
But blyther Patie likes to laugh and sing.

PATIE and ROGER.

SANG I.

TUNE—"The wauking of the faulds."

PATIE.

My Peggy is a young thing,
    Just enter'd in her teens,
Fair as the day, and sweet as May,
Fair as the day, and always gay.
    My Peggy is a young thing,
      And I'm not very auld,
    Yet well I like to meet her at
      The wauking of the fauld.

My Peggy speaks sae sweetly,
    Whene'er we meet alane,

I wish nae mair to lay my care,
I wish nae mair of a' that's rare.
  My Peggy speaks sae sweetly,
    To all the lave I'm cauld ;
  But she gars a' my spirits glow
    At wauking of the fauld.

  My Peggy smiles sae kindly
    Whene'er I whisper love,
That I look down on a' the town,
That I look down upon a crown.
  My Peggy smiles sae kindly,
    It makes me blyth and bauld ;
  And naething gi'es me sic delight
    As wauking of the fauld.

  My Peggy sings sae saftly
    When on my pipe I play,
By a' the rest it is confest,
By a' the rest that she sings best.
  My Peggy sings sae saftly,
    And in her sangs are tald,
With innocence the wale of sense,
    At wauking of the fauld.

PATIE.

This sunny morning, Roger, cheers my blood,
And puts all nature in a jovial mood.
How heartsome is 't to see the rising plants,
To hear the birds chirm o'er their pleasing rants !
How halesome is 't to snuff the cauler air,
And all the sweets it bears, when void of care !
What ails thee, Roger, then ? what gars thee grane ?
Tell me the cause of thy ill-season'd pain.

ROGER.

I'm born, O Patie ! to a thrawart fate ;
I'm born to strive with hardships sad and great :

Tempest may cease to jaw the rowan flood,
Corbies and tods to grein for lambkins' blood ;
But I, opprest with never-ending grief,
Maun ay despair of lighting on relief.

PATIE.

The bees shall loath the flow'r, and quit the hive,
The saughs on boggie ground shall cease to thrive,
Ere scornfu' queans, or loss of warldly gear,
Shall spill my rest, or ever force a tear.

ROGER.

Sae might I say ; but it 's no easy done
By ane whase saul's sae sadly out of tune.
Ye have sae saft a voice, and slid a tongue,
You are the darling baith of auld and young.
If I but ettle at a sang, or speak,
They dit their lugs, syne up their leglens cleek,
And jeer me hameward frae the loan or bught,
While I 'm confus'd with mony a vexing thought :
Yet I am tall and as well built as thee,
Nor mair unlikely to a lass's ee.
For ilka sheep ye have I'll number ten,
And should, as ane may think, come farer ben.

PATIE.

But ablins, neibour, ye have not a heart,
And downa eithly wi' your cunzie part ;
If that be true, what signifies your gear ?
A mind that 's scrimpit never wants some care.

ROGER.

My byre tumbled, nine braw nowt were smoor'd,
Three elf-shot were, yet I these ills endur'd :
In winter last my cares were very sma',
Tho' scores of wethers perish'd in the snaw.

PATIE.

Were your bien rooms as thinly stock'd as mine,
Less ye wad loss and less ye wad repine.
He that has just enough can soundly sleep ;
The o'ercome only fashes fowk to keep.

ROGER.

May plenty flow upon thee for a cross,
That thou may'st thole the pangs of mony a loss :
O may'st thou doat on some fair paughty wench
That ne'er will lout thy lowan drowth to quench.
'Till bris'd beneath the burden, thou cry dool !
And awn that ane may fret that is nae fool.

PATIE.

Sax good fat lambs, I sauld them ilka clute
At the West Port, and bought a winsome flute,
Of plum-tree made, with iv'ry virles round ;
A dainty whistle, with a pleasant sound :
I 'll be mair canty wi' 't, and ne'er cry dool,
Than you with all your cash, ye dowie fool !

ROGER.

Na, Patie, na ! I'm nae sic churlish beast,
Some other thing lies heavier at my breast :
I dream'd a dreary dream this hinder night,
That gars my flesh a' creep yet with the fright.

PATIE.

Now, to a friend, how silly 's this pretence,
To ane wha you and a' your secrets kens :
Daft are your dreams, as daftly wad ye hide
Your well-seen love and dorty Jenny's pride.
Take courage, Roger, me your sorrows tell,
And safely think nane kens them but yoursell.

ROGER.

Indeed now, Patie, ye have guess'd ower true ;
And there is naething I'll keep up frae you.
Me dorty Jenny looks upon asquint ;
To speak but till her I dare hardly mint.
In ilka place she jeers me air and late,
And gars me look bombaz'd and unco blate.
But yesterday I met her yont a knowe,
She fled as frae a shelly-coated cow.
She Bauldy loes, Bauldy that drives the car,
But gecks at me, and says I smell of tar.

PATIE.

But Bauldy lo'es not her ; right well I wat,
He sighs for Neps : sae that may stand for that.

ROGER.

I wish I cou'dna lo'e her ;—but in vain,
I still maun doat, and thole her proud disdain.
My Bawty is a cur I dearly like,
'Till he yowl'd sair she strak the poor dumb tyke ;
If I had fill'd a nook within her breast,
She wad have shewn mair kindness to my beast.
When I begin to tune my stock and horn,
With a' her face she shaws a cauldrife scorn.
Last night I play'd ; ye never heard sic spite ;
"O'er Bogie" was the spring, and her delight :
Yet, tauntingly, she at her cousin speer'd
Gif she could tell what tune I play'd, and sneer'd.
Flocks, wander where ye like, I dinna care,
I'll break my reed, and never whistle mair.

PATIE.

E'en do sae, Roger, wha can help misluck ?
Saebeins she be sic a thrawn-gabbit chuck,

Yonder's a craig, since ye have tint all hope,
Gae till't your ways, and take the lover's lowp.

ROGER.

I needna mak sic speed my blood to spill,
I'll warrant death come soon enough a-will.

PATIE.

Daft gowk! leave aff that silly whingin way ;
Seem careless, there's my hand ye'll win the day.
Hear how I serv'd my lass I love as well
As ye do Jenny, and with heart as leel.
Last morning, I was gay and early out,
Upon a dyke I lean'd, glow'ring about,
I saw my Meg come linkan o'er the lee,—
I saw my Meg, but Meggy saw na me ;
For yet the sun was wading thro' the mist,
And she was close upon me e'er she wist.
Her coats were kiltet, and did sweetly shaw
Her straight bare legs that whiter were than snaw ;
Her cockernony snooded up fou sleek,
Her haffet locks hung waving on her cheek ;
Her cheeks sae ruddy, and her een sae clear ;
And O ! her mouth's like ony hinny pear.
Neat, neat she was, in bustine waistcoat clean,
As she came skiffing o'er the dewy green,—
Blythsome I cry'd, "My bonny Meg, come here,
I ferly wherefore ye're so soon asteer ?
But I can guess, ye're gawn to gather dew."
She scour'd away, and said—"What's that to you ?"
"Then, fare ye well, Meg-Dorts, and e'en 's ye like,"
I careless cry'd, and lap in o'er the dyke.
I trow, when that she saw, within a crack,
She came with a right thieveless errand back ;
Misca'd me first,—then bade me hound my dog,
To wear up three waff ewes stray'd on the bog.

I leugh, and sae did she ; then wi' great haste
I clasp'd my arms about her neck and waist ;
About her yielding waist, and took a fouth
Of sweetest kisses frae her glowing mouth.
While hard and fast I held her in my grips,
My very saul came lowping to my lips.
Sair, sair she flet wi' me 'tween ilka smack,
But weel I kent she meant nae as she spak.
Dear Roger, when your jo puts on her gloom,
Do ye sae too, and never fash your thumb :
Seem to forsake her, soon she'll change her mood ;
Gae woo anither, and she'll gang clean wood.

SANG II.

TUNE—"Fye, gar rub her o'er wi' strae."

Dear Roger, if your Jenny geck,
    And answer kindness with a slight,
Seem unconcern'd at her neglect,
    For women in a man delight.
But them despise who 're soon defeat,
    And, with a simple face, give way
To a repulse,—then be not blate,
    Push bauldly on, and win the day.

When maidens, innocently young,
    Say often what they never mean,
Ne'er mind their pretty lying tongue,
    But tent the language of their een.
If these agree, and she persist
    To answer all your love with hate,
Seek elsewhere to be better blest,
    And let her sigh when 'tis too late.

ROGER.

Kind Patie, now fair fa your honest heart,
Ye're aye sae cadgy, and have sic an art

G

To hearten ane ; for now, as clean's a leek,
Ye've cherish'd me since ye began to speak.
Sae, for your pains, I'll mak ye a propine
My mother (rest her saul !), she made it fine ;
A tartan plaid, spun of good hawslock woo,
Scarlet and green the sets, the borders blue.
With spraings like gowd and siller, cross'd with black ;
I never had it yet upon my back.
Weel are ye wordy o't, wha have sae kind
Redd up my ravel'd doubts, and clear'd my mind.

PATIE.

Well, haud ye there ; and since ye've frankly made
To me a present of your braw new plaid,
My flute 's be yours, and she too that's sae nice,
Shall come a-will, gif ye'll tak my advice.

ROGER.

As ye advise, I'll promise to observ't ;
But ye maun keep the flute, ye best deserv't.
Now tak it out and gie's a bonny spring,
For I'm in tift to hear you play and sing.

PATIE.

But first we'll take a turn up to the height,
And see gif all our flocks be feeding right ;
Be that time, bannocks and a shave of cheese
Will make a breakfast that a laird might please,—
Might please the daintiest gabs, were they sae wise
To season meat with health, instead of spice.
When we have tane the grace drink at this well,
I'll whistle syne, and sing t' ye like mysell.

[*Exeunt.*

SCENE II.

PROLOGUE.

A flowrie howm between twa verdant braes,
Where lasses use to wash and spread their claiths;
A trotting burnie wimpling through the ground,
Its channel peebles, shining, smooth and round.
Here view twa barefoot beauties, clean and clear,—
First please your eye, then gratify your ear;
While Jenny what she wishes discommends,
And Meg, with better sense, true love defends.

PEGGY and JENNY.

JENNY.

Come, Meg, let's fa to wark upon this green,
This shining day will bleach our linen clean;
The water's clear, the lift unclouded blue,
Will mak them like a lily wet with dew.

PEGGY.

Gae farer up the burn to Habbie's How,
Where a' that's sweet in spring and simmer grow;
Between twa birks out o'er a little lin
The water fa's, and makes a singan din;
A pool breast-deep, beneath, as clear as glass,
Kisses with easy whirles the bord'ring grass.
We'll end our washing while the morning's cool,
And when the day grows het we'll to the pool,
There wash oursel's; 'tis healthfu' now in May,
And sweetly cauler on sae warm a day.

JENNY.

Daft lassie, when we're naked, what'll ye say
Giff our twa herds come brattling down the brae,

And see us sae ?—that jeering fellow, Pate,
Wad taunting say, "Haith, lasses, ye 're no blate."

PEGGY.

We 're far frae ony road, and out of sight,
The lads they 're feeding far beyont the height ;
But tell me now, dear Jenny (we're our lane),
What gars ye plague your wooer with disdain ?
The neighbours a' tent this as well as I,
That Roger lo'es ye, yet ye care na by.
What ails ye at him ? Troth, between us twa,
He 's wordy you the best day e'er ye saw.

JENNY.

I dinna like him, Peggy, there 's an end ;
A herd mair sheepish yet I never kend.
He kames his hair, indeed, and gaes right snug,
With ribbon-knots at his blue bonnet lug ;
Whilk pensylie he wears a thought a-jee,
And spreads his garters dic'd beneath his knee.
He falds his owrelay down his breast with care,
And few gang trigger to the kirk or fair.
For a' that, he can neither sing nor say,
Except, "How d' ye ?" or, "There's a bonny day."

PEGGY.

Ye dash the lad with constant slighting pride,
Hatred for love is unco sair to bide ;
But ye'll repent ye, if his love grow cauld—
Wha likes a dorty maiden when she 's auld ?
Like dawted wean that tarrows at its meat,
That for some feckless whim will orp and greet ;
The lave laugh at it till the dinner's past,
And syne the fool-thing is obliged to fast,
Or scart anither's leavings at the last.
Fy, Jenny, think, and dinna sit your time.

SANG III.

TUNE—"Polwart on the green."

The dorty will repent
  If lover's heart grows cauld,
And nane her smiles will tent
  Soon as her face looks auld.

The dawted bairn thus takes the pet,
  Nor eats tho' hunger crave,
Whimpers and tarrows at its meat,
  And 's laught at by the lave.

They jest it till the dinner's past,
  Thus by itself abus'd,
The fool-thing is oblig'd to fast,
  Or eat what they've refus'd.

JENNY.

I never thought a single life a crime.

PEGGY.

Nor I ; but love in whispers lets us ken
That men were made for us, and we for men.

JENNY.

If Roger is my jo, he kens himsell,
For sic a tale I never heard him tell.
He glowrs and sighs, and I can guess the cause ;
But wha's oblig'd to spell his hums and haws ?
Whene'er he likes to tell his mind mair plain,
I'se tell him frankly ne'er to do't again.
They're fools that slav'ry like, and may be free,
The chiels may a' knit up themselves for me.

PEGGY.

Be doing your ways ; for me, I have a mind
To be as yielding as my Patie's kind.

JENNY.

Heh ! lass, how can ye loe that rattle-skull ?
A very deil, that ay maun have his will.
We soon will hear what a poor fechtan life
You twa will lead, sae soon's ye're man and wife.

PEGGY.

I'll rin the risk ; nor have I ony fear,
But rather think ilk langsome day a year,
'Till I with pleasure mount my bridal-bed,
Where on my Patie's breast I'll lay my head.
There he may kiss as lang as kissing's good,
And what we do there's nane dare call it rude.
He's get his will ; why no ? 'tis good my part
To give him that, and he'll give me his heart.

JENNY.

He may, indeed, for ten or fifteen days
Mak meikle o' ye, with an unco fraise,
And daut ye baith afore fowk and your lane ;
But soon as your newfangleness is gane,
He'll look upon you as his tether-stake,
And think he's tint his freedom for your sake.
Instead, then, of lang days of sweet delight,
Ae day be dumb, and a' the neist he'll flyte ;
And may be, in his barlickhoods, ne'er stick
To lend his loving wife a loundering lick.

SANG IV.

TUNE—"O dear mother, what shall I do?"

O dear Peggy, love's beguiling,
We ought not to trust his smiling ;
Better far to do as I do,
Lest a harder luck betide you.

Lasses, when their fancy's carried,
Think of nought but to be marry'd ;
Running to a life destroys
Heartsome, free, and youthfu' joys.

PEGGY.

Sic coarse-spun thoughts as that want pith to move
My settl'd mind ; I'm o'er far gane in love.
Patie to me is dearer than my breath ;
But want of him I dread nae other skaith.
There's nane of a' the herds that tread the green
Has sic a smile, or sic twa glancing een.
And then he speaks with sic a taking art,
His words they thirle like music thro' my heart.
How blythly can he sport and gently rave,
And jest at little fears that fright the lave !
Ilk day that he's alane upon the hill,
He reads fell books that teach him meikle skill ;
He is—but what need I say that or this,
I'd spend a month to tell you what he is !
In a' he says or does there's sic a gate,
The rest seem coofs, compar'd with my dear Pate ;
His better sense will lang his love secure,
Ill-nature hefts in sauls that's weak and poor.

SANG V.

TUNE—" How can I be sad on my wedding-day ?"

How shall I be sad when a husband I hae
That has better sense than ony of thae,
Sour, weak, silly fellows, that study like fools,
To sink their ain joy, and make their wives snools.
The man who is prudent ne'er lightlies his wife,
Or with dull reproaches encourages strife ;
He praises her virtue, and ne'er will abuse
Her for a small failing, but find an excuse.

JENNY.

Hey, " Bonny lass of Branksome !" or 't be lang,
Your witty Pate will put you in a sang.
O 'tis a pleasant thing to be a bride !
Syne whinging gets about your ingle-side,
Yelping for this or that with fasheous din,
To mak' them brats then ye maun toil and spin.
Ae wean fa's sick, an scads itself wi' brue,
Ane breaks his shin, anither tines his shoe ;
The " Deil gaes o'er John Wabster," hame grows hell,
When Pate misca's ye waur than tongue can tell.

PEGGY.

Yes, it's a heartsome thing to be a wife,
When round the ingle-edge young sprouts are rife.
Gif I'm sae happy, I shall have delight
To hear their little plaints, and keep them right.
Wow, Jenny! can there greater pleasure be,
Than see sic we tots toolying at your knee ;
When a' they ettle at, their greatest wish,
Is to be made of, and obtain a kiss ?
Can there be toil in tenting day and night
The like of them, when love makes care delight ?

JENNY.

But poortith, Peggy, is the warst of a',
Gif o'er your heads ill chance should beggary draw ;
There little love or canty cheer can come
Frae duddy doublets and a pantry toom.
Your nowt may die ; the spate may bear away
Frae aff the howms your dainty rucks of bay ;
The thick-blawn wreaths of snaw, or blashy thows,
May smoor your wethers and may rot your ewes :
A dyvour buys your butter, woo, and cheese,
But or the day of payment breaks and flees ;

With glooman brow the laird seeks in his rent,—
'Tis no to gie ; your merchant's to the bent :
His honour maunna want, he poinds your gear ;
Syne driven frae house and hald, where will ye steer ?
Dear Meg, be wise, and lead a single life ;
Troth, it's nae mows to be a married wife.

PEGGY.

  May sic ill luck befa' that silly she
Wha has sic fears, for that was never me.
Let fowk bode weel, and strive to do their best ;
Nae mair's requir'd—let heaven make out the rest.
I've heard my honest uncle aften say
That lads should a' for wives that's virtuous pray ;
For the maist thrifty man could never get
A well-stor'd room, unless his wife wad let.
Wherefore nocht shall be wanting on my part
To gather wealth to raise my shepherd's heart.
Whate'er he wins I'll guide with canny care,
And win the vogue at market, tron, or fair,
For halesome, clean, cheap and sufficient ware.
A flock of lambs, cheese, butter, and some woo,
Shall first be sald to pay the laird his due ;
Syne a' behind's our ain.   Thus without fear,
With love and rowth we thro' the warld will steer ;
And when my Pate in bairns and gear grows rife,
He'll bless the day he gat me for his wife.

JENNY.

  But what if some young giglit on the green,
With dimpled cheeks and twa bewitching een,
Should gar your Patie think his half-worn Meg
And her ken'd kisses, hardly worth a feg ?

PEGGY.

  Nae mair of that.   Dear Jenny, to be free,
There's some men constanter in love than we.

Nor is the ferly great, when nature kind
Has blest them with solidity of mind ;
They'll reason calmly and with kindness smile,
When our short passions wad our peace beguile.
Sae, whensoe'er they slight their maiks at hame,
'Tis ten to ane their wives are maist to blame.
Then I'll employ with pleasure a' my art
To keep him cheerfu', and secure his heart.
At e'en, when he comes weary frae the hill,
I'll have a' things made ready to his will ;
In winter, when he toils thro' wind and rain,
A bleezing-ingle and a clean hearth-stane ;
And soon as he flings by his plaid and staff,
The seething pat's be ready to take aff ;
Clean hag-abag I'll spread upon his board,
And serve him with the best we can afford ;
Good-humour and white bigonets shall be
Guards to my face, to keep his love for me.

JENNY.

A dish of married love right soon grows cauld,
And dosens down to nane, as fowk grow auld.

PEGGY.

But we'll grow auld together, and ne'er find
The loss of youth, when love grows on the mind.
Bairns and their bairns make sure a firmer tie
Than aught in love the like of us can spy.
See yon twa elms that grow up side by side :
Suppose them some years syne bridegroom and bride ;
Nearer and nearer ilka year they've prest,
Till wide their spreading branches are increas'd,
And in their mixture now are fully blest :
This shields the other frae the eastlin blast,
That in return defends it frae the wast.
Sic as stand single (a state sae lik'd by you),
Beneath ilk storm frae every airt maun bow.

JENNY.

I've done. I yield, dear lassie, I maun yield ;
Your better sense has fairly won the field,
With the assistance of a little fae
Lies dern'd within my breast this mony a day.

SANG VI.

Tune—" Nancy's to the greenwood gane."

I yield, dear lassie, you have won,
  And there is nae denying,
That sure as light flows frae the sun,
  Frae love proceeds complying.
For a' that we can do or say
  'Gainst love, nae thinker heeds us ;
They ken our bosoms lodge the fae
  That by the heartstrings leads us.

PEGGY.

Alake, poor pris'ner !—Jenny, that's no fair,
That ye'll no let the wee thing tak the air.
Haste, let him out ; we'll tent as well's we can
Gif he be Bauldy's, or poor Roger's man.

JENNY.

Anither time's as good ; for see ! the sun
Is right far up, and we're not yet begun
To freath the graith. If canker'd Madge, our aunt,
Come up the burn, she'll gie 's a wicked rant :
But when we've done, I'll tell you a' my mind ;
For this seems true—nae lass can be unkind.

                                       [*Exeunt.*

ACT II.

Scene I.

PROLOGUE.

A snug thack house ; before the door a green ;
Hens on the midding, ducks in dubs are seen ;
On this side stands a barn, on that a byre :
A peat stack joins, and forms a rural square.
The house is Glaud's.—There you may see him lean,
And to his divot seat invite his frien.

GLAUD and SYMON.

GLAUD.

Good morrow, nibour Symon !—come, sit down,
And gie's your cracks.—What's a' the news in town ?
They tell me ye was in the ither day,
And sauld your crummock, and her bassand quey.
I'll warrant ye've coft a pund of cut-and-dry :
Lug out your box, and gie 's a pipe to try.

SYMON.

With a' my heart :—and tent me now, auld boy,
I've gather'd news will kittle your mind with joy.
I couldna rest till I came o'er the burn,
To tell ye things have taken sic a turn
Will gar our vile oppressors stend like flaes,
And skulk in hidings on the heather braes.

GLAUD.

Fy, blaw !—Ah ! Symie, rattling chiels ne'er stand
To cleck, and spread the grossest lies aff-hand ;
Whilk soon flies round like wild-fire far and near :
But loose your poke ; be't true or fause let's hear.

SYMON.

Seeing's believing, Glaud ; and I have seen
Hab, that abroad has with our master been ;—
Our brave good master, wha right wisely fled,
And left a fair estate to save his head,
Because, ye ken fou well, he bravely chose
To shine or set in glory with Montrose.
Now Cromwell's gane to Nick, and ane ca'd Monk
Has play'd the Rumple a right slee begunk ;
Restor'd King Charles, and ilka thing's in tune ;
And Habby says, we'll see Sir William soon.

GLAUD.

That makes me blyth indeed ! But dinna flaw ;
Tell o'er your news again, and swear till't a'.
And saw ye Hab ? and what did Halbert say ?
They have been e'en a dreary time away.
Now God be thankèd that our laird's come hame ;
And his estate, say, can he eithly claim ?

SYMON.

They that hag-raid us till our guts did grane,
Like greedy bears, dare nae mair do't again,
And good Sir William sall enjoy his ain.

SANG VII.

TUNE—" Cauld Kail in Aberdeen."

Cauld be the rebels cast,—
    Oppressors base and bloody ;
I hope we'll see them at the last
    Strung a' up in a woody.

Blest be he of worth and sense,
    And ever high in station,
That bravely stands in the defence
    Of conscience, king, and nation.

GLAUD.

And may he lang, for never did he stent
Us in our thriving with a racket rent ;
Nor grumbl'd if ane grew rich, nor shor'd to raise
Our mailens when we put on Sunday claes.

SYMON.

Nor wad he lang, with senseless saucy air,
Allow our lyart noddles to be bare.
" Put on yer bonnet, Symon ; tak a seat :—
How's all at hame ? how's Elspa ? how does Kate ?
How sells black cattle ? what gi'es woo this year ?"
And sic like kindly questions wad he speer.

SANG VIII.

TUNE—" Mucking of Geordy's byre."

The laird who in riches and honour
    Wad thrive, should be kindly and free,
Nor rack the poor tenants who labour
    To rise aboon poverty ;
Else, like the pack-horse that's unfother'd
    And burden'd, will tumble down faint ;
Thus virtue by hardships are smother'd,
    And rackers aft tine their rent.

GLAUD.

Then wad he gar his butler bring bedeen
The nappy bottle ben, and glasses clean,
Whilk in our breast rais'd sic a blythsome flame
As gart me mony a time gae dancing hame.
My heart's e'en raised !—Dear nibour, will ye stay
And tak your dinner here with me the day ?
We'll send for Elspath, too ; and upo' sight
I'll whistle Pate and Roger frae the height.

I'll yoke my sled, and send to the neist town
And bring a draught of ale, baith stout and brown ;
And gar our cottars a',—man, wife, and wean,—
Drink 'till they tine the gate to stand their lane.

SYMON.

I wadna bauk my friend his blyth design,
Gif that it hadna first of a' been mine ;
For here yestreen I brew'd a bow of maut,
Yestreen I slew twa wethers prime and fat.
A furlet of good cakes my Elspa beuk,
And a large ham hangs reesting in the neuk.
I saw mysell, or I came o'er the loan,
Our meikle pot that scads the whey, put on,
A mutton-bouk to boil, and ane we'll roast ;
And on the haggies Elspa spares nae cost.
Small are they shorn, and she can mix fou nice
The gusty ingans with a curn of spice ;
Fat are the puddings,—heads and feet well sung,—
And we've invited nibours, auld and young,
To pass this afternoon with glee and game,
And drink our master's health and welcome hame.
Ye mauna, then, refuse to join the rest,
Since ye're my nearest friend that I like best.
Bring wi' ye a' your family ; and then
Whene'er you please I'll rant wi' you again.

GLAUD.

Spoke like ye'rsell, auld birky ; never fear
But at your banquet I shall first appear.
Faith, we shall bend the bicker, and look bauld,
Till we forget that we are fail'd or auld !—
Auld, said I !—troth, I'm younger be a score
With your good news than what I was before.
I'll dance or e'en !—Hey, Madge ! come forth ; d'ye hear ?

Enter MADGE.

MADGE.

The man's gane gyte !—Dear Symon, welcome here.—
What wad ye, Glaud, with a' this haste and din ?
Ye never let a body sit to spin.

GLAUD.

Spin ! Snuff ! Gae break your wheel, and burn your tow,
And set the meiklest peat-stack in a low ;
Syne dance about the bane-fire till ye die,
Since now again we'll soon Sir William see.

MADGE.

Blyth news indeed ! And wha was't tald you o't ?

GLAUD.

What's that to you ? Gae get my Sunday's coat ;
Wale out the whitest of my bobbit bands,
My white skin hose, and mittens for my hands ;
Then frae their washing cry the bairns in haste,
And mak ye'rsells as trig, head, feet, and waist,
As ye were a' to get young lads or e'en,
For we're gawn o'er to dine with Sym bedeen.

SYMON.

Do, honest Madge ; and, Glaud, I'll o'er the gate
And see that a' be done as I wad hae't.

[*Exeunt.*

SCENE II.

PROLOGUE.

The open field. A cottage in a glen,
An auld wife spinning at the sunny end.
At a small distance, by a blasted tree,
With falded arms and half-rais'd look, ye see

BAULDY *his lane.*

What's this ? I canna bear't ! 'tis war than hell,
To be sae burnt with love, yet darna tell !
O Peggy ! sweeter than the dawning day,
Sweeter than gowany glens or new-mawn hay ;
Blyther than lambs that frisk out o'er the knowes,
Straighter than aught that in the forest grows.
Her een the clearest blob of dew out-shines,
The lily in her breast its beauty tines ;
Her legs, her arms, her cheeks, her mouth, her een,
Will be my deid, that will be shortly seen !
For Pate lo'es her, (waes me !) and she lo'es Pate,
And I with Neps, by some unlucky fate,
Made a daft vow.   O ! but ane be a beast
That makes rash aiths till he's afore the priest.
I darna speak my mind, else a' the three,
But doubt, wad prove ilk ane my enemy.
'Tis sair to thole.—I'll try some witchcraft art
To break with ane, and win the other's heart.
Here Mausy lives,—a witch that for sma' price
Can cast her cantraips, and gi'e me advice.
She can o'ercast the night, and cloud the moon,
And mak the deils obedient to her crune ;
At midnight hours, o'er the kirkyard she raves,
And howks unchristen'd weans out of their graves ;
Boils up their livers in a warlock's pow ;
Rins withershins about the hemlock low ;
And seven times does her prayers backwards pray,

I

Till Plotcock comes with lumps of Lapland clay,
Mixt with the venom of black taids and snakes.
Of this, unsonsy pictures aft she makes
Of any ane she hates, and gars expire
With slow and racking pains afore a fire,
Stuck fou of pins ; the devilish pictures melt ;
The pain by fowk they represent is felt.
And yonder's Mause :—ay, ay, she kens fu weel
When ane like me comes rinning to the deil.
She and her cat sit beeking in her yard ;
To speak my errand, faith, amaist I'm fear'd.
But I maun do't, though I should never thrive ;
They gallop fast that deils and lasses drive.

[*Exit.*

SCENE III.

PROLOGUE.

A green kail-yaird ; a little fount,
    Where water poplin springs ;
There sits a wife with wrinkled front,
    And yet she spins and sings.

MAUSE.

SANG IX.

TUNE—" Carle and the king come."

Peggy, now the king's come ;
Peggy, now the king's come ;
    Thou may dance, and I shall sing,
Peggy, since the king's come.
Nae mair the hawkies shalt thou milk ;
But change thy plaiding-coat for silk,
And be a lady of that ilk,
    Now, Peggy, since the king's come.

Enter BAULDY.

BAULDY.

How does auld honest Lucky of the glen ?
Ye look baith hale and fair at threescore-ten.

MAUSE.

E'en twining out a thread with little din,
And beeking my cauld limbs afore the sun.
What brings my bairn this gate sae air at morn ?
Is there nae muck to lead ? to thresh nae corn ?

BAULDY.

Enough of baith ; but something that requires
Your helping hand employs now all my cares.

MAUSE.

My helping hand ! alake, what can I do,
That underneath baith eild and poortith bow ?

BAULDY.

Ay, but you're wise, and wiser far than we,
Or maist part of the parish tells a lie.

MAUSE.

Of what kind wisdom think ye I'm possest,
That lifts my character aboon the rest ?

BAULDY.

The word that gangs, how ye're sae wise and fell,
Ye'll may be tak it ill gif I sou'd tell.

MAUSE.

What fowk say of me, Bauldy, let me hear ;
Keep naithing up,—ye naithing have to fear.

BAULDY.

Well, since ye bid me, I shall tell ye a'
That ilk ane talks about you, but a flaw.
When last the wind made Glaud a roofless barn ;
When last the burn bore down my mither's yarn ;
When Brawny, elf-shot, never mair came hame ;
When Tibby kirn'd, and there nae butter came ;
When Bessy Freetock's chuffy-cheeked wean
To a fairy turn'd, and couldna stand its lane ;
When Wattie wander'd ae night thro' the shaw,
And tint himsell amaist amang the snaw ;
When Mungo's mare stood still and swat wi' fright,
When he brought east the howdy under night ;
When Bawsy shot to dead upon the green ;
And Sara tint a snood was nae mair seen ;
You, Lucky, gat the wyte of a' fell out,
And ilka ane here dreads ye round about ;
And sae they may that mean to do ye skaith,
For me to wrang ye, I'll be very laith ;
But when I neist make groats, I'll strive to please
You with a firlot of them mixt with pease.

MAUSE.

I thank ye, lad ; now tell me your demand,
And, if I can, I'll lend my helping hand.

BAULDY.

Then, I like Peggy ; Neps is fond of me ;
Peggy likes Pate ; and Patie's bauld and slee,
And loo's sweet Meg ; but Neps I downa see.
Could ye turn Patie's love to Neps, and then
Peggy's to me, I'd be the happiest man.

MAUSE.

I'll try my art to gar the bowls row right ;
Sae gang your ways and come again at night ;

'Gainst that time I'll some simple things prepare
Worth all your pease and groats, tak ye nae care.

BAULDY.

Well, Mause, I'll come, gif I the road can find,
But if ye raise the de'il, he'll raise the wind ;
Syne rain and thunder, may be, when 'tis late,
Will make the night sae mirk, I'll tine the gate.
We're a' to rant in Symie's at the feast ;
O ! will ye come like badrans for a jest ?
And there you can our different haviours spy ;
There's nane shall ken o't there but you and I.

MAUSE.

'Tis like I may ; but let na on what's past
'Tween you and me, else fear a kittle cast.

BAULDY.

If I aught of your secrets e'er advance,
May ye ride on me ilka night to France.

[*Exit* BAULDY.

MAUSE, *her lane.*

This fool imagines, as do mony sic,
That I'm a witch in compact with Auld Nick,
Because by education I was taught
To speak and act aboon their common thought.
Their gross mistake shall quickly now appear ;
Soon shall they ken what brought, what keeps me here.
Now since the royal Charles, and right's restor'd,
A shepherdess is daughter to a lord.
The bonny foundling that's brought up by Glaud,
Wha has an uncle's care on her bestow'd,
Her infant life I sav'd, when a false friend
Bow'd to th' usurper, and her death design'd,
To establish him and his in all these plains
That by right heritage to her pertains.

She's now in her sweet bloom, has blood and charms
Of too much value for a shepherd's arms.
None know't but me—and if the morn were come,
I'll them tales will gar them all sing dumb.

SCENE IV.

PROLOGUE.

Behind a tree upon the plain
    Pate and his Peggy meet,
In love without a vicious stain,
The bonny lass and cheerfu' swain
    Change vows and kisses sweet.

PATIE and PEGGY.

PEGGY.

O Patie ! let me gang ; I mauna stay ;
We're baith cry'd hame, and Jenny she's away.

PATIE.

I'm laith to part sae soon, now we're alane,
And Roger he's away with Jenny gane.
They're as content, for aught I hear or see,
To be alane themselves, I judge, as we.
Here, where primroses thickest paint the green,
Hard by this little burnie let us lean.
Hark how the lav'rocks chant aboon our heads,
How fast the westlin winds sough through the reeds.

PEGGY.

The scented meadows, birds, and healthy breeze,
For aught I ken, may mair than Peggy please.

PATIE.

Ye wrang me sair to doubt my being kind ;
In speaking sae, ye ca' me dull and blind,
Gif I could fancy aught's sae sweet or fair
As my sweet Meg, or worthy of my care.
Thy breath is sweeter than the sweetest brier ;
Thy cheek and breast the finest flow'rs appear ;
Thy words excel the maist delightfu' notes
That warble through the merle or mavis' throats ;
With thee I tent nae flowers that busk the field,
Or ripest berries that our mountains yield ;
The sweetest fruits that hing upon the tree
Are far inferior to a kiss of thee.

PEGGY.

But Patrick for some wicked end may fleech,
And lambs should tremble when the foxes preach.
I darna stay ; ye joker, let me gang,
Or swear ye'll never 'tempt to do me wrang.

PATIE.

Sooner a mother shall her fondness drap,
And wrang the bairn sits smiling on her lap ;
The sun shall change, the moon to change shall cease ;
The gaits to climb, the sheep to yield the fleece ;
Ere aught by me be either said or done
Shall do thee wrang ;—I swear by all aboon.

PEGGY.

Then keep your aith.   But mony lads will swear,
And be mansworn to twa in half a year.
Now I believe ye like me wonder weel ;
But if anither lass your heart should steal,
Your Meg, forsaken, bootless might relate
How she was dauted anes by faithless Pate.

PATIE.

I'm sure I canna change ; ye needna fear,
Tho' we're but young, I've lo'ed ye mony a year.
I mind it well, when thou could'st hardly gang,
Or lisp out words, I choos'd thee frae the thrang
Of a' the bairns, and led thee by the hand,
Aft to the tansy knowe or rashy strand,
Thou smiling by my side.   I took delight
To pu' the rashes green with roots sae white,
Of which, as well as my young fancy could,
For thee I plet the flow'ry belt and snood.

PEGGY.

When first thou gaed with shepherds to the hill,
And I to milk the ewes first tried my skill,
To bear a leglen was nae toil to me,
When at the bught at ev'n I met with thee.

SANG X.

TUNE—" Winter was cauld, and my claithing was thin."

PEGGY.

When first my dear laddie gaed to the green hill,
And I at ewe-milking first sey'd my young skill,
To bear the milk bowie no pain was to me,
When I at the bughting forgather'd with thee.

PATIE.

When corn-riggs wav'd yellow, and blue heather-bells
Bloom'd bonny on moorland and sweet rising fells,
Nae birns, brier, or breckens, gave trouble to me,
If I found the berries right ripen'd for thee.

PEGGY.

When thou ran, or wrestled, or putted the stane,
And came off the victor, my heart was ay fain ;
Thy ilka sport manly gave pleasure to me ;
For nane can putt, wrestle, or run swift as thee.

PATIE.

Our Jenny sings saftly the " Cowden broom knowes ;"
And Rosie lilts sweetly the "Milking the ewes ;"
There's few " Jenny Nettles " like Nansy can sing ;
At " Thro' the wood, laddie," Bess gars our lugs ring.
But when my dear Peggy sings, with better skill,
The " Boatman," " Tweed-side," or the " Lass of the mill,"
'Tis mony times sweeter and pleasing to me,
For tho' they sing nicely, they cannot like thee.

PEGGY.

How easy can lasses trow what they desire !
And praises sae kindly increases love's fire ;
Give me still this pleasure, my study shall be
To make myself better and sweeter for thee.

PATIE.

When corns grew yellow, and the heatherbells
Bloom'd bonny on the moor and rising fells,
Nae birns, or briers, or whins e'er troubled me,
Gif I could find blae-berries ripe for thee.

PEGGY.

When thou didst wrestle, run, or putt the stane,
And wan the day, my heart was flightering fain.
At all these sports thou still gave joy to me,
For nane can wrestle, run, or putt with thee.

PATIE.

Jenny sings saft the " Broom of Cowdenknowes ;"
And Rosie lilts the " Milking of the Ewes ;"

There's nane like Nansy " Jenny Nettles " sings ;
At turns in " Maggy Lauder" Marion dings.
But when my Peggy sings with sweeter skill
The " Boatman," or the " Lass of Patie's mill,"
It is a thousand times mair sweet to me ;
Tho' they sing well, they canna sing like thee.

PEGGY.

How eith can lasses trow what they desire !
And, rees'd by them we love, blaws up that fire.
But wha loves best let time and carriage try ;
Be constant, and my love shall time defy.
Be still as now, and a' my care shall be
How to contrive what pleasant is for thee.

PATIE.

Wert thou a giglit gawky like the lave
That little better than our nowt behave ;
At naught they'll ferly, senseless tales believe,
Be blythe for silly hechts, for trifles grieve ;
Sic ne'er could win my heart that kenna how
Either to keep a prize, or yet prove true ;
But thou in better sense without a flaw,
As in thy beauty, far excels them a'.
Continue kind, and a' my care shall be
How to contrive what pleasing is for thee.

PEGGY.

Agreed ; but hearken, yon's auld aunty's cry,
I ken they'll wonder what can make us stay.

PATIE.

And let them ferly.—Now, a kindly kiss,
Or fivescore good anes wad not be amiss ;
And syne we'll sing the sang, with tunefu' glee,
That I made up last owk on you and me.

PEGGY.

Sing first, syne claim your hire.

PATIE.

Well, I agree.

SANG XI.

To its awn tune.

By the delicious warmness of thy mouth,
And rowing eye that, smiling, tells the truth,
I guess, my lassie, that, as well as I,
Ye're made for love, and why should ye deny?

PEGGY.

But ken ye lad, gif we confess o'er soon
Ye think us cheap, and syne the wooing's done;
The maiden that o'er quickly tines her pow'r,
Like unripe fruit, will taste but hard and sour.

PATIE.

But gin they hing o'er lang upon the tree,
Their sweetness they may tyne, and say may ye.
Red-cheeked, ye completely ripe appear,
And I have thol'd and woo'd a lang half year.

PEGGY

(Falling into Patie's arms).

Then dinna pu me, gently thus I fa'
Into my Patie's arms for good and a';
But stint your wishes to this kind embrace,
And mint nae farther till we've got the grace.

PATIE.

(With his left hand about her waist).

O charming armfu' !—Hence, ye cares, away !
I'll kiss my treasure a' the live lang day !
All night I'll dream my kisses o'er again
Till that day come that ye'll be a' my ain.

BOTH.

Sun, gallop down the westlin skies,
Gang soon to bed, and quickly rise.
O lash your steeds, post time away,
And haste about our bridal-day;
And if you're weary'd, honest light,
Sleep, gin ye like, a week that night.

[Curtain falls while they kiss.

ACT III.

Scene I.

PROLOGUE.

Now turn your eyes beyond yon spreading lime,
And tent a man whase beard seems bleach'd with time ;
Ane elwand fills his hand, his habit mean,
Nae doubt ye'll think he has a pedlar been ;
But whist, it is the knight in masquerade
That comes hid in this cloud to see his lad.
Observe how pleas'd the loyal suff'rer moves
Thro' his auld av'nues, anes delightfu' groves.

Sir William, *solus.*

The gentleman thus hid in low disguise,
I'll for a space, unknown, delight mine eyes
With a full view of ev'ry fertile plain,
Which once I lost, which now are mine again.
Yet, 'midst my joy, some prospects pain renew,
Whilst I my once fair seat in ruins view.
Yonder, ah me ! it desolately stands,
Without a roof, the gates fall'n from their bands ;
The casements all broke down, no chimney left,
The naked walls of tapestry all bereft.
My stables and pavilions, broken walls,
That with each rainy blast decaying falls ;
My gardens once adorn'd the most complete,
With all that nature, all that art makes sweet ;
Where round the figur'd green and pebble walks,
The dewy flow'rs hung nodding on their stalks ;
But overgrown with nettles, docks, and brier,
No hyacinths or eglantines appear.
Here fail'd and broke's the rising ample shade,
Where peach and nec'trine trees their branches spread,

Basking in rays, and early did produce
Fruit fair to view, delightful to the use.
All round in gaps the walls in ruin lie,
And from what stands the wither'd branches fly.
These soon shall be repair'd ; and now my joy
Forbids all grief, when I'm to see my boy,
My only prop, and object of my care,
Since heav'n too soon call'd home his mother fair.
Him, ere the rays of reason clear'd his thought,
I secretly to faithful Symon brought,
And charg'd him strictly to conceal his birth
Till we should see what changing times brought forth.
Hid from himself, he starts up by the dawn,
And ranges careless o'er the height and lawn,
After his fleecy charge serenely gay,
With other shepherds whistling o'er the day.
Thrice happy life ! that's from ambition free,
Remov'd from crowns, and courts, how cheerfully
A calm, contented mortal spends his time,
In health, his soul unstain'd with crime !

SANG XII.

TUNE—"Happy Clown."

Hid from himself, now by the dawn
He starts as fresh as roses blawn,
And ranges o'er the heights and lawn,
  After his bleating flocks.

Healthful, and innocently gay,
He chaunts and whistles out the day ;
Untaught to smile and then betray,
  Like courtly weathercocks.

Life happy, from ambition free,
Envy, and vile hypocrisy,

When truth and love with joy agree,
　　Unsully'd with a crime.

Unmov'd with what disturbs the great,
In propping of their pride and state,
He lives, and, unafraid of fate,
　　Contented spends his time.

Now tow'rds good Symon's house I'll bend my way,
And see what makes yon gamboling to-day ;
All on the green in a fair wanton ring
My youthful tenants gaily dance and sing.

　　　　　　　　　　　　　　　　　　[Exit.

SCENE II.

PROLOGUE.

'Tis Symon's house, please to step in,
　　And visy't round and round ;
There's nought superfluous to give pain,
　　Or costly to be found.
Yet, all is clean ; a clear peat ingle
　　Glances amidst the floor ;
The green horn-spoons, beech luggies mingle,
　　On skelfs forgainst the door.
While the young brood sport on the green,
　　The auld anes think it best
With the brown cow to clear their een,
　　Snuff, crack, and take their rest.

SYMON, GLAUD, and ELSPA.

GLAUD.

We anes were young oursells ; I like to see
The bairns bob round with other merrylie.

Troth, Symon, Patie's grown a strapan lad,
And better looks than his I never bade ;
Amang our lads he bears the gree awa',
And tells his tale the clev'rest of them a'.

ELSPA.

Poor man ! he's a great comfort to us baith ;
God made him good, and hide him ay frae skaith ;
He is a bairn, I'll say't, well worth our care,
That gae us ne'er vexation late or air.

GLAUD.

I trow, goodwife, if I be not mistane,
He seems to be with Peggy's beauty tane ;
And troth my niece is a right dainty wean,
As ye well ken ; a bonnier needna be,
Nor better, be't she were nae kin to me.

SYMON.

Ha, Glaud, I doubt that ne'er will be a match,
My Patie's wild, and will be ill to catch ;
And or he were, for reasons I'll not tell,
I'd rather be mixt with the mools mysell.

GLAUD.

What reason can ye have ? there's nane, I'm sure,
Unless ye may cast up that she's but poor.
But gif the lassie marry to my mind
I'll be to her as my ain Jenny kind.
Fourscore of breeding ewes of my ain birn,
Five kye that at ae milking fills a kirn,
I'll gie to Peggy that day she's a bride ;
By and attour, if my good luck abide,
Ten lambs at spaining time as lang's I live,
And twa quey cawfs I'll yearly to them give.

ELSPA.

Ye offer fair, kind Glaud, but dinna speer
What may be is not fit ye yet should hear.

SYMON.

Or this day eight days likely he shall learn
That our denial disna slight his bairn.

GLAUD.

We'll nae mair o't ; come, gies the other bend,
We'll drink their healths, whatever way it end.

[Their healths gae round.]

SYMON.

But will ye tell me, Glaud ?   By some 'tis said,
Your niece is but a fundling, that was laid
Down at your hallon-side ae morn in May,
Right clean row'd up, and bedded on dry hay.

GLAUD.

That clattern Madge, my titty, tells sic flaws
Whene'er our Meg her cankart humour gaws.

Enter JENNY.

O father, there's an auld man on the green,
The fellest fortune-teller e'er was seen ;
He tents our loofs, and syne whops out a book,
Turns owre the leaves, and gies our brows a look ;
Syne tells the oddest tales that e'er ye heard ;
His head is grey, and lang and grey his beard.

SYMON.

Gae bring him in, we'll hear what he can say,
Nane shall gang hungry by my house to-day.

[*Exit* JENNY.

L

But for his telling fortunes, troth, I fear
He kens nae mair of that than my grey mare.

GLAUD.

Spae-men ! the truth of a' their saws I doubt,
For greater liars never ran thereout.

Re-enter JENNY, *bringing in* SIR WILLIAM ; PATIE *following.*

SYMON.

Ye're welcome, honest carle.   Here tak a seat.

SIR WILLIAM.

I give thee thanks, good man, I'se no be blate.

GLAUD.

(Drinks.)

Come, t'ye, friend.   How far came ye the day ?

SIR WILLIAM.

I pledge ye, nibour.   E'en but a little way ;
Rousted with eild, a wee piece gate seems lang ;
Twa mile or three's the maist that I do gang.

SYMON.

Ye're welcome here to stay all night with me,
And tak sic bed and board as we can gi'e.

SIR WILLIAM.

That's kind unsought.   Well, 'gin ye have a bairn
That ye like well, and wad his fortune learn,
I shall employ the farthest of my skill
To spae it faithfully, be't good or ill.

SYMON.

(Pointing to PATIE.)

Only that lad.   Alack ! I have nae mae,
Either to make me joyful now or wae.

SIR WILLIAM.

Young man, let's see your hand.   What gars ye sneer ?

PATIE.

Because your skill's but little worth, I fear.

SIR WILLIAM.

Ye cut before the point.   But, billy, bide,
I'll wager there's a mouse-mark on your side.

ELSPA.

Betooch-us-to ! and well I wat that's true ;
Awa ! awa ! the deil's owre grit wi' you.
Four inch aneath his oxter is the mark,
Scarce ever seen since he first wore a sark.

SIR WILLIAM.

I'll tell ye mair ; if this young lad be spared
But a short while, he'll be a braw rich laird.

ELSPA.

A laird ! Hear ye, goodman, what think ye now ?

SYMON.

I dinna ken.   Strange auld man, wha art thou ?
Fair fa' your heart, 'tis good to bode of wealth.
Come, turn the timmer to laird Patie's health.

[PATIE's health gaes round.]

PATIE.

A laird of twa good whistles and a kent,
Twa curs, my trusty tenants on the bent,
Is all my great estate, and like to be ;
Sae, cunning carle, ne'er break your jokes on me.

SYMON.

Whist, Patie, let the man look ow're your hand ;
Aftimes as broken a ship has come to land.

> [SIR WILLIAM looks a little at PATIE'S hand, then counterfeits
> falling into a trance.—While they endeavour to lay him
> right.]

ELSPA.

Preserve s ! the man's a warlock, or possest
With some nae good, or second-sight at least.
Where is he now ?

GLAUD.

He's seeing a' that's done
In ilka place beneath or yont the moon.

ELSPA.

These second-sighted fowks (his peace be here !)
See things far aff, and things to come, as clear,
As I can see my thumb.   Wow ! can he tell
(Speer at him soon as he comes to himsell,)
How soon we'll see Sir William ? Whisht, he heaves,
And speaks out broken words like ane that raves.

SYMON.

He'll soon grow better.—Elspa, haste ye, gae
And fill him up a tass of usquebæ.

SIR WILLIAM.

(Starts up and speaks.)

A knight that for a lion fought
    Against a herd of bears,
Was to lang toil and trouble brought,
    In which some thousands shares.
But now again the lion rares,
    And joy spreads o'er the plain ;
The lion has defeat the bears,
    The knight returns again.

That knight in a few days shall bring
    A shepherd frae the fauld,
And shall present him to the king,
    A subject true and bauld.
He Mr. Patrick shall be call'd ;
    All you that hear me now
May well believe what I have tald,
    For it shall happen true.

SYMON.

Friend, may your spaeing happen soon and weel ;
But, faith, I'm redd you've bargain'd with the deil,
To tell some tales that fowks wad secret keep ;
Or do you get them tald you in your sleep ?

SIR WILLIAM.

Howe'er I get them never fash your beard,
Nor come I to redd fortunes for reward ;
But I'll lay ten to one with ony here
That all I prophesy shall soon appear.

SYMON.

You prophesying fowks are odd kind men !
They're here that ken, and here that disna ken

The wimpled meaning of your unco tale,
Whilk soon will mak a noise o'er moor and dale.

GLAUD.

'Tis nae sma' sport to hear how Sym believes,
And takes't for gospel what the spae-man gives
Of flawing fortunes, whilk he evens to Pate ;
But what we wish we trow at ony rate.

SIR WILLIAM.

Whisht, doubtfu' carle ; for ere the sun
　Has driven twice down to the sea,
What I have said ye shall see done
　In part, or nae mair credit me.

GLAUD.

Well, be't sae, friend ; I shall say naething mair,
But I've twa sonsy lasses, young and fair,
Plump, ripe for men ; I wish ye could foresee
Sic fortunes for them might bring joy to me.

SIR WILLIAM.

Nae mair thro' secrets can I sift,
　Till darkness black the bent ;
I have but anes a day that gift,
　Sae rest a while content.

SYMON.

Elspa, cast on the claith, fetch butt some meat,
And of your best gar this auld stranger eat.

SIR WILLIAM.

Delay a while your hospitable care ;
I'd rather enjoy this evening calm and fair,
Around yon ruin'd tower to fetch a walk,
With you, kind friend, to have some private talk.

SYMON.

Soon as you please I'll answer your desire ;
And, Glaud, you'll tak your pipe beside the fire ;
We'll but gae round the place, and soon be back,
Syne sup together, and tak our pint and crack.

GLAUD.

I'll out a while, and see the young anes play ;
My heart's still light, albeit my locks be grey.

[*Exeunt.*

SCENE III.

PROLOGUE.

Jenny pretends an errand hame,
Young Roger draps the rest,
To whisper out his melting flame,
And thow his lassie's breast.
Behind a bush well hid frae sight they meet ;
See, Jenny's laughing ; Roger's like to greet.
Poor shepherd !

ROGER and JENNY.

ROGER.

Dear Jenny, I wad speak t' ye; wad ye let ;
And yet I ergh, ye'r ay sae scornfu' set.

JENNY.

And what wad Roger say, gif he could speak ?
Am I oblig'd to guess what ye're to seek ?

ROGER.

Yes, ye may guess right eith for what I grein,
Baith by my service, sighs, and langing een ;
And I maun out wi't, tho' I risk your scorn,
Ye're never frae my thoughts baith e'en and morn.
Ah ! could I loo ye less, I'd happy be ;
But happier far, could ye but fancy me.

JENNY.

And wha kens, honest lad, but that I may ?
Ye canna say that e'er I said ye nay.

ROGER.

Alake ! my frighted heart begins to fail
Whene'er I mint to tell ye out my tale,
For fear some tighter lad, mair rich than I,
Has win your love, and near your heart may lie.

JENNY.

I loo my father,—cousin Meg I love,—
But to this day nae man my heart could move.
Except my kin, ilk lad's alike to me,
And frae ye a' I best had keep me free.

ROGER.

How lang, dear Jenny ? Sayna that again.
What pleasure can ye tak in giving pain ?
I'm glad, however, that ye yet stand free ;
Wha kens but ye may rue, and pity me ?

JENNY.

Ye have my pity else, to see you set
On that whilk makes our sweetness soon forget.
Wow ! but we're bonny, good, and everything !
How sweet we breathe whene'er we kiss or sing !

But we're nae sooner fools to give consent,
Than we our daffin and tint power repent;
When prison'd in four wa's, a wife right tame,
Altho' the first, the greatest drudge at hame.

ROGER.

That only happens when, for sake of gear,
Ane wales a wife as he wad buy a mare;
Or, when dull parents bairns together bind
Of different tempers, that can ne'er prove kind.
But love, true, downright love, engages me
(Tho' thou should scorn) still to delight in thee.

JENNY.

What sugar'd words frae wooer's lips can fa'!
But girning marriage comes and ends them a'.
I've seen with shining fair the morning rise,
And soon the fleecy clouds mirk a' the skies;
I've seen the silver spring a while rin clear,
And soon the mossy puddles disappear.
The bridegroom may rejoice, the bride may smile,
But soon contentions a' their joys beguile.

ROGER.

I've seen the morning rise with fairest light,
The day unclouded sink in calmest night.
I've seen the spring rin wimpling thro' the plain
Increase and join the ocean without stain;
The bridegroom may be blyth, the bride may smile,
Rejoice thro' life and all your fears beguile.

JENNY.

Were I but sure ye lang would love maintain,
The fewest words my easy heart could gain;
For I maun own, since now at last your free,
Altho' I jok'd, I lov'd your company;

M

And ever had a warmness in my breast
That made ye dearer to me than the rest.

ROGER.

I'm happy now ! o'er happy ! haud my head !
This gush of pleasure's like to be my dead.
Come to my arms ! or strike me ! I'm all fir'd
With wond'ring love ! Let's kiss till we be tir'd.
Kiss, kiss ; we'll kiss the sun and starns away,
And ferly at the quick return of day.
O Jenny ! let my arms about thee twine,
And briz thy bonny breasts and lips to mine.

[They embrace.

SANG XIII.

Tune—" Leith Wynd."

JENNY.

Were I assur'd you'll constant prove,
    You should nae mair complain ;
The easy maid beset with love
    Few words will quickly gain.
For I must own now, since you're free,
    This too fond heart of mine
Has lang, a black-sole true to thee,
    Wish'd to be pair'd with thine.

ROGER.

I'm happy now ; ah ! let my head
    Upon thy breast recline ;
The pleasure strikes me near-hand dead ;
    Is Jenny then sae kind ?
O let me briz thee to my heart,
    And round my arms entwine ;
Delytfu' thought ! we'll never part,
    Come, press thy mouth to mine.

JENNY.

With equal joy my safter heart does yield,
To own thy well-try'd love has won the field.
Now by these warmest kisses thou hast tane,
Swear thus to love me when by vows made ane.

ROGER.

I swear by fifty thousand yet to come,
Or may the first ane strike me deaf and dumb,
There shall not be a kindlier dawted wife,
If you agree with me to lead your life.

JENNY.

Well, I agree.   Neist to my parent gae,
Get his consent,—he'll hardly say ye nae ;
Ye have what will commend ye to him weel,
Auld fowks like them that want na milk and meal.

SANG XIV.

TUNE—"O'er Bogie."

JENNY.

Well, I agree, ye're sure of me.
    Next to my father gae ;
Make him content to give consent,—
    He'll hardly sae ye nay.
For ye have what he wad be at,
    And will commend you weel,
Since parents auld think love grows cauld,
    Where bairns want milk and meal.

Should he deny, I carena by,
    He'd contradict in vain ;
Tho' a' my kin had said and sworn,
    But thee I will have nane.

Then never range nor learn to change,
　Like those in high degree;
And if you faithful prove in love,
　You'll find nae fault in me.

ROGER.

My faulds contain twice fifteen farrow nowt,—
As mony newcal in my byres rowt;
Five pack of woo I can at Lammas sell,
Shorn frae my bob-tail'd bleaters on the fell.
Good twenty pair of blankets for our bed,
With meikle care my thrifty mither made;
Ilk thing that makes a heartsome house and tight,
Was still her care, my father's great delight.
They left me all, which now gi'es joy to me,
Because I can give a', my dear, to thee,
And had I fifty times as meikle mair
Nane but my Jenny should the samen skair;
My love and all is yours; now haud them fast,
And guide them as ye like to gar them last.

JENNY.

I'll do my best; but see wha comes this way,
Patie and Meg; besides, I maunna stay.
Let's steal frae ither now and meet the morn;
If we be seen we'll dree a deal of scorn.

ROGER.

To where the saugh-tree shades the menin pool,
I'll frae the hill come down when day grows cool;
Keep tryst and meet me there, there let us meet
To kiss and tell our loves; there's nought sae sweet.

[*Exeunt.*

SCENE IV.

PROLOGUE.

This scene presents the Knight and Sym
   Within a gallery of the place,
Where all looks ruinous and grim;
   Nor has the Baron shown his face,
But joking with his shepherd leel,
   Aft speers the gate he kens fu' weel.

SIR WILLIAM and SYMON.

SIR WILLIAM.

To whom belongs this house so much decay'd?

SYMON.

To ane that lost it, lending gen'rous aid
To bear the head up, when rebellious tale,
Against the laws of nature did prevail.
Sir William Worthy is our master's name,
Whilk fills us with joy, now he's come hame.

PROLOGUE.

(Sir William draps his masking beard;
   Symon, transported, sees
The welcome knight, with fond regard,
   And grasps him round the knees.)

My master! my dear master! do I breathe,
To see him healthy, strong, and free frae skaith,
Return'd to cheer his wishing tenant's sight';
To bless his son, my charge, the world's delight?

SIR WILLIAM.

Rise, faithful Symon, in my arms enjoy
A place thy due, kind guardian of my boy.
I came to view thy care in this disguise,
And am confirm'd thy conduct has been wise ;
Since still the secret thou'st securely seal'd,
And ne'er to him his real birth reveal'd.

SYMON.

The due obedience to your strict command
Was the first lock. Neist, my ain judgment fand
Out reasons plenty ; since, without estate,
A youth, tho' sprung frae kings, looks baugh and blate.

SIR WILLIAM.

And aften vain and idly spend their time,
Till grown unfit for action, past their prime,
Hang on their friends ; which gi'es their sauls a cast
That turns them downright beggars at the last.

SYMON.

Now well I wat, sir, you have spoken true ;
For there's laird Kytie's son, that's loo'd by few,—
His father steght his fortune in his wame,
And left his heir nought but a gentle name.
He gangs about sornan frae place to place
As scrimpt of manners as of sense and grace ;
Oppressing a', as punishment o' their sin,
That are within his tenth degree of kin ;
Rins in ilk trader's debt, wha's sae unjust
To his ain family as to gi'e him trust.

SIR WILLIAM.

Such useless branches of a commonwealth
Should be lopt off, to give a state mair health.—

Unworthy bare reflection.—Symon, run
O'er all your observations on my son.
A parent's fondness easily finds excuse ;
But do not with indulgence truth abuse.

SYMON.

To speak his praise, the langest simmer day
Wad be owre short, could I them right display.
In word and deed he can sae well behave,
That out of sight he rins before the lave ;
And when there's e'er a quarrel or contest,
Patrick's made judge, to tell whase cause is best ;
And his decree stands good ;—he'll gar it stand,
Wha dares to grumble finds his correcting hand.
With a firm look, and commanding way,
He gars the proudest of our herds obey.

SIR WILLIAM.

Your tale much pleases ; my good friend proceed.
What learning has he ? Can he read and write ?

SYMON.

Baith wonder well, for troth I didna spare
To gie him at the school enough of lear ;
And he delights in books ; he reads and speaks
With fowks that ken them, Latin words and Greeks.

SIR WILLIAM.

Where gets he books to read, and of what kind ?
Tho' some give light, some blindly lead the blind.

SYMON.

Whene'er he drives our sheep to Edinburgh Port
He buys some books of history, sangs, or sport ;
Nor does he want of them a rowth at will,
And carries ay a pouchfu' to the hill.

About ane Shakespar and a famous Ben
He aften speaks, and ca's them best of men.
How sweetly Hawthornden and Stirling sing,
And ane caw'd Cowley, loyal to his King,
He kens fou well, and gars their verses ring.
I sometimes thought that he made o'er great fraise
About fine poems, histories, and plays.
When I reprov'd him anes, a book he brings ;
" With this," quoth he, " on braes I crack with kings."

SIR WILLIAM.

He answer'd well ; and much ye glad my ear,
When such accounts I of my shepherd hear.
Reading such books can raise a peasant's mind
Above a lord's that is not thus inclin'd.

SYMON.

What ken we better, that sae sindle look,
Except on rainy Sundays, on a book ?
When we a leaf or twa half read, half spell,
Till a' the rest sleep round as weel's oursell.

SIR WILLIAM.

Well jested, Symon.—But one question more
I'll only ask ye now, and then give o'er.
The youth 's arriv'd the age when little loves
Flighter around young hearts like cooing doves ;
Has nae young lassie, with inviting mien
And rosy cheek,—the wonder of the green,—
Engag'd his look, and caught his youthfu' heart ?

SYMON.

I fear'd the warst, but ken'd the smallest part ;
Till late, I saw him twa three times mair sweet
With Glaud's fair niece than I thought right or meet.

I had my fears, but now have nought to fear
Since, like yourself, your son will soon appear ;
A gentleman, enrich'd with all those charms,
May bless the fairest best-born lady's arms.

SIR WILLIAM.

This night will end his unambitious fire,
When higher views shall greater thoughts inspire.
Go, Symon, bring him quickly here to me ;
None but yourself shall our first meeting see.
Yonder's my horse and servant nigh at hand,—
They come just at the time I gave command.
Straight in my own apparel I'll go dress ;
Now ye the secret may to all confess.

SYMON.

With how much joy I on this errand flee,
There's nane can know that is not downright me !

[*Exit.*

SIR WILLIAM, *solus.*

Whene'er th' event of hope's success appears,
One happy hour cancels the toil of years ;
A thousand toils are lost in Lethe's stream,
And cares evanish like a morning dream ;
When wish'd-for pleasures rise like morning light,
The pain that's past enhances the delight.
Those joys I feel, that words can ill express,
I ne'er had known, without my late distress ;
But, from his rustic business and love
I must in haste my Patrick soon remove
To·courts and camps, that may his soul improve.
Like the rough diamond, as it leaves the mine,
    Only in little breakings shews its light,
Till artful polishing has made it shine ;
    Thus education makes the genius bright.

N

SANG XV.

TUNE—"Wat ye wha I met yestreen."

Now from rusticity and love,
   Whose flames but over lowly burn,
My gentle shepherd must be drove,
   His soul must take another turn.
As the rough diamond from the mine
   In breakings only shews its light,
Till polishing has made it shine,—
   Thus learning makes the genius bright.

[Exit.

ACT IV.

Scene I.

PROLOGUE.

The scene describ'd in former page,
Glaud's onset.—Enter Mause and Madge.

MAUSE.

Our laird come hame !—and owns young Pate his heir !—
That's news indeed !

MADGE.

As true as ye stand there.
As they were dancing all in Symon's yard,
Sir William, like a warlock, with a beard
Five nieves in length, and white as driven snaw,
Amang us came, cry'd—" Haud ye merry a'!"
We ferly'd meikle at his unco look,
While, frae his pouch, he whirl'd forth a book.
As we stood round about him on the green,
He view'd us a', but fix'd on Pate his een ;
Then pawkily pretended he could spae,
Yet, for his pains and skill, wad naithing hae.

MAUSE.

Then sure the lasses, and ilk gaping coof,
Wad rin about him, and haud out their loof.

MADGE.

As fast as fleas skip to the tate of woo,
Whilk slee tod-lowrie hads without his mow,
When he to drown them, and his hips to cool,
In summer days slides backward in a pool !

In short, he did for Pate braw things foretell,
Without the help of conjuring or spell.
At last, when well diverted, he withdrew,
Pou'd off his beard to Symon.—Symon knew
His welcome master ;—round his knees he gat,
Hang at his coat, and syne for blythness grat.
Patrick was sent for :—Happy lad is he !—
Symon told Elspa—Elspa tald it me.
Ye'll hear out a' the secret story soon ;
And troth 'tis e'en right odd, when a' is done,
To think how Symon ne'er afore wad tell,
Na, no sae meikle as to Pate himsell.
Our Meg, poor thing, alake ! has lost her jo.

MAUSE.

It may be sae, wha kens, and may be no.
To lift a love that's rooted is great pain ;
E'en kings have tane a queen out of the plain,—
And what has been before may be again.

MADGE.

Sic nonsense !—Love tak' root, but tocher-good,
'Tween a herd's bairn and ane of gentle blood !—
Sic fashions in King Bruce's days might be,
But siccan ferlies now we never see.

MAUSE.

Gif Pate forsakes her, Bauldy she may gain.—
Yonder he comes ; and wow ! but he looks fain.
Nae doubt he thinks that Peggy's now his ain.

MADGE.

He get her ! slaverin doof ! it sets him weel
To yoke a plough where Patrick thought to till !
Gif I were Meg, I'd let young master see——

MAUSE.

Ye'd be as dorty in your choice as he ;
And so wad I !   But whisht ! here Bauldy comes.

Enter BAULDY

(Singing).

Jock said to Jenny—"Jenny, wilt thou do't ?"
" Ne'er a fit," quoth Jenny, " for my tocher-good ;
For my tocher-good, I winna marry thee !"
" E'ens ye like," quoth Jocky, " ye may let it be."

MADGE.

Weel liltet, Bauldy, that's a dainty sang.

BAULDY.

I'll gie ye't a',—'tis better than 'tis lang !

(Sings again).

" I hae gowd and gear ; I hae land eneugh ;
I have seven good owsen ganging in a pleugh.
Ganging in a pleugh, and linkan o'er the lee ;
And gin ye winna tak me, I can let ye be.

I hae a good ha' house, a barn, and a byer,
A peatstack 'fore the door,—will mak a rantin fire.
I'll mak a rantin fire, and merry sall we be ;
And gin ye winna tak me, I can let ye be."

Jenny said to Jocky,—" Gin ye winna tell,
Ye sall be the lad,—I'll be the lass mysell.
Ye're a bonny lad, and I'm a lassie free ;
Ye're welcomer to tak me than to let me be."

I trow sae.   Lasses will come to at last,
Tho' for a while they maun their snaw-baws cast.

MAUSE.

Well, Bauldy, how gaes a' ?

BAULDY.

Faith, unco right ;
I hope we'll a' sleep sound but ane this night.

MADGE.

And wha's the unlucky ane, if we may ask ?

BAULDY.

To find out that is nae difficult task,—
Poor, bonny Peggy ; wha maun think nae mair
On Pate, turn'd Patrick, and Sir William's heir.
Now, now, good Madge, and honest Mause, stand be ;
While Meg 's in dumps, put in a word for me.
I'll be as kind as ever Pate could prove,
Less wilfu', and ay constant in my love.

MADGE.

As Neps can witness, and the bushy thorn
Where mony a time to her your heart was sworn !
Fy, Bauldy, blush ! and vows of love regard.
What other lass will trow a mansworn herd ?
The curse of heaven hings ay aboon their heads
That's ever guilty of sic sinfu' deeds.
I'll ne'er advise my niece sae grey a gate ;
Nor will she be advis'd, fou well I wat.

BAULDY.

Sae grey a gate ! mansworn ! and a' the rest !—
Ye lied, auld roudes ; and in faith had best
Eat in your words, else I shall gar you stand,
With a het face, afore the haly band.

MADGE.

Ye'll gar me stand ! ye shevelling-gabbit brock !
Speak that again, and trembling dread my rock,
And ten sharp nails, that, when my hands are in,
Can flyp the skin o' ye'r cheeks out o'er your chin.

BAULDY.

I take ye witness, Mause, ye heard her say
That I'm mansworn.—I winna let it gae.

MADGE.

Ye're witness, too, he ca'd me bonny names,
And should be serv'd as his good-breeding claims.
Ye filthy dog!

> [Flees to his hair like a fury.—A stout battle.—Mause
> endeavours to redd them.]

MAUSE.

Let gang your grips!—Fye, Madge!—Howt, Bauldy, lean!—
I wadna wish this tulzie had been seen,
'Tis sae daft like——

> [Bauldy gets out of Madge's clutches with a bleeding nose.]

MADGE.

'Tis dafter like to thole
An ether-cap like him to blaw the coal!
It set him well, with vile, unscrapit tongue,
To cast up whether I be auld or young.
They're aulder yet than I have married been,
And, or they died, their bairns' bairns have seen.

MAUSE.

That's true; and Bauldy, ye was far to blame,
To ca' Madge ought but her ain christen'd name.

BAULDY.

My lugs, my nose, and noddle finds the same.

MADGE.

" Auld roudes!"—filthy fellow, I shall auld ye!

MAUSE.

Howt, no ! Ye'll e'en be friends with honest Bauldy.
Come, come, shake hands ; this maun nae farder gae ;
Ye man forgi'e e'm.   I see the lad looks wae.

BAULDY.

In troth now, Mause, I have at Madge nae spite ;
But she abusing first, was a' the wyte
Of what has happen'd, and should therefore crave
My pardon first, and shall acquittance have.

MADGE.

I crave your pardon, gallows-face !—Gae greet,
And own your faut to her that ye wad cheat ;
Gae, or be blasted in your health and gear,
Till ye learn to perform as well as swear.
Vow and lowp back !—was e'er the like heard tell ?
Swith tak him deel, he's our lang out of hell !

BAULDY.

His presence be about us ! Curst were he
That were condemn'd for life to live with thee.

[*Runs off.*

MADGE.

(Laughing.)

I think I have towzled his harigalds a wee !
He'll no soon grein to tell his love to me.
He's but a rascal that would mint to serve
A lassie sae, he does but ill deserve !

MAUSE.

Ye towin'd him tightly.   I commend ye for't.
His bleeding snout gae me nae little sport ;

For this forenoon he had that scant of grace
And breeding baith, to tell me to my face
He hop'd I was a witch, and wadna stand
To lend him in this case my helping hand.

MADGE.

A witch ! how had ye patience this to bear,
And leave him een to see, or lugs to hear ?

MAUSE.

Auld wither'd hands and feeble joints like mine
Obliges fowk resentment to decline,
Till aft 'tis seen, when vigour fails, that we
With cunning can the lack of pith supply.
Thus I pat off revenge till it was dark,
Syne bade him come, and we should gang to wark.
I'm sure he'll keep his tryst ; and I came here
To seek your help that we the fool may fear.

MADGE.

And special sport we'll hae, as I protest;
Ye'll be the witch, and I shall play the ghaist.
A linen sheet wound round me like ane dead,
I'll cawk my face, and grane, and shake my head;
We'll fleg him sae, he'll mint nae mair to gang
A conjuring to do a lassie wrang.

MAUSE.

Then let us go ; for see, 'tis hard on night,—
The westlin cloud shines with a setting light.

[*Exeunt.*

SCENE II.

PROLOGUE.

When birds begin to nod upon the bough,
And the green swaird grows damp with falling dew,
While good Sir William is to rest retir'd,
The Gentle Shepherd, tenderly inspir'd,
Walks through the broom with Roger ever leel,
To meet, to comfort Meg, and tak fareweel.

PATIE and ROGER.

ROGER.

Wow ! but I'm cadgie, and my heart lowps light ;
O, Mr. Patrick, ay your thoughts were right !
Sure gentle fowks are farer seen than we,
That naething hae to brag of pedigree.
My Jenny now, who brak my heart this morn,
Is perfect yielding, sweet, and nae mair scorn :
I spak my mind—she heard—I spak again—
She smil'd—I kiss'd—I woo'd, nor woo'd in vain.

PATIE.

I'm glad to hear 't.—But O ! my change this day
Heaves up my joy ;—and yet I'm sometimes wae.
I've found a father, gently kind as brave,
And an estate that lifts me boon the lave ;
With looks all kindness, words that love confest,
He all the father to my soul exprest,
While close he held me to his manly breast :
" Such were the eyes," he said, " thus smil'd the mouth
Of thy lov'd mother, blessing o' my youth,
Wha set too soon !"—And while he praise bestow'd,
Adown his gracefu' cheeks a torrent flow'd.
My new-born joys, and this his tender tale,
Did, mingled thus, o'er a' my thoughts prevail ;
That, speechless, lang my late-ken'd sire I view'd,
While gushing tears my panting breast bedew'd :

Unusual transports made my head turn round,
Whilst I myself with rising raptures found
The happy son of ane sae much renown'd.
But he has heard!—Too faithful Symon's fear
Has brought my love for Peggy to his ear ;
Which he forbids :—ah ! this confounds my peace,
While thus to beat my heart must sooner cease.

ROGER.

How to advise ye, troth, I'm at a stand ;
But were 't my case, ye'd clear it up aff hand.

PATIE.

Duty and haflin reason plead his cause ;
But love rebels against all bounding laws;
Fixt in my soul the shepherdess excels,
And part of my new happiness repels.

SANG XVI.

TUNE—"Kirk wad let me be."

Duty and part of reason
    Plead strong on the parent's side ;
Which love superior calls treason ;
    The strongest must be obey'd.

For now, tho' I'm one of the gentry,
    My constancy falsehood repels ;
For change in my heart is no entry,
    Still there my dear Peggy excels.

ROGER.

Enjoy them baith.   Sir William will be won.
Your Peggy's bonny ; you're his only son.

PATIE.

She's mine by vows and stronger ties of love,
And frae these bands nae fate my mind shall move.
I'll wed nane else, thro' life I will be true,
But still obedience is a parent's due.

ROGER.

Is not our master and yourself to stay
Amang us here ? Or are ye gawn away
To London court, or ither far aff parts,
To leave your ain poor us with broken hearts ?

PATIE.

To Edinburgh straight to-morrow we advance,
To London neist, and afterwards to France,
Where I must stay some years, and learn to dance,
And twa three other monkey tricks. That done,
I come hame strutting in my red-heel'd shoon.
Then 'tis designed, when I can well behave,
That I maun be some petted thing's dull slave,
For some few bags of cash, that I wat weel,
I nae mair need nor carts do a third wheel.
But Peggy, dearer to me than my breath,
Sooner than hear sic news, shall hear my death.

ROGER.

"They wha have just enough can soundly sleep,
The owrecome only fashes fowk to keep."—
Good master Patrick, take your ain tale hame.

PATIE.

What was my morning thought, at night's the same;
The poor and rich but differ in the name.
Content's the greatest bliss we can procure
Frae 'boon the lift ; without it kings are poor.

ROGER.

But an estate like yours yields braw content,
When we but pick it scantly on the bent.
Fine claes, saft beds, sweet houses, sparkling wine,
Good cheer, and witty friends, whene'er ye dine ;
Submissive servants, honour, wealth, and ease,—
Wha's no content with these are ill to please.

PATIE.

Sae Roger thinks, and thinks not far amiss,
But mony a cloud hings hovering o'er their bliss ;
The passions rule the roast,—and if they're sour,
Like the lean kye, they'll soon the fat devour.
The spleen, tint honour, and affronted pride,
Stang like the sharpest goads in gentry's side.
The gouts and gravels, and the ill disease,
Are frequentest with fowk owrelaid with ease ;
While o'er the moor the shepherd, with less care,
Enjoys his sober wish and halesome air.

ROGER.

Lord, man, I wonder, ay, and it delights
My heart, whene'er I hearken to your flights ;
How gat ye a' that sense I fain wad lear,
That I may easier disappointments bear ?

PATIE.

Frae books, the wale of books, I gat some skill ;
These best can teach what's real good and ill.
Ne'er grudge ilk year to ware some stanes of cheese,
To gain these silent friends that ever please.

ROGER.

I'll do 't, and ye shall tell me which to buy ;
Faith I'se hae books, tho' I should sell my kye.
But now let's hear how you're design'd to move
Between Sir William's will and Peggy's love ?

PATIE.

Then here it lies.   His will maun be obey'd.
My vows I'll keep, and she shall be my bride ;—
But I some time this last design maun hide.
Keep you the secret close, and leave me here ;
I sent for Peggy,—yonder comes my dear.

ROGER.

Pleased that ye trust me with the secret, I
To wyle it frae me a' the deils defy.

Exit ROGER.

PATIE, *solus.*

With what a struggle must I now impart
My father's will to her that hauds my heart !
I ken she loves, and her saft soul will sink
While it stands trembling on the hated brink
Of disappointment.—Heav'n support my fair,
And let her comfort claim your tender care !—
Her eyes are red !—

Enter PEGGY.

——My Peggy, why in tears ?
Smile as ye wont, allow nae room for fears ;
Tho' I'm nae mair a shepherd, yet I'm thine.

PEGGY.

I dare not think sae high !   I now repine
At the unhappy chance that made not me
A gentle match, or still a herd kept thee.
Wha can withouten pain see, frae the coast,
The ship that bears his all like to be lost ?

Like to be carried by some reiver's hand,
Far frae his wishes, to some distant land ?

PATIE.

Ne'er quarrel fate, whilst it with me remains
To raise thee up, or still attend these plains.
My father has forbid our loves, I own ;
But love 's superior to a parent's frown.
I falsehood hate.   Come, kiss thy cares away ;
I ken to love as well as to obey.
Sir William's generous.—Leave the task to me
To make strict duty and true love agree.

PEGGY.

Speak on, speak ever thus, and still my grief ;
But short I dare to hope the fond relief.
New thoughts a gentler face will soon inspire,
That with nice airs swims round in silk attire ;
Then I, poor me ! with sighs may ban my fate,
When the young laird 's nae mair my heartsome Pate.
Nae mair again to hear sweet tales exprest
By the blyth shepherd that excell'd the rest,—
Nae mair be envied by the tattling gang
When Patie kiss'd me when I danc'd or sang,—
Nae mair, alake ! we'll on the meadows play,
And rin haff-breathless round the rucks of hay,
As aft-times I have fled from thee right fain
And fa'n on purpose that I might be tane,—
Nae mair around the foggy knowe I'll creep,
To watch and stare upon thee while asleep.
But hear my vow—'twill help to give me ease—
May sudden death, or deadly sair disease,
And warst of ills, attend my wretched life,
If e'er to ane but you I be a wife.

SANG XVII.

TUNE—" Wae's my heart that we should sunder."

Speak on, speak thus, and still my grief,
   Hold up a heart that's sinking under
These fears, that soon will want relief,
   When Pate must from his Peggy sunder.
A gentler face and silk attire,
   A lady rich in beauty's blossom,
Alake, poor me ! will now conspire
   To steal thee from thy Peggy's bosom.

No more the shepherd who excell'd
   The rest, whose wit made them to wonder,
Shall now his Peggy's praises tell,—
   Ah ! I can die, but never sunder.
Ye meadows where we often stray'd,
   Ye banks where we were wont to wander,
Sweet-scented rucks round which we play'd,—
   You'll lose your sweets when we're asunder.

Again, ah ! shall I never creep
   Around the knowe with silent duty,
Kindly to watch thee while asleep,
   And wonder at thy manly beauty ?
Hear, heav'n, while solemnly I vow,
   Tho' thou shouldst prove a wand'ring lover,
Thro' life, to thee I shall prove true,
   Nor be a wife to any other.

PATIE.

Sure heaven approves ; and be assur'd of me
I'll ne'er gang back of what I've sworn to thee.
And time (tho' time maun interpose a while,
And I maun leave my Peggy and this isle),—
Yet time, nor distance, nor the fairest face
(If there's a fairer), e'er shall fill thy place.

I'd hate my rising fortune, should it move
The fair foundation of our faithfu' love.
If at my foot were crowns and sceptres laid
To bribe my soul frae thee, delightful maid,
For thee I'd soon leave these inferior things
To sic as have the patience to be kings.—
Wherefore that tear? Believe, and calm thy mind.

PEGGY.

I greet for joy to hear thy words sae kind.
When hopes were sunk, and nought but mirk despair
Made me think life was little worth my care,
My heart was like to burst; but now I see
Thy gen'rous thoughts will save thy heart for me.
With patience, then, I'll wait each wheeling year,
Dream thro' that night, till my day-star appear;
And all the while, I'll study gentler charms
To make me fitter for my trav'ler's arms.
I'll gain on Uncle Glaud, he's far frae fool,
And will not grudge to put me through ilk school
Where I may manners learn.

SANG XVIII.

TUNE—"Tweedside."

When hope was quite sunk in despair,
    My heart it was going to break;
My life appear'd worthless my care,
    But now I will save 't for thy sake.
Where'er my love travels by day,
    Wherever he lodges by night,
With me his dear image shall stay,
    And my soul keep him ever in sight.

P

With patience, I'll wait the long year
　And study the gentlest charms,
Hope time away till thou appear,—
　To lock thee for ay in those arms.
Whilst thou wast a shepherd, I priz'd
　No higher degree in this life ;
But now, I'll endeavour to rise
　To a height is becoming thy wife.

For beauty that's only skin deep
　Must fade like the gowans of May ;
But, inwardly rooted, will keep
　For ever, without a decay.
Nor age, nor the changes of life,
　Can quench the fair fire of love,
If virtue's ingrain'd in the wife,
　And the husband have sense to approve.

PATIE.

That's wisely said ;
And what he wares that way shall be well paid.
Tho' without a' the little helps of art
Thy native sweets might gain a prince's heart,
Yet now, lest in our station we offend,
We must learn modes to innocence unken'd :—
Affect aft-times to like the thing we hate,
And drap serenity, to keep up state ;
Laugh when we're sad ; speak when we've nought to say ;
And for the fashion, when we're blyth, seem wae ;
Pay compliments to them we aft have scorn'd,
Then scandalize them when their backs are turn'd.

PEGGY.

If this is gentry, I had rather be
What I am still.　But I'll be ought with thee.

PATIE.

No, no, my Peggy, I but only jest
With gentry's apes ; for still, amang the best,
Good manners give integrity a bleeze,
When native virtues join the arts to please.

PEGGY.

Since with nae hazard and sae small expense
My lad frae books can gather siccan sense,
Then why, ah ! why should the tempestuous sea
Endanger thy dear life, and frighten me ?
Sir William's cruel, that wad force his son
For watna-whats, sae great a risk to run.

PATIE.

There is nae doubt but travelling does improve ;
Yet I would shun it for thy sake, my love.
But soon as I've shook aff my landwart cast
In foreign cities, hame to thee I'll haste.

PEGGY.

With every setting day and rising morn,
I'll kneel to heaven and ask thy safe return,
Under that tree, and on the suckler brae,
Where aft we wont, when bairns, to run and play ;
And to the hazel shaw, where first ye vow'd
Ye wad be mine, and I as eithly trow'd,
I'll aften gang, and tell the trees and flow'rs—
With joy—that they'll bear witness I am yours.

SANG XIX.

TUNE—" Bush aboon Traquair."

At setting day and rising morn,
    With soul that still shall love thee,
I'll ask of heaven thy safe return,
    With all that can improve thee.

I'll visit aft the birken bush
    Where first thou kindly told me
Sweet tales of love, and hid my blush
    Whilst round thou didst enfold me.

To all our haunts I will repair,
    By greenwood shaw or fountain ;
Or where the summer day I'd share
    With thee upon yon mountain.
There will I tell the trees and flow'rs,
    From thoughts unfeign'd and tender ;
By vows you're mine, by love is yours,
    A heart which cannot wander.

PATIE.

My dear, allow me from thy temples fair
A shining ringlet of thy flowing hair,
Which, as a sample of each lovely charm,
I'll aften kiss, and wear about my arm.

PEGGY.

Were ilka hair that appertains to me
Worth an estate, they all belong to thee.
My shears are ready, take what you demand,
And aught what love with virtue may command.

PATIE.

Nae mair we'll ask : but since we've little time,
To ware 't on words, wad border on a crime ;
Love's safter meaning better is exprest,
When 'tis with kisses on the heart imprest.

               [They embrace while the curtain is let down.

ACT V.

Scene I.

PROLOGUE.

See how poor Bauldy stares like ane possest,
And roars up Symon frae his kindly rest:
Bare-legg'd, with night-cap, and unbutton'd coat,
See the auld man comes forward to the sot.

SYMON and BAULDY.

SYMON.

What want ye, Bauldy, at this early hour,
When nature nods beneath the drowsy pow'r?
Far to the north, the scant approaching light
Stands equal 'twixt the morning and the night.
What gars ye shake, and glowre, and look sae wan?
Your teeth they chitter, hair like bristles stand.

BAULDY.

O len' me soon some water, milk, or ale,
My head's grown giddy,—legs with shaking fail:—
I'll ne'er dare venture forth at night my lane.
Alake! I'll never be mysell again;
I'll ne'er o'erput it.—Symon! O, Symon! O!

[Symon gives him a drink.

SYMON.

What ails thee, gowk, to make so loud ado?
You've wak'd Sir William, he has left his bed.
He comes, I fear ill-pleas'd; I hear his tread.

Enter SIR WILLIAM.

SIR WILLIAM.

How goes the night? does day-light yet appear?
Symon, you're very timeously asteer.

SYMON.

I'm sorry, Sir, that we've disturb'd your rest ;
But some strange thing has Bauldy's sp'rit opprest,
He's seen some witch, or wrestled with a ghaist.

BAULDY.

O ! ay ; dear Sir, in troth, 'tis very true ;
And I am come to make my plaint to you.

SIR WILLIAM.
(Smiling.)

I lang to hear't.

BAULDY.

                Ah ! Sir, the witch ca'd Mause,
That wins aboon the mill amang the haws,
First promis'd that she'd help me with her art,
To gain a bonny thrawart lassie's heart.
As she had trysted, I met wi'er this night ;
But may nae friend of mine get sic a fright !
For the curst hag, instead of doing me good,
(The very thought o't 's like to freeze my blood !)
Rais'd up a ghaist, or deil, I kenna whilk,
Like a dead corse in sheet as white as milk ;
Black hands it had, and face as wan as death.
Upon me fast the witch and it fell baith,
Lows'd down my breeks, while I, like a great fool,
Was labour'd as I wont to be at school.
My heart out of its hool was like to loup,
I pithless grew with fear, and had nae hope ;
Till, with an elritch laugh, they vanish'd quite.
Syne I, half dead with anger, fear, and spite,
Crap up, and fled straight frae them, Sir, to you,
Hoping your help to gi'e the deil his due.
I'm sure my heart will ne'er gi'e o'er to dunt,
Till in a fat tar-barrel Mause be burnt.

SIR WILLIAM.

Well, Bauldy, whate'er 's just shall granted be ;
Let Mause be brought this morning down to me.

BAULDY.

Thanks to your honour, soon shall I obey ;
But first I'll Roger raise, and twa three mae,
To catch her fast, or she get leave to squeel,
And cast her cantrips that bring up the deil.

[*Exit* BAULDY.

SIR WILLIAM.

Troth, Symon, Bauldy's mair afraid than hurt,
The witch and ghaist have made themselves good sport.
What silly notions crowd the clouded mind,
That is through want of education blind !

SYMON.

But does your honour think there's nae sic thing
As witches raising deils up through a ring ?
Syne playing tricks, a thousand I could tell,
Could never be contriv'd on this side hell.

SIR WILLIAM.

Such as the devil's dancing in a moor,
Amongst a few old women craz'd and poor,
Who were rejoic'd to see him frisk and lowp
O'er braes and bogs, with candles in his dowp ;
Appearing sometimes like a black horn'd cow,
Aft-times like Bawty, Badrans, or a Sow ;
Then with his train through airy paths to glide,
While they on cats, or clowns, or broomstaffs ride ;
Or in an egg-shell skim out o'er the main,
To drink their leader's health in France or Spain :
Then aft by night bumbaze hare-hearted fools,
By tumbling down their cupboards, chairs, and stools.

Whate'er 's in spells, or if there witches be,
Such whimsies seem the most absurd to me.

SYMON.

'Tis true enough, we ne'er heard that a witch
Had either meikle sense, or yet was rich :
But Mause, tho' poor, is a sagacious wife,
And lives a quiet and very honest life ;
That gars me think this hobleshew that 's past
Will end in nothing but a joke at last.

SIR WILLIAM.

I'm sure it will,—but see increasing light
Commands the imps of darkness down to night.
Bid raise my servants, and my horse prepare,
Whilst I walk out to take the morning air.

SANG XX.

TUNE—" Bonny grey-ey'd morn."

The bonny grey-ey'd morn begins to peep,
  And darkness flies before the rising ray,
The hearty hynd starts from his lazy sleep,
  To follow healthfu' labours of the day.
Without a guilty sting to wrinkle his brow,
  The lark and the linnet 'tend his levee,
And he joins the concert, driving the plow,
  From toil of grimace and pageantry free.

While fluster'd with wine, or madden'd with loss
  Of half an estate, the prey of a "main,"
The drunkard and gamester tumble and toss,
  Wishing for calmness and slumber in vain.
Be my portion health and quietness of mind,
  Plac'd at a due distance from parties and state ;
Where neither ambition, nor avarice blind,
  Reach him who has happiness link'd to his fate.

[*Exeunt.*

Scene II.

PROLOGUE.

While Peggy laces up her bosom fair,
With a blue snood Jenny binds up her hair :
Glaud by his morning ingle takes a beek ;
The rising sun shines motty through the reek ;
A pipe his mouth, the lasses please his een,
And now and then his joke maun intervene.

GLAUD.

I wish, my bairns, it may keep fair till night,
Ye do not use so soon to see the light :
Nae doubt now ye intend to mix the thrang,
To take your leave of Patrick or he gang ;
But do you think that now, when he's a laird,
That he poor landwart lasses will regard ?

JENNY.

Tho' he's young master now, I'm very sure
He has mair sense than slight auld friends, tho' poor ;
But yesterday he ga'e us mony a tug,
And kiss'd my cousin there frae lug to lug.

GLAUD.

Ay, ay, nae doubt o't, and he'll do't again !
But be advis'd, his company refrain.
Before, he as a shepherd sought a wife,
With her to live a chaste and frugal life ;
But now grown gentle, soon he will forsake
Sic godly thoughts, and brag of being a rake.

PEGGY.

A rake ! what's that ?—Sure, if it means ought ill,
He'll never be't, else I have tint my skill.

GLAUD.

Daft lassie, you ken nought of the affair ;
Ane young, and good, and gentle's unco rare.
A rake's a graceless spark, that thinks nae shame
To do what like of us thinks sin to name.
Sic are sae void of shame, they'll never stap
To brag how aften they have had the clap ;
They'll tempt young things like you with youdith flush'd,
Syne mak ye a' their jest when you're debauch'd.
Be wary then, I say, and never gi'e
Encouragement, or bourd with sic as he.

PEGGY.

Sir William's virtuous, and of gentle blood ;
And may not Patrick too, like him, be good ?

GLAUD.

That's true, and mony gentry mae than he,
As they are wiser, better are than we ;
But thinner sawn : they're sae puft up with pride,
There's mony of them mocks ilk haly guide
That shaws the gate to heav'n.   I've heard mysell
Some of them laugh at doomsday, sin, and hell.

JENNY.

Watch o'er us, father !—heh, that's very odd ;
Sure him that doubts a doomsday, doubts a God.

GLAUD.

Doubt ! why they neither doubt, nor judge, nor think,
Nor hope, nor fear ; but curse, debauch, and drink.—
But I'm no saying this, as if I thought
That Patrick to sic gates will e'er be brought.

PEGGY.

The Lord forbid !   Na, he kens better things.
But here comes aunt ; her face some ferly brings.

Enter MADGE.

MADGE.

Haste, haste ye ! We're a' sent for owre the gate,
To hear, and help to redd some odd debate
'Tween Mause and Bauldy, 'bout some witchcraft spell,
At Symon's house ; the knight sits judge himsell.

GLAUD.

Lend me my staff. Madge, lock the outer door.
And bring the lasses wi' ye ; I'll step before.

[Exit GLAUD.

MADGE.

Poor Meg !—Look, Jenny, was the like e'er seen ?
How bleer'd and red with greeting look her een !
This day her brankan wooer taks his horse,
To strut a gentle spark at Edinburgh cross :
To change his kent cut frae the branchy plane,
For a nice sword, and glancing headed cane ;
To leave his ram-horn spoons, and kitted whey,
For gentler tea that smells like new-won hay ;
To leave the green-sward dance, when we gae milk,
To rustle amang the beauties clad in silk.
But Meg, poor Meg ! maun with the shepherds stay,
And tak what God will send, in hodden grey.

PEGGY.

Dear aunt, what needs ye fash us wi' your scorn ?
That's no my faut that I'm nae gentler born.
Gif I the daughter of some laird had been,
I ne'er had notic'd Patie on the green :
Now since he rises, why should I repine ?
If he's made for another, he'll ne'er be mine :
And then, the like has been, if the decree
Designs him mine, I yet his wife may be.

MADGE.

A bonny story, troth !—But we delay ;
Prin up your aprons baith, and come away.

[Exeunt.

Scene III.

PROLOGUE.

Sir William fills the twa-arm'd chair,
  While Symon, Roger, Glaud, and Mause,
Attend, and with loud laughter hear
  Daft Bauldy bluntly plead his cause :—
For now it's tell'd him that the tawse
  Was handled by revengefu' Madge,
Because he brak good breeding's laws,
  And with his nonsense rais'd their rage.

Enter SIR WILLIAM, PATIE, ROGER, SYMON, GLAUD, BAULDY, and
MAUSE.

SIR WILLIAM.

And was that all ?—Well, Archibald, you was serv'd
No otherwise than what ye well deserv'd.
Was it so small a matter to defame
And thus abuse an honest woman's name ?
Besides your going about to have betray'd,
By perjury, an innocent young maid.

BAULDY.

Sir, I confess my faut thro' a' the steps,
And ne'er again shall be untrue to Neps.

MAUSE.

Thus far, Sir, he oblig'd me on the score,
I ken'd not that they thought me sic before.

BAULDY.

An't like your Honour, I believ'd it weel ;
But troth I was e'en doilt to seek the deil.

Yet, with your Honour's leave, tho' she's nae witch,
She's baith a slee and a revengfu' ——,
And that my some place finds.   But I had best
Haud in my tongue, for yonder comes the ghaist,
And the young bonny witch whase rosie cheek
Sent me without my wit the deil to seek.

Enter MADGE, PEGGY, *and* JENNY.

SIR WILLIAM.
(Looking at PEGGY.)
   Whose daughter's she that wears th' Aurora gown,
With face so fair, and locks a lovely brown ?—
How sparkling are her eyes ?—What's this I find !
The girl brings all my sister to my mind :
Such were the features once adorn'd a face,
Which death too soon depriv'd of sweetest grace.
Is this your daughter, Glaud ?

GLAUD.
                              Sir, she's my niece ;—
And yet she's not ;—but I should hald my peace.

SIR WILLIAM.
   This is a contradiction ; what d'ye mean ?—
She is, and she is not !—pray, Glaud, explain.

GLAUD.
   Because I doubt if I should make appear
What I have kept a secret thirteen year.

MAUSE.
You may reveal what I can fully clear.

SIR WILLIAM.
Speak soon ; I'm all impatience.

PATIE.

So am I ;
For much I hope ; and hardly yet know why.

GLAUD.

Then since my master orders, I obey :—
This bonny foundling, ae clear morn of May,
Close by the lee-side of my door I found,
All sweet and clean, and carefully hapt round
In infant weeds of rich and gentle make.—
What could they be (thought I) did thee forsake ?
Wha, warse than brutes, could leave expos'd to air
Sae much of innocence, sae sweetly fair,
Sae helpless young ;—for she appear'd to me
Only about twa towmonds auld to be.
I took her in my arms—the bairnie smil'd
With sic a look wad made a savage mild.
I hid the story, and she pass'd sincesyne
As a poor orphan, and a niece of mine.
Nor do I rue my care about the wean,
For she's well worth the pains that I have tane.
Ye see she's bonny ; I can swear she's good,
And am right sure she's come of gentle blood :—
Of whom I kenna :—naithing ken I mair,
Than what I to your Honour now declare.

SIR WILLIAM.

This tale seems strange !

PATIE.

The tale delights my ear.

SIR WILLIAM.

Command your joys, young man, till truth appear.

MAUSE.

That be my task.—Now, Sir, bid all be hush ;
Peggy may smile, thou hast no cause to blush.

Lang have I wish'd to see this happy day,
That I might safely to the truth give way ;
That I may now Sir William Worthy name
The best and nearest friend that she can claim.
He saw 't at first, and with quick eye did trace
His sister's beauties in her daughter's face.

SIR WILLIAM.

Old woman, do not rave ; prove what you say ;
'Tis dangerous in affairs like this to play.

PATIE.

What reason, Sir, can an old woman have
To tell a lie, when she's sae near her grave ?—
But how or why it should be truth, I grant,
I everything looks like a reason want.

OMNES.

The story's odd !—we wish we heard it out.

SIR WILLIAM.

Make haste, good woman, and resolve each doubt.

MAUSE.

(Leading PEGGY to SIR WILLIAM.)

Sir, view me well.   Has fifteen years so plew'd
A wrinkled face that you have often view'd,
That here I as an unknown stranger stand,
Who nurs'd her mother that now holds my hand ?
Yet stronger proofs I'll give if you demand.

SIR WILLIAM.

Ha, honest nurse !—where were my eyes before ?
I know thy faithfulness, and need no more :
Yet from the lab'rinth to lead out my mind,
Say, to expose her who was so unkind ?—

[SIR WILLIAM embraces PEGGY, and makes her sit by him.]

Yes, surely thou'rt my niece !—Truth must prevail !—
But no more words till Mause relate her tale.

PATIE.

Good nurse, dispatch thy story wing'd with blisses,
That I may give my cousin fifty kisses.

MAUSE.

Then it was I that sav'd her infant life,
Her death being threaten'd by an uncle's wife.
The story's lang :—but I the secret knew,
How they pursu'd with avaricious view
Her rich estate, of which they're now possest.
All this to me a confident confest.
I heard with horror, and with trembling dread
They'd smoor the sakeless orphan in her bed.
That very night, when all were sunk in rest,
At midnight hour the floor I saftly prest,
And staw the sleeping innocent away,
With whom I travell'd some few miles ere day.
All day I hid me ;—when the day was done,
I kept my journey, lighted by the moon ;
Till eastward fifty miles I reach'd these plains,
Where needful plenty glads your cheerful swains,
For fear of being found out, and to secure
My charge, I laid her at this shepherd's door ;
And took a neighbouring cottage here, that I,
Whate'er should happen to her, might be by.
Here honest Glaud, himsell, and Symon may
Remember well, how I that very day
Frae Roger's father took my little crove.

GLAUD.

(With tears of joy running down his beard.)

I well remember't.—Lord reward your love !—
Lang have I wish'd for this ; for aft I thought
Sic knowledge some time should about be brought.

PATIE.

'Tis now a crime to doubt !   My joys are full,
With due obedience to my parent's will.
Sir, with paternal love survey her charms ;
And blame me not for rushing to her arms ;
She's mine by vows, and would, tho' still unknown,
Have been my wife, when I my vows durst own.

SIR WILLIAM.

My niece, my daughter, welcome to my care ;
Sweet image of thy mother, good and fair !
Equal with Patrick :—now my greatest aim
Shall be to aid your joys, and well-match'd flame.
My boy, receive her from your father's hand,
With as good will as either would demand.

[PATIE and PEGGY embrace, and kneel to SIR WILLIAM.]

PATIE.

With as much joy this blessing I receive,
As ane wad life that's sinking in a wave.

SIR WILLIAM.

(Raises them.)

I give you both my blessing.   May your love
Produce a happy race, and still improve.

PEGGY.

My wishes are complete ; my joys arise,
While I'm half dizzy with the blest surprise !
And am I then a match for my ain lad,
That for me so much generous kindness had ?
Lang may Sir William bless these happy plains,
Happy while heaven grant he on them remains.

R

PATIE.

Be lang our guardian, still our master be,
We'll only crave what you shall please to gi'e ;
Th' estate be yours, my Peggy's ane to me.

GLAUD.

I hope your Honour now will take amends
Of them that sought her life for wicked ends.

SIR WILLIAM.

The base unnatural villain soon shall know
That eyes above watch the affairs below.
I'll strip him soon of all to her pertains,
And make him reimburse his ill-got gains.

PEGGY.

To me the views of wealth and an estate
Seem light, when put in balance with my Pate ;
For his sake only I'll ay thankful bow
For such a kindness, best of men, to you.

SYMON.

What double blythness wakens up this day !—
I hope now, sir, you'll no soon haste away.
Shall I unsaddle your horse, and gar prepare
A dinner for ye of hale country fare ?
See how much joy unwrinkles every brow,
Our looks hing on the twa, and doat on you ;
Even Bauldy, the bewitch'd, has quite forgot
Fell Madge's tawse, and pawky Mause's plot.

SIR WILLIAM.

Kindly old man ! remain with you this day !
I never from these fields again will stray.
Masons and wrights shall soon my house repair,
And busy gardeners shall new planting rear ;

My father's hearty table soon you'll see
Restor'd, and my best friends rejoice with me.

SYMON.

That's the best news I've heard this twenty year ;
New day breaks up,—rough times begin to clear.

GLAUD.

God save the king ! and save Sir William lang
To enjoy their ain, and raise the shepherd's sang !

ROGER.

Wha winna dance ? Wha will refuse to sing ?
What shepherd's whistle winna lilt the spring ?

BAULDY.

I'm friends with Mause; with very Madge I'm gree'd ;
Altho' they skelpit me when woodly fleid.
I'm now fu' blyth, and frankly can forgive
To join and sing,—" Lang may Sir William live !"

MADGE.

Lang may he live !   And, Bauldy, learn to steek
Your gab a wee, and think before ye speak ;
And never ca' her auld that wants a man,
Else ye may yet some witch's fingers ban.
This day I'll with the youngest of you rant,
And brag for ay that I was ca'd the aunt
Of our young lady, my dear bonny bairn !

PEGGY.

No other name I'll ever for you learn.
And, my good nurse, how shall I gratefu' be
For a' thy matchless kindness done for me ?

MAUSE.

The flowing pleasure of this happy day
Does fully all I can require repay.

SIR WILLIAM.

To faithful Symon, and, kind Glaud, to you,
And to your heirs, I give in endless feu
The mailens ye possess, as justly due,
For acting like kind fathers to the pair,
Who have enough besides, and these can spare.
Mause, in my house in calmness close your days,
With nought to do but sing your Maker's praise.

OMNES.

The Lord of heaven return your Honour's love,
Confirm your joys, and a' your blessings roove !

PATIE.
(Presenting ROGER to SIR WILLIAM.)

Sir, here's my trusty friend that always shar'd
My bosom secrets, ere I was a laird.
Glaud's daughter, Janet, (Jenny, think nae shame),
Rais'd and maintains in him a lover's flame.
Lang was he dumb, at last he spak and won,
And hopes to be our honest uncle's son ;
Be pleas'd to speak to Glaud for his consent,
That nane may wear a face of discontent.

SIR WILLIAM.

My son's demand is fair.   Glaud, let me crave
That trusty Roger may your daughter have
With frank consent ; and while he does remain
Upon these fields, I make him chamberlain.

GLAUD.

You crowd your bounties, Sir !—what can we say,
But that we're dyvours that can ne'er repay ?—

Whate'er your Honour wills I shall obey.
Roger, my daughter with my blessing take,
And still our master's right your business make ;
Please him, be faithful, and this auld grey head
Shall nod with quietness down among the dead.

ROGER.

I ne'er was good at speaking a' my days,
Or ever loo'd to make o'er great a fraise ;
But for my master, father, and my wife,
I will employ the cares of all my life.

SIR WILLIAM.

My friends, I'm satisfy'd you'll all behave,
Each in his station, as I'd wish or crave.
Be ever virtuous, soon or late ye'll find
Reward and satisfaction to your mind.
The maze of life sometimes looks dark and wild,
And oft when hopes are highest we're beguil'd ;
Aft when we stand on brinks of dark despair
Some happy turn with joy dispels our care.
Now all's at rights, who sings best let me hear.

PEGGY.

When you demand, I readiest should obey.
I'll sing you ane,—the newest that I hae.

SANG XXI.

TUNE—"Corn-riggs are bonny."

My Patie is a lover gay,
    His mind is never muddy,
His breath is sweeter than new hay,
    His face is fair and ruddy ;
His shape is handsome,—middle size,—
    He's comely in his wauking,

The shining of his een surprise,
   'Tis heaven to hear him tauking.

Last night, I met him on a bawk
   Where yellow corn was growing,
There, mony a kindly word he spak
   That set my heart a-glowing.
He kiss'd, and vow'd he wad be mine,
   And loo'd me best of ony ;
That gars me like to sing sinsyne,—
   O corn-riggs are bonny !

Let lasses of a silly mind
   Refuse what maist they're wanting,
Since we for yielding were design'd,
   We chastely should be granting.
Then I'll comply and marry Pate,
   And syne my cockernony
He's free to touzle air and late,
   Where corn-riggs are bonny.

                    [*Exeunt* OMNES.

L Y R I C.

XI

THE DEDICATION

PREFIXED TO

THE TEA-TABLE MISCELLANY;

A COLLECTION OF SONGS,

From which the following, composed by ALLAN RAMSAY, *are extracted.*

1724—1727.

Behold, and listen, while the fair
Breaks in sweet sounds the willing air,
And with her own breath fans the fire
Which her bright eyes do first inspire :
What reason can that love control,
Which more than one way courts the soul?

E. W.

TO

Ilka lovely British lass,
   Frae ladies Charlotte, Anne, and Jean,
Down to ilka bonny singing Bess
   Wha dances barefoot on the green.

DEAR LASSES,
YOUR most humble slave,
   Wha ne'er to serve you shall decline,
Kneeling wad your acceptance crave,
   When he presents this sma' propine :—

S

Then take it kindly to your care,
    Revive it with your tunefu' notes ;
Its beauties will look sweet and fair,
    Arising saftly thro' your throats.

The wanton wee thing will rejoice,
    When tented by a sparkling eye,
The spinnet tinkling with her voice,
    It lying on her lovely knee.

While kettles dringe on ingles dour,
    Or clashes stay the lazy lass,
Their sangs may ward ye frae the sour,
    And gaily vacant minutes pass.

E'en while the tea's filled reeking round,
    Rather than plot a tender tongue,
Treat a' the circling lugs wi' sound,
    Syne safely sip when ye have sung.

May happiness haud up your hearts,
    And warm ye lang with loving fires !
May powers propitious play their parts,
    In matching you to your desires !

                                        A. RAMSAY.

EDINBURGH, January 1st, 1724.

XII.

WINE AND MUSIC.

1721.

SYMON.

O COLIN ! how dull is't to be,
    When a soul is sinking wi' pain,
To one who is pained like me ;
      My life's grown a load,
      And my faculties nod,
    While I sigh for cold Jeanie in vain.
By beauty and scorn I am slain,
    The wound it is mortal and deep,
My pulses beat low in each vein,
    And threaten eternal sleep.

COLIN.

Come, here are the best cures for thy wounds ;
    O boy, the cordial bowl !
With soft harmonious sounds ;
Wounds ! these can cure all wounds,
    With soft harmonious sounds,
    And pull of the cordial bowl.
O Symon ! sink thy care, and tune up thy drooping soul.

Above, the gods beinly bouze,
    When round they meet in a ring ;
They cast away care, and carouse
    Their nectar, while they sing.
    Then drink and cheerfully sing,
These make the blood circle fine ;
      Strike up the music,
      The safest physic,
Compounded with sparkling wine.

XIII.

HORACE TO VIRGIL.

O Cyprian goddess ! twinkle clear,
And Helen's brithers ay appear ;
Ye stars wha shed a lucky light,
Auspicious ay keep in a sight.
King Æol, grant a tydie tirl,
But boast the blasts that rudely whirl.
Dear ship, be canny with your care,
At Athens land my Virgil fair,
Syne soon and safe, baith lith and spaul,
Bring hame the tae haff o' my saul.

Daring and unco' stout he was,
With heart hool'd in three sloughs of brass,
Wha ventur'd first on the rough sea
With hempen branks and horse of tree.
Wha in the weak machine durst ride
Thro' tempests and a rairing tide ;
Not clinty craigs, nor hurricane
That drives the Adriatic main,
And gars the ocean gowl and quake,
Could e'er a soul sae sturdy shake.
The man wha could sic rubs win o'er,
Without a wink, at death might glow'r,
Wha, unconcern'd, can take his sleep
Amang the monsters of the deep.

Jove vainly twin'd the sea and eard,
Since mariners are not afraid
With laws of nature to dispense,
And impiously treat Providence.
Audacious men at nought will stand,
When vicious passions have command.
Prometheus ventur'd up, and staw
A lowan coal frae heav'n's high ha' ;

Unsonsy theft, which fevers brought
In bikes, which fowks like sybows hought ;
Then death, erst slaw, began to ling,
And fast as haps to dart his sting.
Neist, Dedalus must contradict
Nature, forsooth, and feathers stick
Upon his back, syne upward streek,
And in at Jove's high winnocks keek ;
While Hercules, wi's timber-mell,
Plays rap upo' the yates of hell.

What is't man winna ettle at ?
E'en wi' the gods he'll bell the cat.
Tho' Jove be very laith to kill,
They winna let his bowt lye still.

XIV.

AN ODE TO MR. F——.

1721.

Now gowans sprout and lavrocks sing,
And welcome west winds warm the spring,
O'er hill and dale they saftly blaw,
And drive the winter's cauld awa.
The ships, lang gyzen'd at the peer,
Now spread their sails and smoothly steer ;
The nags and nowt hate wissen'd strae,
And frisking to the fields they gae ;
Nor hinds wi' elson and hemp lingle,
Sit soleing shoon out o'er the ingle.
Now bonny haughs their verdure boast,
That late were clad wi' snaw and frost.
With her gay train, the Paphian queen
By moonlight dances on the green ;
She leads, while nymphs and graces sing,
And trip around the fairy ring.

Meantime, poor Vulcan, hard at thrift,
Gets mony a sair and heavy lift,
Whilst rinnen down, his haff-blind lads
Blaw up the fire, and thump the gads.

Now leave your fitsted on the dew,
And busk yersell in habit new;
Be gratefu' to the guiding pow'rs,
And blythly spend your easy hours.
O canny F——! tutor time,
And live as lang's y're in your prime;
That ill-bred Death has nae regard
To king or cottar, or a laird.
As soon a castle he'll attack,
As wa's of divots, roof'd wi' thack.
Immediately, we'll a' take flight
Unto the mirk realms of night,
As stories gang, with ghaists to roam
In gloomy Pluto's gousty dome;
Bid fair good-day to pleasure, syne
Of bonny lasses and red wine.

Then deem ilk little care a crime,
Dares waste an hour of precious time;
And since our life's sae unco short,
Enjoy it a', ye've nae mair for't.

———————

XV.

AN ODE TO THE PH——.

1721.

LOOK up to Pentland's tow'ring top,
    Buried beneath great wreaths of snaw,
O'er ilka cleugh, ilk scar, and slap,
    As high as ony Roman wa'.

Driving their baws frae whins or tee,
   There's no nae gowfer to be seen,
Nor dousser fowk wysing a-jee
   The byast bouls on Tamson's green.

Then fling on coals, and ripe the ribs,
   And beek the house baith but and ben,
That mutchkin stoup it hauds but dribs,
   Then let's get in the tappit hen.

Good claret best keeps out the cauld,
   And drives away the winter soon;
It makes a man baith gash and bauld,
   And heaves his saul beyond the moon.

Leave to the gods your ilka care,
   If that they think us worth their while
They can a' rowth of blessings spare,
   Which will our fasheous fears beguile.

For what they have a mind to do,
   That will they do, should we gang wud;
If they command the storms to blaw,
   Then upo' sight the hailstanes thud.

But soon as e'er they cry—" Be quiet,"
   The blatt'ring winds dare nae mair move,
But cour into their caves, and wait
   The high command of supreme Jove.

Let neist day come as it thinks fit,
   The present minute's only ours;
On pleasure let's employ our wit,
   And laugh at fortune's feckless powers.

Be sure ye dinna quat the grip
   Of ilka joy when ye are young,

Before auld age your vitals nip,
    And lay ye twafald o'er a rung.

Sweet youth's a blyth and heartsome time;
    Then, lads and lasses, while it's May,
Gae pou the gowan in its prime
    Before it wither and decay.

Watch the saft minutes of delyte
    When Jenny speaks beneath her breath,
And kisses, laying a' the wyte
    On you, if she keap ony skaith.

" Haith, ye're ill-bred," she'll smiling say,
    " Ye'll worry me, you greedy rook ;"
Syne frae your arms she'll rin away,
    And hide hersell in some dark nook.

Her laugh will lead you to the place
    Where lies the happiness you want,
And plainly tells you to your face
    Nineteen nay says are ha'f a grant.

Now to her heaving bosom cling,
    And sweetly toolie for a kiss,
Frae her fair finger whop a ring,
    As taiken of a future bliss.

These bennisons, I'm very sure,
    Are of the gods' indulgent grant;
Then, surly carles, whisht,—forbear
    To plague us with your whining cant.

XVI.

A BALLAD ON BONNY KATE.
1728.

CEASE, poets, your cunning devising
   Of rhymes that low beauties o'er-rate ;
They all, like the stars at the rising
   Of Phœbus, must yield to fair Kate.

We sing, and we think it our duty
   To admire the kind blessings of fate,
That has favour'd the earth with such beauty
   As shines so divinely in Kate.

In her smiles, in her features and glances,
   The graces shine forth in full state,
While the god of love dang'rously dances
   On the neck and white bosom of Kate.

How straight, how well-turn'd and genteel, are
   Her limbs ! and how graceful her gait !
Their hearts made of stone or of steel are,
   That are not adorers of Kate.

But ah ! what a sad palpitation
   Feels the heart, and how simple and blate
Must he look, almost dead with vexation,
   Whose love is fixt hopeless on Kate ?

Had I all the charms of Adonis,
   And galeons freighted with plate,
As Solomon wise, I'd think none is,
   So worthy of all as dear Kate.

Ah ! had she for me the same passion,
   I'd tune the lyre early and late ;
The sage's song on his Circassian
   Should yield to my sonnets on Kate.

His pleasure each moment shall blossom
   Unfading, gets her for his mate ;

T

He'll grasp ev'ry bliss in his bosom,
   That's linked by Hymen to Kate.

Pale Envy may raise up false stories,
   And hell may prompt malice and hate ;
But nothing shall sully their glories
   Who are shielded with virtue like Kate.

" This name," say ye, "many a lass has,
   " And t' apply it may raise a debate ;"
But sure he as dull as an ass is,
   That cannot join Cochran to Kate.

XVII.

TO DR. J. C.

WHO GOT THE FOREGOING TO GIVE THE YOUNG LADY.

HERE, happy Doctor, take this sonnet,
   Bear to the fair the faithful strains ;
Bow, make a leg, and doff your bonnet,
   And get a kiss for Allan's pains.

For such a ravishing reward,
   The Cloud-Compeller's self would try
To imitate a British bard,
   And bear his ballads from the sky.

XVIII.

AN ODE ON DRINKING.

HENCE every thing that can
Disturb the quiet of man !
   Be blyth, my soul,
   In a full bowl
   Drown thy care,
   And repair
   The vital stream,

Since life's a dream,
Let wine abound,
And healths go round,
We'll sleep more sound ;
And let the dull, unthinking mob pursue
Each endless wish, and still their care renew.

XIX.

THE LAST TIME I CAME O'ER THE MOOR.

THE last time I came o'er the moor,
I left my love behind me.
Ye pow'rs ! what pain do I endure,
When soft ideas mind me !
Soon as the ruddy morn display'd
The beaming day ensuing,
I met betimes my lovely maid,
In fit retreats for wooing.

Beneath the cooling shade we lay,
Gazing and chastely sporting ;
We kiss'd and promis'd time away,
Till night spread her black curtain.
I pity'd all beneath the skies,
E'en kings, when she was nigh me ;
In raptures I beheld her eyes,
Which could but ill deny me.

Should I be call'd where cannons roar,
Where mortal steel may wound me ;
Or cast upon some foreign shore,
Where dangers may surround me ;
Yet hopes again to see my love,
To feast on glowing kisses,
Shall make my cares at distance move,
In prospect of such blisses.

In all my soul there's not one place
　To let a rival enter ;
Since she excels in ev'ry grace,
　In her my love shall centre.
Sooner the seas shall cease to flow,
　Their waves the Alps shall cover,
On Greenland ice shall roses grow,
　Before I cease to love her.

The next time I go o'er the moor,
　She shall a lover find me ;
And that my faith is firm and pure,
　Tho' I left her behind me.
Then Hymen's sacred bonds shall chain
　My heart to her fair bosom,
There, while my being does remain,
　My love more fresh shall blossom.

XX.

THE LASS OF PATIE'S MILL.

THE lass of Patie's mill,
　So bonny, blyth, and gay,
In spite of all my skill,
　She stole my heart away.
When tedding of the hay,
　Bareheaded on the green,
Love 'midst her locks did play,
　And wanton'd in her een.

Her arms white, round, and smooth,
　Breasts rising in their dawn,
To age it would give youth
　To press 'em with his hand.
Thro' all my spirits ran
　An ecstasy of bliss,

When I such sweetness fand
   Wrapt in a balmy kiss.

Without the help of art,
   Like flowers which grace the wild,
She did her sweets impart
   Whene'er she spoke or smil'd.
Her looks they were so mild,
   Free from affected pride,
She me to love beguil'd,—
   I wish'd her for my bride.

O had I all the wealth
   Hopeton's high mountains* fill,
Insur'd lang life and health,
   And pleasure at my will;
I'd promise and fulfil
   That none but bonny she,
The lass of Patie's mill,
   Should share the same wi' me.

XXI.

YE WATCHFUL GUARDIANS OF THE FAIR.

YE watchful guardians of the fair,
Who skiff on wings of ambient air,
Of my dear Delia take a care,
   And represent her lover
With all the gaiety of youth,
With honour, justice, love, and truth,—
Till I return her passions sooth,
   For me in whispers move her.

---

* Thirty-three miles south-west of Edinburgh, where the Earl of Hopeton's mines of gold and lead are.

Be careful no base sordid slave,
With soul sunk in a golden grave,
Who knows no virtue but to save,
        With glaring gold bewitch her ;
Tell her for me she was design'd,
For me who know how to be kind,
And have more plenty in my mind
        Than one who's ten times richer.

Let all the world turn upside down,
And fools run an eternal round,
In quest of what can ne'er be found,
        To please their vain ambition.
Let little minds great charms espy
In shadows which at distance lie,
Whose hop'd-for pleasure, when come nigh,
        Proves nothing in fruition.

But cast into a mould divine,
Fair Delia does with lustre shine,
Her virtuous soul's an ample mine,
        Which yields a constant treasure.
Let poets in sublimest lays
Employ their skill her fame to raise ;
Let sons of music pass whole days,
        With well-tun'd reeds to please her.

XXII.

THE YELLOW HAIRED LADDIE.

In April, when primroses paint the sweet plain,
And summer approaching rejoiceth the swain,
The yellow-hair'd laddie would oftentimes go
To wilds and deep glens where the hawthorn trees grow.

There, under the shade of an old sacred thorn,
With freedom he sang his loves ev'ning and morn ;

He sang with so soft and enchanting a sound,
That sylvans and fairies unseen danc'd around.

The shepherd thus sung :—Tho' young Maya be fair,
Her beauty is dash'd with a scornful proud air ;
But Susie was handsome, and sweetly could sing,
Her breath, like the breezes, perfum'd in the spring.

That Madia in all the gay bloom of her youth,
Like the moon was inconstant, and never spoke truth ;
But Susie was faithful, good-humour'd and free,
And fair as the goddess who sprung from the sea.

That mamma's fine daughter, with all her great dow'r,
Was awkwardly airy, and frequently sour :
Then sighing, he wish'd, would parents agree,
The witty sweet Susie his mistress might be.

XXIII.

NANNY O.

WHILE some for pleasure pawn their health,
    'Twixt Lais * and the bagnio,
I'll save myself, and without stealth
    Kiss and caress my Nanny O.
She bids more fair to engage a Jove,
    Than Leda did or Danae O †
Were I to paint the queen of love,
    None else should sit but Nanny O.

How joyfully my spirits rise,
    When dancing she moves finely O ;
I guess what heav'n is by her eyes,
    Which sparkle so divinely O.

---

* A famous Corinthian courtezan.
† Two beauties to whom Jove made love ; to one in the figure of a swan, to the other in a golden shower.

Attend my vow, ye gods, while I
　　Breathe in the blest Britannio,
None's happiness I shall envy,
　　As long's ye grant me Nanny O.

Chorus.
My bonny bonny Nanny O,
My loving charming Nanny O,
I care not tho' the world do know
How dearly I love Nanny O.

XXIV.

BONNY JEAN.

LOVE's goddess, in a myrtle grove,
　　Said, " Cupid, bend thy bow with speed,
Nor let the shaft at random rove,
　　For Jenny's haughty heart must bleed."
The smiling boy, with divine art,
　　From Paphos shot an arrow keen,
Which flew unerring to the heart,
　　And kill'd the pride of bonny Jean.

No more the nymph, with haughty air,
　　Refuses Willie's kind address ;
Her yielding blushes shew no care,
　　But too much fondness to suppress.
No more the youth is sullen now,
　　But looks the gayest on the green,
Whilst every day he spies some new
　　Surprising charms in bonny Jean.

A thousand transports crowd his breast,
　　He moves as light as fleeting wind,
His former sorrows seem a jest,
　　Now when his Jeanie is turn'd kind.

Riches he looks on with disdain,
    The glorious fields of war look mean,
The cheerful hound and horn give pain,
    If absent from his bonny Jean.

The day he spends in am'rous gaze,
    Which, e'en in summer, shorten'd seems,
When sunk in down, with glad amaze,
    He wonders at her in his dreams.
All charms disclos'd, she looks more bright
    Than Troy's fair prize—the Spartan queen ;
With breaking day, he lifts his sight
    And pants to be with bonny Jean.

XXV.

AULD LANGSYNE.

SHOULD auld acquaintance be forgot,
    Tho' they return with scars ?
These are the noblest hero's lot
    Obtain'd in glorious wars.
Welcome, my Varo, to my breast,
    Thy arms about me twine,
And make me once again as blest
    As I was langsyne.

Methinks around us on each bough
    A thousand Cupids play,
Whilst thro' the groves I walk with you,
    Each object makes me gay.
Since your return, the sun and moon
    With brighter beams do shine,
Streams murmur soft notes while they run,
    As they did langsyne.

Despise the court and din of state ;
    Let that to their share fall

Who can esteem such slav'ry great,
   While bounded like a ball.
But sunk in love, upon my arms
   Let your brave head recline ;
We'll please ourselves with mutual charms,
   As we did langsyne.

O'er moor and dale with your gay friend
   You may pursue the chase,
And, after a blyth bottle, end
   All cares in my embrace.
And in a vacant rainy day
   You shall be wholly mine ;
We'll make the hours run smooth away,
   And laugh at langsyne.

The hero, pleas'd with the sweet air
   And signs of gen'rous love
Which had been utter'd by the fair,
   Bow'd to the pow'rs above.
Next day, with glad consent and haste,
   Th' approach'd the sacred shrine,
Where the good priest the couple blest,
   And put them out of pine.

XXVI.

THE PENITENT.

Tune—"The Lass of Livingston."

PAIN'D with her slighting Jamie's love
   Bell dropt a tear, Bell dropt a tear,
The gods descended from above,
   Well pleas'd to hear, well pleas'd to hear.
They heard the praises of the youth
   From her own tongue, from her own tongue,

Who now converted was to truth ;
    And thus she sung, and thus she sung :—

" Blest days when our ingenuous sex
    More frank and kind, more frank and kind,
Did not their lov'd adorers vex,
    But spoke their mind, but spoke their mind.
Repenting now, she promis'd fair,
    Would he return, would he return,
She ne'er again would give him care,
    Or cause to mourn, or cause to mourn.

Why lov'd I the deserving swain,
    Yet still thought shame, yet still thought shame,
When he my yielding heart did gain,
    To own my flame, to own my flame ?
Why took I pleasure to torment,
    And seem'd too coy, and seem'd too coy ?
Which makes me now, alas ! lament
    My slighted joy, my slighted joy.

Ye fair, while beauty's in its spring,
    Own your desire, own your desire,
While Love's young power with his soft wing
    Fans up the fire, fans up the fire.
O do not with a silly pride,
    Or low design, or low design,
Refuse to be a happy bride,
    But answer plain, but answer plain."

Thus the fair mourner wail'd her crime
    With flowing eyes, with flowing eyes ;
Glad Jamie heard her all the time
    With sweet surprise, with sweet surprise.
Some god had led him to the grove,
    His mind unchang'd, his mind unchang'd,—
Flew to her arms, and cry'd—" My love,
    I am reveng'd, I am reveng'd."

XXVII.

LOVE'S CURE.

TUNE—"Peggy, I must love thee."

As from a rock, past all relief,
    The shipwrecked Colin spying
His native home, o'ercome with grief,
    Half sunk in waves, and dying ;
With the next morning sun he spies
A ship, which gives unhop'd surprise,
New life springs up, he lifts his eyes
    With joy, and waits her motion,—

So when, by her whom I long lov'd,
    I scorn'd was and deserted,
Low with despair my spirits mov'd
    To be for ever parted.
Thus drooped I, till diviner grace
I found in Peggy's mind and face ;
Ingratitude appear'd then base,
    But virtue more engaging.

Then, now, since happily I've hit,
    I'll have no more delaying ;
Let beauty yield to manly wit,
    We lose ourselves in staying :
I'll haste dull courtship to a close
Since marriage can my fears oppose,
Why should we happy minutes lose,
    Since, Peggy, I must love thee ?

Men may be foolish, if they please,
    And deem't a lover's duty
To sigh and sacrifice their ease,
    Doating on a proud beauty:
Such was my case for many a year,
Still hope succeeded to my fear,
False Betty's charms now disappear
    Since Peggy's far outshine them.

XXVIII.

BESSY BELL AND MARY GRAY.

O, Bessy Bell and Mary Gray !
    They are twa bonny lasses ;
They bigg'd a bower on yon burnbrae,
    And theck'd it o'er with rashes.
Fair Bessy Bell I loo'd yestreen,
    And thought I ne'er could alter ;
But Mary Gray's twa pawky een
    They gar my fancy falter.

Now Bessy's hair 's like a lint tap,
    She smiles like a May morning,
When Phœbus starts frae Thetis' lap
    The hills with rays adorning.
White is her neck, saft is her hand,
    Her waist and feet's fou genty,
With ilka grace she can command,
    Her lips, O wow ! they're dainty.

And Mary's locks are like the craw,
    Her eyes like diamonds' glances ;
She's ay sae clean redd up and braw,
    She kills whene'er she dances.
Blyth as a kid, with wit at will,
    She blooming, tight, and tall is ;
And guides her airs sae gracefu' still,—
    O Jove ! she's like thy Pallas.

Dear Bessy Bell and Mary Gray,
    Ye unco sair oppress us,
Our fancies jee between you twae,—
    Ye are sic bonny lasses.
Wae's me ! for baith I canna get,
    To ane by law we're stinted ;
Then I'll draw cuts, and take my fate,
    And be with ane contented.

XXIX.

THE YOUNG LAIRD AND EDINBURGH KATY.

Now wat ye wha I met yestreen
    Coming down the street, my jo?
My mistress, in her tartan screen,
    Fou bonny, braw, and sweet, my jo.
"My dear," (quoth I), "thanks to the night,
    That never wish'd a lover ill;
Since ye're out of your mother's sight
    Let's tak a walk up to the hill.

" O Katy! wiltu gang wi' me,
    And leave the dinsome town awhile?
The blossom's sprouting frae the tree
    And a' the simmer's gawn to smile.
The mavis, nightingale, and lark,—
    The bleeting lambs and whistling hynd,—
In ilka dale, green, shaw, and park,
    Will nourish health, and glad ye'r mind.

" Soon as the clear goodman of day
    Does bend his morning draught of dew,
We'll gae to some burnside and play,
    And gather flow'rs to busk ye'r brow.
We'll pou the daisies on the green,
    The lucken gowans frae the bog;
Between hands now and then we'll lean,
    And sport upo' the velvet fog.

There's up into a pleasant glen,
    A wee piece frae my father's tower,
A canny, saft, and flow'ry den,
    Which circling birks has form'd a bower:
Whene'er the sun grows high and warm,
    We'll to the cawler shade remove;
There will I lock thee in mine arms,
    And love and kiss, and kiss and love.

XXX.

KATY'S ANSWER.

My mither's ay glowran o'er me,
Though she did the same before me ;
    I canna get leave
    To look to my love,
Or else she'll be like to devour me.

Right fain wad I take ye'r offer,
Sweet Sir, but I'll tine my tocher ;
    Then, Sandy, ye'll fret,
    And wyte ye'r poor Kate,
Whene'er ye keek in your toom coffer.

For though my father has plenty
Of siller and plenishing dainty,
    Yet he's unco sweer
    To twin wi' his gear ;
And sae we hae need to be tenty.

Tutor my parents wi' caution,
Be wylie in ilka motion ;
    Brag well o' ye'r land,
    And there's my leal hand,
Win them, I'll be at your devotion.

XXXI.

MARY SCOTT.

Happy's the love which meets return,
When in soft flames souls equal burn ;
But words are wanting to discover
The torments of a hopeless lover.
Ye registers of heav'n, relate,
If looking o'er the rolls of fate,
Did you there see, mark'd for my marrow,
Mary Scott, the flower of Yarrow ?

Ah, no ! her form's too heav'nly fair,
Her love the gods above must share,
While mortals with despair explore her,
And at a distance due adore her.
O, lovely maid ! my doubts beguile,
Revive and bless me with a smile ;
Alas ! if not, you'll soon debar a
Sighing swain the banks of Yarrow.

Be hush, ye fears ! I'll not despair,
My Mary's tender as she's fair ;
Then I'll go tell her all my anguish,
She is too good to let me languish.
With success crown'd, I'll not envy
The folks who dwell above the sky ;
When Mary Scott's become my marrow,
We'll make a paradise on Yarrow.

XXXII.

O'ER BOGIE.

I WILL awa wi' my love,
    I will awa wi' her,
Tho' a' my kin had sworn and said
    I'll o'er Bogie wi' her.
If I can get but her consent,
    I dinna care a strae
Tho' ilka ane be discontent,
    Awa wi' her I'll gae.
        I will awa, &c.

For now she's mistress of my heart,
    And worthy of my hand,
And, well I wat, we shanna part
    For siller or for land.

Let rakes delyte to swear and drink,
  And beaux admire fine lace,
But my chief pleasure is to blink
  On Bessy's bonny face.
    I will awa, &c.

There a' the beauties do combine,
  Of colour, traits, and air,
The saul that sparkles in her een
  Makes her a jewel rare ;
Her flowing wit gives shining life
  To a' her other charms ;
How blest I'll be when she's my wife,
  And locked up in my arms.
    I will awa, &c.

There blythly will I rant and sing
  While o'er her sweets I range,
I'll cry—" Your humble servant, king,
  Shamefa' them that wad change.
A kiss of Betty and a smile,
  Ab'eet ye wad lay down
The right ye hae to Britain's isle,
  And offer me your crown.
    I will awa, &c.

XXXIII.

O'ER THE MOOR TO MAGGY.

AND I'll o'er the moor to Maggy,
  Her wit and sweetness call me,
Then to my fair I'll show my mind,
  Whatever may befall me.

V

If she love mirth, I'll learn to sing ;
　　Or likes the Nine to follow,
I'll lay my lugs in Pindus' spring,
　　And invocate Apollo.

If she admire a martial mind,
　　I'll sheath my limbs in armour ;
If to the softer dance inclin'd,
　　With gayest airs I'll charm her ;
If she love grandeur, day and night
　　I'll plot my nation's glory,
Find favour in my prince's sight,
　　And shine in future story.

Beauty can wonders work with ease,
　　Where wit is corresponding,
And bravest men know best to please
　　With complaisance abounding.
My bonny Maggy's love can turn
　　Me to what shape she pleases,
If in her breast that flame shall burn,
　　Which in my bosom bleezes.

XXXIV.

I'LL NEVER LEAVE THEE.

JONNY.

　Tho' for seven years and mair honour should reave me
To fields where cannons rair, thou needna grieve thee ;
For deep in my spirit thy sweets are indented,
And love shall preserve ay what love has imprinted.
Leave thee, leave thee ! I'll never leave thee,
Gang the warld as it will, dearest, believe me.

NELLY.

O Jonny, I'm jealous whene'er ye discover
My sentiments yielding, ye'll turn a loose rover ;
And nought i' the warld wad vex my heart sairer,
If you prove inconstant, and fancy ane fairer.
Grieve me, grieve me ! Oh, it wad grieve me
A' the lang night and day, if you deceive me.

JONNY.

My Nelly, let never sic fancies oppress thee,
For while my blood's warm I'll kindly caress ye ;
Your blooming saft beauties first beeted love's fire,
Your virtue and wit make it flame ay the higher.
Leave thee, leave thee ! I'll never leave thee,
Gang the warld as it will, dearest, believe me.

NELLY.

Then, Jonny, I'll frankly this minute allow ye
To think me your mistress, for love gars me trow ye ;
And gin ye prove false, to ye'rsell be it said then,
Ye'll win but sma' honour to wrang a kind maiden.
Reave me, reave me, heav'ns ! it wad reave me
Of my rest night and day, if ye deceive me.

JONNY.

Bid icicles hammer red gauds on the studdy,
And fair simmer mornings nae mair appear ruddy ;
Bid Britons think ae gate ; and when they obey ye,
But never till that time, believe I'll betray ye.
Leave thee, leave thee ! I'll never leave thee,
The stars shall gang withershins e'er I deceive thee.

XXXV.

POLWART ON THE GREEN.

At Polwart on the green
 If you'll meet me the morn,
Where lasses do convene
 To dance about the thorn,
A kindly welcome ye shall meet
 Frae her wha likes to view
A lover and a lad complete—
 The lad and lover you.

Let dorty dames say na,
 As lang as e'er they please,
Seem caulder than the sna',
 While inwardly they bleeze ;
But I will frankly shaw my mind,
 And yield my heart to thee ;
Be ever to the captive kind,
 That langs na to be free.

At Polwart on the green,
 Amang the new-mawn hay,
With sangs and dancing keen,
 We'll pass the heartsome day ;
At night, if beds be o'er thrang laid,
 And thou be twin'd of thine,
Thou shalt be welcome, my dear lad,
 To take a part of mine.

XXXVI.

JOHN HAY'S BONNY LASSIE.

By smooth winding Tay a swain was reclining,
Aft cry'd he—" O hey ! maun I still living pining
Mysell thus away, and darna discover
To my bonny Hay that I am her lover.

" Nae mair it will hide,—the flame waxes stranger,—
  If she's not my bride, my days are nae langer ;
Then I'll take a heart, and try at a venture,
  May be, ere we part, my vows may content her.

" She's fresh as the Spring, and sweet as Aurora,
  When birds mount and sing, bidding day a good morrow ;
The sward of the mead, enamell'd with daisies,
  Looks wither'd and dead when twin'd of her graces.

" But if she appear where verdures invite her,
  The fountains run clear, and flowers smell the sweeter ;
'Tis heaven to be by when her wit is a-flowing,
  Her smiles and bright eyes set my spirits a-glowing.

" The mair that I gaze the deeper I'm wounded,
  Struck dumb with amaze, my mind is confounded ;
I'm all in a fire, dear maid, to caress ye,
  For a' my desire is Hay's bonny lassie."

XXXVII.

GENTY TIBBY AND SONSY NELLY.

Tibby has a store of charms,
Her genty shape our fancy warms,
How starkly can her sma' white arms
  Fetter the lad wha looks but at her !
Frae ancle to her slender waist
  These sweets conceal'd invite to dawt her,
Her rosy cheek and rising breast
  Gar ane's mouth gush bowt fou' o' water.

Nelly's gawsy, saft and gay,
Fresh as the lucken flowers in May,
Ilk ane that sees her, cries—" Ah hey !
  She's bonny, O I wonder at her !

The dimples of her chin and cheek,
    And limbs sae plump, invite to dawt her;
Her lips sae sweet, and skin sae sleek,
    Gar mony mouths beside mine water.

Now strike my finger in a bore,
My wyzen with the maiden shore,*
Gin I can tell whilk I am for
    When these twa stars appear thegither.
O love! why dost thou gi'e thy fires
    Sae large, while we're obliged to nither
Our spacious sauls' immense desires,
    And ay be in a hankerin swither?

Tibby's shape and airs are fine,
And Nelly's beauties are divine;
But since they canna baith be mine,
    Ye gods! give ear to my petition,—
Provide a good lad for the tane;
    But let it be with this provision,
I get the other to my lane,
    In prospect plano and fruition.

XXXVIII.

UP IN THE AIR.

Now the sun's gane out o' sight,
Beet the ingle, and snuff the light;
In glens the fairies skip and dance,
And witches wallop o'er to France.
        Up in the air,
        On my bonny grey mare,
And I see her yet, and I see her yet,
        Up in, &c.

---

* *Divide my windpipe with the maiden.*—The maiden was an engine for beheading formerly used in Scotland. It was of a construction similar to that of the guillotine.

The wind's drifting hail and sna'
O'er frozen hags like a footba',
Nae starns keek thro' the azure slit,
'Tis cauld and mirk as ony pit.
   The man i' the moon
   Is carousing aboon,
D' ye see, d' ye see, d' ye see him yet ?
   The man, &c.

Take your glass to clear your een,
'Tis the elixir hales the spleen,
Baith wit and mirth it will inspire,
And gently puff the lover's fire.
   Up in the air,
   It drives away care ;
Ha'e wi' ye, ha'e wi' ye, and ha'e wi' ye, lads, yet,
   Up in, &c.

Steek the doors, keep out the frost,
Come, Willy, gi'e's about ye'r toast ;
Tilt it, lads, and lilt it out,
And let us ha'e a blythsome bowt.
   Up wi't there, there,
   Dinna cheat, but drink fair ;
Huzza ! huzza ! and huzza ! lads, yet,
   Up wi't, &c.

XXXIX.

TO MRS. E. C.

"NOW PHŒBUS ADVANCES ON HIGH."

Now Phœbus advances on high,
 No footsteps of winter are seen ;
The birds carol sweet in the sky,
 And lambkins dance reels on the green.

Thro' groves and by rivulets clear
   We wander for pleasure and health,
Where buddings and blossoms appear,
   Giving prospects of joy and of wealth.

View every gay scene all around,
   That are, and that promise to be;
Yet in them all nothing is found
   So perfect, Eliza, as thee.

Thine eyes the clear fountains excel;
   Thy locks they out-rival the grove;
When zephyrs these pleasingly swell,
   Each wave makes a captive to love.

The roses and lilies combin'd,
   And flowers of most delicate hue,
By thy cheeks and thy breasts are outshin'd,
   Their tinctures are nothing so true.

What can we compare with thy voice,
   And what with thy humour so sweet?
No music can bless with such joys,—
   Sure angels are just so complete.

Fair blossom of every delight,
   Whose beauties ten thousands outshine,
Thy sweets shall be lastingly bright,
   Being mixed with so many divine.

Ye powers! who have given such charms
   To Eliza, your image below,
O save her from all human harms,
   And make her hours happily flow.

XL.

TO CALISTA.

"SHE SUNG; THE YOUTH ATTENTION GAVE."

SHE sung; the youth attention gave,
    And charms on charms espies,
Then, all in raptures, falls a slave
    Both to her voice and eyes !
So spoke and smil'd the eastern maid,
    Like thine, seraphic were her charms,
That in Circassia's vineyards stray'd,
    And blest the wisest monarch's arms.

A thousand fair of high desert
    Strave to enchant the amorous king,
But the Circassian gain'd his heart,
    And taught the royal hand to sing.
Calista thus our sang inspires,
    And claims the smooth and highest lays ;
But while each charm our bosom fires,
    Words seem too few to sound her praise.

Her mind, in ev'ry grace complete,
    To paint, surpasses human skill ;
Her majesty mixed with the sweet,—
    Let seraphs sing her if they will :
Whilst wond'ring, with a ravish'd eye
    We all that's perfect in her view,
Viewing a sister of the sky,
    To whom an adoration's due.

W

XLI.

GIVE ME A LASS WITH A LUMP OF LAND.

Gi'e me a lass with a lump of land,
    And we for life shall gang thegither;
Tho' daft or wise I'll never demand,
    Or black or fair it maks na whether.
I'm aff with wit, and beauty will fade,
    And blood alane is no worth a shilling;
But she that's rich her market's made,
    For ilka charm about her is killing.

Gi'e me a lass with a lump of land,
    And in my bosom I'll hug my treasure;
Gin I had anes her gear in my hand,
    Should love turn dowf, it will find pleasure.
Laugh on wha likes, but there's my hand,
    I hate with poortith, tho' bonny, to meddle;
Unless they bring cash or a lump of land,
    They'se never get me to dance to their fiddle.

There's meikle good love in bands and bags,
    And siller and gowd's a sweet complexion;
But beauty, and wit, and virtue in rags,
    Have tint the art of gaining affection.
Love tips his arrows with woods and parks,
    And castles, and riggs, and moors, and meadows;
And naithing can catch our modern sparks,
    But well-tocher'd lasses or jointur'd widows.

XLII.

LOCHABER NO MORE.

FAREWELL to Lochaber, and farewell my Jean,
Where heartsome with thee I've mony day been;
For Lochaber no more, Lochaber no more,
We'll maybe return to Lochaber no more.
These tears that I shed they are a' for my dear,
And no for the dangers attending on wear,
Tho' bore on rough seas to a far bloody shore,
Maybe to return to Lochaber no more.

Tho' hurricanes arise, and rise ev'ry wind,
They'll ne'er make a tempest like that in my mind;
Tho' loudest of thunder on louder waves roar,
That's naething like leaving my love on the shore.
To leave thee behind me my heart is sair pain'd,—
By ease that's inglorious no fame can be gain'd,—
And beauty and love's the reward of the brave,
And I must deserve it before I can crave.

Then glory, my Jeany, maun plead my excuse!
Since honour commands me, how can I refuse;
Without it, I ne'er can have merit for thee,
And without thy favour I'd better not be.
I gae then, my lass, to win honour and fame,
And if I should luck to come gloriously hame,
I'll bring a heart to thee with love running o'er,
And then I'll leave thee and Lochaber no more.

XLIII.

VIRTUE AND WIT.

THE PRESERVATIVE OF LOVE AND BEAUTY.

CONFESS thy love, fair blushing maid ;
  For since thine eyes consenting,
Thy safter thoughts are a' betray'd,
  And naysays no worth tenting.
Why aims thou to oppose thy mind
  With words, thy wish denying ?
Since nature made thee to be kind,
  Reason allows complying.

Nature and reason's joint consent
  Make love a sacred blessing ;
Then happily that time is spent
  That's war'd on kind caressing.
Come then, my Katie, to my arms,
  I'll be nae mair a rover,
But find out heav'n in a' thy charms,
  And prove a faithful lover.

SHE.

What you design by nature's law
  Is fleeting inclination ;
That willy-wisp bewilds us a'
  By its infatuation.
When that gaes out, caresses tire
  And love's nae mair in season,
Syne weakly we blaw up the fire
  With all our boasted reason.

HE.

The beauties of inferior cast
  May start this just reflection,
But charms like thine maun always last
  Where wit has the protection.

Virtue and wit, like April rays,
   Make beauty rise the sweeter ;
The langer then on thee I gaze,
   My love will grow completer.

XLIV.

ADIEU FOR A WHILE MY NATIVE GREEN PLAINS.

HE.

Adieu for a while my native green plains,
My nearest relations, and neighbouring swains ;
Dear Nelly, frae these I'd start easily free
Were minutes not ages while absent frae thee.

SHE.

Then tell me the reason thou dost not obey
The pleading of love, but thus hurries away ;
Alake ! thou deceiver, o'er plainly I see
A lover sae roving will never mind me.

HE.

The reason unhappy is owing to fate,
That gave me a being without an estate ;
Which lays a necessity now upon me
To purchase a fortune for pleasure to thee.

SHE.

Small fortune may serve where love has the sway,
Then, Johny, be counsell'd nae langer to stray ;
For while thou proves constant in kindness to me,
Contented I'll ay find a treasure in thee.

HE.

Cease, my dear charmer, else soon I'll betray
A weakness unmanly, and quickly give way
To fondness, which may prove a ruin to thee,
A pain to us baith, and dishonour to me.

Bear witness ye streams, and witness ye flow'rs,
Bear witness ye watchful, invisible pow'rs,
If ever my heart be unfaithful to thee,
May nothing propitious e'er smile upon me.

XLV.

AND I'LL AWA' TO BONNY TWEEDSIDE.

AND I'll awa'
To bonny Tweedside,
And see my deary come throw,
And he sall be mine
Gif sae he incline,
For I hate to lead apes below.

While young and fair,
I'll make it my care
To secure mysell in a jo;
I'm no sic a fool
To let my blood cool,
And syne gae lead apes below.

Few words, bonny lad,
Will eithly persuade,
Tho' blushing, I daftly sae no;
Gae on with your strain,
And doubt not to gain,
For I hate to lead apes below.

Unty'd to a man,
Do whate'er we can
We never can thrive or dow;
Then I will do well,
Do better wha will,
And let them lead apes below.

Our time is precious,
And gods are gracious,
That beauties upon us bestow;
'Tis not to be thought
We got them for nought,
Or to be set up for a show.

'Tis carry'd by votes;
Come, kilt up your coats,
And let us to Edinburgh go;
Where she that's bonny
May catch a Johny,
And never lead apes below.

XLVI.

THE WIDOW.

THE widow can bake and the widow can brew,
The widow can shape and the widow can sew,
And mony braw things the widow can do,—
Then have at the widow, my laddie.

With courage attack her baith early and late;
To kiss and clap her ye maunna be blate,—
Speak well, and do better; for that's the best gate
To win a young widow, my laddie.

The widow she's youthfu', and never a hair
The waur of the wearing, and has a good skair
Of every thing lovely; she's witty and fair
And has a rich jointure, my laddie.

What could ye wish better, your pleasure to crown,
Than a widow the bonniest toast in the town,
With naething but draw in your stool and sit down,
And sport with the widow, my laddie.

Then till her, and kill her with courtesy dead,
Tho' stark love and kindness be all ye can plead;
Be heartsome and airy, and hope to succeed
    With a bonny gay widow, my laddie.

Strike iron while 'tis het, if ye'd have it to wald,—
For fortune ay favours the active and bauld,
But ruins the wooer that's thowless and cauld,
    Unfit for the widow, my laddie.

XLVII.

THE STEP-DAUGHTER'S RELIEF.

I WAS anes a well-tocher'd lass,
    My mither left dollars to me;
But now I'm brought to a poor pass,
    My step-dame has gart them flee.

My father he's aften frae hame,
    And she plays the deel with his gear;
She neither has lawtith nor shame,
    And keeps the hale house in a steer.

She's barmy-fac'd, thriftless, and bauld,
    And gars me aft fret and repine,
While hungry, half-naked, and cauld,
    I see her destroy what's mine.

But soon I might hope a revenge,
    And soon of my sorrows be free,
My poortith to plenty wad change
    If she were hung up on a tree.

Quoth Ringan,—wha lang time had loo'd
    This bonny lass tenderly,—
" I'll take thee, sweet May, in thy snood,
    Gif thou wilt gae hame with me.

'Tis only yoursell that I want ;
　　Your kindness is better to me
Than a' that your step-mother, scant
　　Of grace, now has taken frae thee.

" I'm but a young farmer, 'tis true,
　　And ye are the sprout of a laird,
But I have milk-cattle enow
　　And rowth of good rucks in my yard.
Ye shall have naething to fash ye,—
　　Sax servants shall jouk to thee ;
Then kilt up your coats, my lassie,
　　And gae thy ways hame with me."

The maiden her reason employed,
　　Not thinking the offer amiss,
Consented ; while Ringan, o'erjoy'd,
　　Receiv'd her with mony a kiss.
And now she sits blythly singan,
　　And joking her drunken step-dame,
Delighted with her dear Ringan
　　That makes her goodwife at hame.

XLVIII.

BONNY CHIRSTY.

How sweetly smells the simmer green !
　　Sweet taste the peach and cherry ;
Painting and order please our een,
　　And claret makes us merry :
But finest colours, fruits and flowers,
　　And wine, tho' I be thirsty,
Lose a' their charms and weaker powers,
　　Compar'd with those of Chirsty.

When wand'ring o'er the flow'ry park,
    No nat'ral beauty wanting,
How lightsome is 't to hear the lark,
    And birds in concert chanting !
But if my Chirsty tunes her voice,
    I'm wrapt in admiration,
My thoughts with ecstasies rejoice,
    And drap the hale creation.

Whene'er she smiles a kindly glance,
    I take the happy omen,
And aften mint to make advance,
    Hoping she'll prove a woman ;
But dubious of my ain desert,
    My sentiments I smother,
With secret sighs I vex my heart,
    For fear she love another.

Thus sang blate Edie by a burn,
    His Chirsty did o'erhear him ;
She doughtna let her lover mourn,
    But, ere he wist, drew near him.
She spake her favour with a look,
    Which left nae room to doubt her :
He wisely this white minute took,
    And flang his arms about her.

My Chirsty !—witness, bonny stream,
    Sic joys frae tears arising !
I wish this may not be a dream ;
    O love the maist surprising !
Time was too precious now for tauk ;
    This point of a his wishes
He wadna with set speeches bauk,
    But wair'd it a' on kisses.

XLIX.

THE SOGER LADDIE.

My soger laddie is over the sea,
And he will bring gold and money to me ;
And when he comes hame, he'll make me a lady :
My blessing gang with my soger laddie.

My doughty laddie is handsome and brave,
And can as a soger and lover behave ;
True to his country, to love he is steady,
There 's few to compare with my soger laddie.

Shield him, ye angels, frae death in alarms,
Return him with laurels to my langing arms ;
Syne frae all my care ye'll pleasantly free me,
When back to my wishes my soger ye gi'e me.

O ! soon may his honours bloom fair on his brow,
As quickly they must if he get his due ;
For in noble actions his courage is ready,
Which makes me delight in my soger laddie.

L.

THE BONNY SCOT.

Tune—" The Boatman."

Ye gales that gently wave the sea,
    And please the canny boatman,
Bear me frae hence, or bring to me
    My brave, my bonny Scotman.
        In haly bands
        We join'd our hands,
    Yet may not this discover,
        While parents rate
        A large estate
    Before a faithful lover.

But I lure chuse in Highland glens
　　To herd the kid and goat—man,
Ere I could for sic little ends
　　Refuse my bonny Scotman.
　　　　Wae worth the man
　　　　Wha first began
　　The base ungenerous fashion,
　　　　Frae greedy views,
　　　　Love's art to use,
　　While strangers to its passion.

Frae foreign fields, my lovely youth,
　　Haste to thy longing lassie,
Wha pants to press thy bawmy mouth,
　　And in her bosom hawse thee.
　　　　Love gi'es the word,
　　　　Then haste on board ;
　　Fair winds and tenty boatman,
　　　　Waft o'er, waft o'er,
　　　　Frae yonder shore,
　　My blyth, my bonny Scot—man.

LI.

LOVE INVITING REASON.

WHEN innocent pastime our pleasure did crown,
　　Upon a green meadow, or under a tree,
Ere Annie became a fine lady in town,
　　How lovely, and loving, and bonny was she !
Rouse up thy reason, my beautifu' Annie,
　　Let ne'er a new whim ding thy fancy a-jee ;
O ! as thou art bonny, be faithfu' and canny,
　　And favour thy Jamie, wha doats upon thee.

Does the death of a lintwhite give Annie the spleen ?
　　Can tyning of trifles be uneasy to thee ?

Can lapdogs and monkeys draw tears frae these een
 That look with indifference on poor dying me ?
Rouse up thy reason, my beautifu' Annie,
 And dinna prefer a paroquet to me ;
O ! as thou art bonny, be prudent and canny,
 And think on thy Jamie, wha doats upon thee.

Ah ! should a new gown or a Flanders-lace head,
 Or yet a wee coatie, tho' never sae fine,
Gar thee grow forgetfu', and let his heart bleed,
 That anes had some hope of purchasing thine ?
Rouse up thy reason, my beautifu' Annie,
 And dinna prefer your fleegeries to me ;
O ! as thou art bonny, be solid and canny,
 And tent a true lover that doats upon thee.

Shall a Paris edition of new-fangle Sanny,
 Tho' gilt o'er wi' laces and fringes he be,
By adoring himself, be admir'd by fair Annie,
 And aim at these bennisons promis'd to me ?
Rouse up thy reason, my beautifu' Annie,
 And never prefer a light dancer to me ;
O ! as thou art bonny, be constant and canny,
 Love only thy Jamie, wha doats upon thee.

O ! think, my dear charmer, on ilka sweet hour
 That slade away saftly between thee and me,
Ere squirrels, or beaux, or fopp'ry had power
 To rival my love, and impose upon thee.
Rouse up thy reason, my beautifu' Annie,
 And let thy desires be a' center'd in me ;
O ! as thou art bonny, be faithfu' and canny,
 And love him wha's langing to centre in thee.

LII.

THE BOB OF DUNBLANE.

LASSIE, lend me your braw hemp heckle,
  And I'll lend you my thripling kame ;
For fainness, deary, I'll gar ye keckle,
  If ye'll go dance the Bob of Dunblane.
Haste ye, gang to the ground of ye'r trunkies,
  Busk ye braw, and dinna think shame ;
Consider in time, if leading of monkies
  Be better than dancing the Bob of Dunblane.

Be frank, my lassie, lest I grow fickle,
  And take my word and offer again ;
Syne ye may chance to repent it meikle
  Ye did na accept of the Bob of Dumblane.
The dinner, the piper, and priest shall be ready,
  And I'm grown dowie with lying my lane ;
Away then, leave baith minny and daddy,
  And try with me the Bob of Dunblane.

LIII.

THROW THE WOOD, LADDIE.

O SANDY, why leaves thou thy Nelly to mourn ?
    Thy presence could ease me,
    When naething could please me ;
Now dowie I sigh on the bank of the burn,
Or throw the wood, laddie, until thou return.

Tho' woods now are bonny, and mornings are clear,
    While lavrocks are singing,
    And primroses springing,
Yet nane of them pleases my eye or my ear,
When throw the wood, laddie, ye dinna appear.

That I am forsaken some spare no to tell ;
  I'm fash'd wi' their scorning,
  Baith ev'ning and morning ;
Their jeering gaes aft to my heart wi' a knell,
When throw the wood, laddie, I wander mysel.

Then stay, my dear Sandy, nae langer away,
  But quick as an arrow,
  Haste here to thy marrow,
Wha's living in languor till that happy day,
When throw the wood, laddie, we'll dance, sing, and play.

LIV.

AN THOU WERE MY AIN THING.

An thou were my ain thing,
  I would love thee, I would love thee ;
An thou were my ain thing
  How dearly would I love thee.

Like bees that suck the morning dew
Frae flowers of sweetest scent and hue,
Sae wad I dwell upo' thy mou,
  And gar the gods envy me.
    An thou were, &c.

Sae lang's I had the use of light
I'd on thy beauties feast my sight,
Syne, in saft whispers through the night
  I'd tell how much I loo'd thee.
    An thou were, &c.

How fair and ruddy is my Jean !
She moves a goddess o'er the green.

Were I a king, thou should be queen,—
Nane but myself aboon thee.

An thou were, &c.

I'd grasp thee to this breast of mine,
Whilst thou like ivy or the vine
Around my stronger limbs should twine,
Form'd hardy to defend thee.

An thou were, &c.

Time 's on the wing and will not stay,
In shining youth let's make our hay;
Since love admits of no delay,
O ! let na scorn undo thee.

An thou were, &c.

While love does at his altar stand,
Hae, there's my heart, gi'e me thy hand,
And with ilk smile thou shalt command
The will of him wha loves thee.

An thou were, &c.

LV.

THERE'S MY THUMB I'LL NE'ER BEGUILE THEE.

My sweetest May, let love incline thee
T' accept a heart which he designs thee ;
And as your constant slave regard it,
Syne for its faithfulness reward it :
'Tis proof a shot to birth or money,
But yields to what is sweet or bonny.
Receive it, then, with a kiss and smily,—
There 's my thumb it will ne'er beguile thee.

How tempting sweet these lips of thine are !
Thy bosom white and legs sae fine are,
That when in pools I see thee clean 'em,
They carry away my heart between 'em.
I wish, and I wish, while it gaes duntin,
O gin I had thee on a mountain ;
Tho kith and kin and a' should revile thee,
There's my thumb I'll ne'er beguile thee.

Alane thro' flow'ry hows I dander,
Tenting my flocks, lest they should wander ;
Gin thou 'll gae alang I'll dawt thee gaylie,
And gi'e my thumb I'll ne'er beguile thee.
O my dear lassie, it is but daffin
To had thy wooer up ay niff naffin :
That na, na, na, I hate it most vilely ;
O say yes, and I'll ne'er beguile thee.

LVI.

THE HIGHLAND LADDIE.

The Lawland lads think they are fine,
　　But O they 're vain and idly gaudy ;
How much unlike that gracefu' mien
　　And manly looks of my Highland laddie !
O my bonny, bonny Highland laddie !
My handsome, charming Highland laddie !
May heaven still guard, and love reward,
Our Lawland lass and her Highland laddie !

If I were free at will to chuse
　　To be the wealthiest Lawland lady,

Y

I'd take young Donald without trews,
  With bonnet blue and belted plaidy.
    O my bonny, &c.

The brawest beau in borrows town,
  In a' his airs with art made ready,
Compar'd to him he's but a clown ;
  He's finer far in 's tartan plaidy.
    O my bonny, &c.

O'er benty hill with him I'll run,
  And leave my Lawland kin and daddy ;
Frae winter's cauld and summer's sun,
  He'll screen me with his Highland plaidy.
    O my bonny, &c.

A painted room and silken bed
  May please a Lawland laird and lady,
But I can kiss and be as glad,
  Behind a bush, in 's Highland plaidy.
    O my bonny, &c.

Few compliments between us pass,
  I ca' him my dear Highland laddie ;
And he ca's me his Lawland lass,
  Syne rows me in his Highland plaidy.
    O my bonny, &c.

Nae greater joy I'll e'er pretend
  Than that his love prove true and steady,
Like mine to him, which ne'er shall end
  While Heaven preserves my Highland laddie.
    O my bonny, &c.

LVII

THE COALIER'S DAUGHTER.

THE coalier has a daughter,
   And O she's wonder bonny !
A laird he was that sought her,
   Rich baith in lands and money.
The tutors watch'd the motion
   Of this young honest lover ;
But love is like the ocean,—
   Wha can its depths discover ?

He had the art to please ye,
   And was by a' respected ;
His airs sat round him easy,—
   Genteel, but unaffected.
The coalier's bonny lassie,
   Fair as the new-blown lily,
Ay sweet and never saucy,
   Secur'd the heart of Willy.

He lov'd beyond expression
   The charms that were about her,
And panted for possession ;
   His life was dull without her.
After mature resolving,
   Close to his breast he held her,
In saftest flames dissolving,
   He tenderly thus tell'd her :

My bonny coalier's daughter,
   Let naething discompose ye,
'Tis not your scanty tocher
   Shall ever make me lose ye ;
For I have gear in plenty,
   And love says, 'tis my duty
To ware what heaven has lent me
   Upon your wit and beauty.

LVIII.

THE MILL, MILL-O.

BENEATH a green shade I fand a fair maid
    Was sleeping sound and still-O,
A' lowing wi' love, my fancy did rove
    Around her with good will-O :
Her bosom I press'd, but, sunk in her rest,
    She stir'd na my joy to spill-O :
While kindly she slept, close to her I crept,
    And kiss'd, and kiss'd her my fill-O.

Oblig'd by command in Flanders to land,
    T' employ my courage and skill-O,
Frae 'er quietly I staw, hois'd sails and awa,
    For wind blew fair on the hill-O.
Twa years brought me hame, where loud-frasing fame
    Tald me with a voice right shrill-O,
My lass, like a fool, had mounted the stool,*
    Nor kend wha'd done her the ill-O.

Mair fond of her charms, with my son in her arms,
    I ferlying speer'd how she fell-O ;
Wi' the tear in her eye, quoth she, Let me die,
    Sweet Sir, gin I can tell-O.
Love gae the command, I took her by the hand,
    And bad her a' fears expel-O,
And nae mair look wan, for I was the man
    Wha had done her the deed mysell-O.

My bonny sweet lass, on the gowany grass,
    Beneath the Shilling-hill-O ; †
If I did offence, I'se make ye amends
    Before I leave Peggy's mill-O.

---

* Of repentance.   † Where they winnow the chaff from the corn.

O ! the mill, mill-O, and the kill, kill-O,
    And the cogging of the wheel-O,
The sack and the sieve, a' thae ye maun leave,
    And round with a soger reel-O.

LIX.

COLIN AND GRISY PARTING.

WITH broken words and downcast eyes,
    Poor Colin spoke his passion tender,
And parting with his Grisy, cries,
    Ah ! woe's my heart that we should sunder.

To others I am cold as snow,
    But kindle with thine eyes like tinder ;
From thee with pain I'm forc'd to go,
    It breaks my heart that we should sunder.

Chain'd to thy charms, I cannot range,
    No beauty new my love shall hinder,
Nor time nor place shall ever change
    My vows, tho' we're oblig'd to sunder.

The image of thy graceful air,
    And beauties which invite our wonder,
Thy lively wit, and prudence rare,
    Shall still be present, tho' we sunder.

Dear nymph, believe thy swain in this,
    You'll ne'er engage a heart that's kinder ;
Then seal a promise with a kiss,
    Always to love me, tho' we sunder.

Ye gods ! take care of my dear lass,
That as I leave her I may find her,
When that blest time shall come to pass,
We'll meet again, and never sunder.

LX.

TO L. L. IN MOURNING.

TUNE—"Where Helen lies."

AH ! why those tears in Nelly's eyes ?
To hear thy tender sighs and cries,
The gods stand list'ning from the skies,
    Pleas'd with thy piety.
To mourn the dead, dear nymph, forbear,
And of one dying take a care,
Who views thee as an angel fair,
    Or some divinity.

O ! be less graceful, or more kind,
And cool this fever of my mind,
Caus'd by the boy severe and blind,
    Wounded I sigh for thee ;
While hardly dare I hope to rise
To such a height by Hymen's ties,
To lay me down where Helen lies,
    And with thy charms be free.

Then must I hide my love and die,
When such a sov'reign cure is by ?
No, she can love, and I'll go try,
    Whate'er my fate may be.
Which soon I'll read in her bright eyes;
With those dear agents I'll advise,
They tell the truth, when tongues tell lies
    The least believ'd by me.

LXI.

A SCOTS CANTATA.

Music by L. BOCCHI.

RECITATIVE.

BLATE Jonny faintly tald fair Jean his mind ;
　Jeany took pleasure to deny him lang ;
He thought her scorn came frae a heart unkind,
　Which gart him in despair tune up this sang.

AIR.

O bonny lassie, since 'tis sae
　That I'm despis'd by thee,
I hate to live ; but O ! I'm wae
　And unco sweer to die.
Dear Jeany, think what dowy hours
　I thole by your disdain ;
Ah ! should a breast sae saft as yours
　Contain a heart of stane ?

RECITATIVE.

These tender notes did a' her pity move ;
　With melting heart she listen'd to the boy.
O'ercome, she smil'd, and promis'd him her love ;
　He, in return, thus sang his rising joy :—

AIR.

Hence frae my breast, contentious care !
　Ye've tint the power to pine ;
My Jeany's good, my Jeany's fair,
　And a' her sweets are mine.
O ! spread thine arms, and gi'e me fowth
　Of dear enchanting bliss,
A thousand joys around thy mouth
　Gi'e heaven with ilka kiss.

LXII.

THE TOAST.

Come, let's ha'e mair wine in,
Bacchus hates repining,
Venus lo'es nae dwining,—
    Let's be blyth and free.
Away with dull ! here t' ye, sir,
Ye'r mistress, Robie, gie's her ;
We'll drink her health with pleasure,
    Wha's belov'd by thee.

Then let Peggy warm ye,
That's a lass can charm ye
And to joys alarm ye ;
    Sweet is she to me :
Some angel ye wad ca' her,
And never wish ane brawer,
If ye bare-headed saw her,
    Kilted to the knee.

Peggy a dainty lass is,
Come, let's join our glasses,
And refresh our hauses
    With a health to thee.
Let coofs their cash be clinking,
Be statesmen tint in thinking,
While we with love and drinking
    Give our cares the lie.

LXIII.

A SOUTH SEA SANG.

Tune—"For our lang biding here."

When we came to London town,
    We dream'd of gowd in gowpings here,

And rantin'ly ran up and down,
   In rising stocks to buy a skair :
We daftly thought to row in rowth,
   But for our daffin paid right dear ;
The lave will fare the waur in trouth,
   For our lang biding here.

But when we fand our purses toom,
   And dainty stocks began to fa',
We hang our lugs, and wi' a gloom,
   Girn'd at stock-jobbing ane and a'.
If we gang near the South Sea house,
   The whillywhas will grip ye'r gear,
Syne a' the lave will fare the waur,
   For our lang biding here.

LXIV.

HAP ME WITH THY PETTICOAT.

O Bell ! thy looks have kill'd my heart,
   I pass the day in pain,
When night returns I feel the smart,
   And wish for thee in vain.
I'm starving cold, while thou art warm ;
   Have pity and incline,
And grant me for a hap that charm-
   ing petticoat of thine.

My ravish'd fancy in amaze
   Still wanders o'er thy charms ;
Delusive dreams ten thousand ways
   Present thee to my arms :

z

But waking, think what I endure,
 While cruel you decline
Those pleasures which can only cure
 This panting breast of mine.

I faint, I fail, and wildly rove,
 Because you still deny
The just reward that's due to love,
 And let true passion die.
O ! turn and let compassion seize
 That lovely breast of thine ;
Thy petticoat could give me ease,
 If thou and it were mine.

Sure heaven has fitted for delight
 That beauteous form of thine,
And thou'rt too good its laws to slight,
 By hind'ring the design.
May all the powers of love agree
 At length to make thee mine ;
Or loose my chains, and set me free
 From ev'ry charm of thine.

LXV.

FY GAR RUB HER O'ER WI' STRAE.

GIN ye meet a bonny lassie,
 Gi'e her a kiss, and let her gae ;
But if ye meet a dirty hussy,
 Fy gar rub her o'er wi' strae.

Be sure ye dinna quat the grip
 Of ilka joy, when ye are young,

Before auld age your vitals nip,
    And lay ye twafald o'er a rung.

Sweet youth's a blyth and heartsome time ;
    Then, lads and lasses, while 'tis May,
Gae pu' the gowan in its prime,
    Before it wither and decay.

Watch the saft minutes of delyte,
    When Jenny speaks beneath her breath,
And kisses, laying a' the wyte
    On you, if she kepp ony skaith.

" Haith, ye're ill-bred," she'll smiling say,
    " Ye'll worry me, ye greedy rook."
Syne frae your arms she'll rin away,
    And hide herself in some dark nook.

Her laugh will lead you to the place,
    Where lies the happiness ye want,
And plainly tell you to your face,
    Nineteen na-says are half a grant.

Now to her heaving bosom cling,
    And sweetly toolie for a kiss ;
Frae her fair finger whoop a ring,
    As taiken of a future bliss.

These bennisons, I'm very sure,
    Are of the gods' indulgent grant :
Then, surly carles, whisht, forbear
    To plague us with your whining cant.

LXVI.

THE CORDIAL.

HE.

WHERE wad bonny Anne ly ?
Alane ye nae mair man ly :
Wad ye a goodman try ?
   Is that the thing ye're laking ?

SHE.

Can a lass sae young as I
Venture on the bridal tye,
Syne down with a goodman ly ?
   I'm fleed he'd keep me wauking.

HE.

Never judge until ye try,
Mak me your goodman, I
Shanna hinder you to ly,
   And sleep till ye be weary.

SHE.

What if I should wauking ly,
When the hautboys are gawn by,
Will ye tent me when I cry,
   My dear, I'm faint and iry ?

HE.

In my bosom thou shalt ly,
When thou waukrife art or dry,
Healthy cordial standing by,
   Shall presently revive thee.

SHE.

To your will I then comply,
Join us, priest, and let me try
How I'll wi' a goodman ly,
Wha can a cordial gi' me.

LXVII.

ALLAN WATER.

WHAT numbers shall the muse repeat,
What verse be found to praise my Annie ?
On her ten thousand graces wait,
Each swain admires, and owns she's bonny.
Since first she trod the happy plain,
She set each youthful heart on fire ;
Each nymph does to her swain complain,
That Annie kindles new desire.

This lovely darling, dearest care,
This new delight, this charming Annie,
Like summer's dawn she's fresh and fair,
When Flora's fragrant breezes fan ye.
All day the am'rous youths conveen,
Joyous they sport and play before her ;
All night, when she no more is seen,
In blissful dreams they still adore her.

Among the crowd Amyntor came,
He look'd, he lov'd, he bow'd to Annie ;
His rising sighs express his flame,
His words were few, his wishes many.
With smiles the lovely maid reply'd,
Kind shepherd, why should I deceive ye ?

Alas ! your love must be deny'd,
    This destin'd breast can ne'er relieve ye.

Young Damon came with Cupid's art,
    His wiles, his smiles, his charms beguiling,
He stole away my virgin heart ;
    Cease, poor Amyntor, cease bewailing.
Some brighter beauty you may find,
    On yonder plain the nymphs are many ;
Then chuse some heart that's unconfin'd,
    And leave to Damon his own Annie.

LXVIII.

O MARY ! THY GRACES AND GLANCES.

O MARY ! thy graces and glances,
    Thy smiles so enchantingly gay,
And thoughts so divinely harmonious,
    Clear wit and good humour display.
But say not thou'lt imitate angels
    Ought farrer, tho' scarcely (ah me !)
Can be found equalizing thy merit,
    A match amongst mortals for thee.

Thy many fair beauties shed fires
    May warm up ten thousand to love,
Who, despairing, may fly to some other,
    While I may despair, but ne'er rove.
What a mixture of sighing and joys
    This distant adoring of thee
Gives to a fond heart too aspiring,
    Who loves in sad silence like me ?

Thus looks the poor beggar on treasure;
   And shipwreck'd on landscapes on shore :
Be still more divine, and have pity ;
   I die soon as hope is no more.
For, Mary, my soul is thy captive,
   Nor loves nor expects to be free ;
Thy beauties are fetters delightful,
   Thy slavery's a pleasure to me.

LXIX.

THIS IS NO MY AIN HOUSE.

THIS is no my ain house,
   I ken by the rigging o't;
Since with my love I've changed my vows,
   I dinna like the bigging o't:
For now that I'm young Robie's bride,
And mistress of his fire-side,
Mine ain house I'll like to guide,
   And please me with the trigging o't.

Then farewell to my father's house,
   I gang where love invites me ;
The strictest duty this allows,
   When love with honour meets me.
When Hymen moulds us into ane,
My Robie's nearer than my kin,
And to refuse him were a sin,
   Sae lang's he kindly treats me.

When I'm in mine ain house,
   True love shall be at hand ay,
To make me still a prudent spouse,
   And let my man command ay ;

Avoiding ilka cause of strife,
The common pest of married life,
That makes ane wearied of his wife,
    And breaks the kindly band ay.

LXX.

MY DADDY FORBAD, MY MINNY FORBAD.

When I think on my lad,
    I sigh and am sad,
For now he is far frae me :
    My daddy was harsh,
    My minny was warse,
That gart him gae yont the sea :
    Without an estate,
    That made him look blate,
And yet a brave lad is he :
    Gin safe he come hame,
    In spite of my dame,
He'll ever be welcome to me.

Love speers nae advice
    Of parent's o'erwise,
That have but ae bairn like me,
    That looks upon cash
    As naithing but trash,
That shackles what should be free.
    And tho' my dear lad
    Not ae penny had,
Since qualities better has he,
    Abeit I'm an heiress,
    I think it but fair is
To love him, since he loves me.

Then my dear Jamie,
　To thy kind Jeanie
Haste, haste thee in o'er the sea,
　To her wha can find
　Nae ease in her mind,
Without a blyth sight of thee.
　Tho' my daddy forbad,
　And my minny forbad,
Forbidden I will not be ;
　For since thou alone
　My favour hast won,
Nane else shall e'er get it for me.

Yet them I'll not grieve,
　Or without their leave,
Gi'e my hand as a wife to thee :
　Be content with a heart
　That can never desert,
Till they cease to oppose or be.
　My parents may prove
　Yet friends to our love,
When our firm resolves they see ;
　Then I with pleasure
　Will yield up my treasure,
And a' that love orders, to thee.

LXXI.

STEER HER UP AND HAUD HER GAWN.

O STEER her up and haud her gawn,
　Her mither's at the mill, jo ;
But gin she winna tak a man,
　E'en let her tak her will, jo.

Pray thee, lad, leave silly thinking,
    Cast thy cares of love away ;
Let's our sorrows drown in drinking,
    'Tis daffin langer to delay.

See that shining glass of claret,
    How invitingly it looks !
Take it aff, and let's have mair o't,
    Pox on fighting, trade, and books.
Let's have pleasure while we're able,
    Bring us in the meikle bowl,
Place't on the middle of the table,
    And let wind and weather gowl.

Call the drawer, let him fill it
    Fou as ever it can hold ;
O tak tent ye dinna spill it,
    'Tis mair precious far than gold.
By you've drunk a dozen bumpers,
    Bacchus will begin to prove,
Spite of Venus and her mumpers,
    Drinking better is than love.

LXXII.

CLOUT THE CALDRON.

HAVE you any pots or pans,
    Or any broken chandlers ?
I am a tinkler to my trade,
    And newly come frae Flanders :
As scant of siller as of grace,
    Disbanded, we've a bad run ;
Gae tell the lady of the place,
    I'm come to clout her caldron.
        Fa adrie, didle, didle, &c.,

Madam, if you have wark for me,
 I'll do't to your contentment,
And dinna care a single flea
 For any man's resentment:
For, lady fair, tho' I appear
 To every ane a tinkler,
Yet to yoursell I'm bauld to tell,
 I am a gentle jinker.
   Fa adrie, didle, didle, &c.

Love Jupiter into a swan
 Turn'd, for his lovely Leda;
He like a bull o'er meadows ran
 To carry off Europa:
Then may not I as well as he,
 To cheat your Argos blinker,
And win your love, like mighty Jove,
 Thus hide me in a tinkler?
   Fa adrie, didle, didle, &c.

Sir, ye appear a cunning man,
 But this fine plot you'll fail in,
For there is neither pot nor pan
 Of mine you'll drive a nail in.
Then bind your budget on your back,
 And nails up in your apron,
For I've a tinkler under tack,
 That's us'd to clout my caldron.
   Fa adrie, didle, didle, &c.

LXXIII.

THE MALTMAN.

THE maltman comes on Monday,
     He craves wonder sair,
Cries, Dame, come gi'e me my siller,
     Or malt ye sall never get mair.
I took him into the pantry,
     And gave him some good cock-broo,
Syne paid him upon a gantree,
     As hostler wives should do.

When maltmen come for siller,
     And gaugers with wands o'er soon,
Wives, tak them a' down to the cellar,
     And clear them as I have done.
This bewith, when cunzie is scanty,
     Will keep them frae making din,
The knack I learn'd frae an auld aunty,
     The snackest of a' my kin.

The maltman is right cunning,
     But I can be as slee,
And he may crack of his winning,
     When he clears scores with me :
For come when he likes, I'm ready ;
     But if frae hame I be,
Let him wait on our kind lady,
     She'll answer a bill for me.

LXXIV.

BONNY BESSY.

BESSY's beauties shine sae bright,
  Were her many virtues fewer,
She wad ever give delight,
  And in transport make me view her.
Bonny Bessie, thee alane
  Love I, naithing else but thee;
With thy comeliness I'm tane,
  And langer cannot live without thee.

Bessy's bosom's saft and warm,
  Milk-white fingers still employ'd;
He who takes her to his arm,
  Of her sweets can ne'er be cloy'd.
My dear Bessy, when the roses
  Leave thy cheek, as thou grows aulder,
Virtue, which thy mind discloses,
  Will keep love frae growing caulder.

Bessy's tocher is but scanty,
  Yet her face and saul discovers
These enchanting sweets in plenty
  Must entice a thousand lovers.
It's not money, but a woman
  Of a temper kind and easy,
That gives happiness uncommon;
  Petted things can nought but teez ye.

LXXV.

THE QUADRUPLE ALLIANCE.

Swift, Sandy, Young, and Gay,
  Are still my heart's delight,
I sing their sangs by day,
    And read their tales at night.
      If frae their books I be,
      'Tis dulness then with me;
      But when these stars appear,
      Jokes, smiles, and wit shine clear.

Swift, with uncommon style,
  And wit that flows with ease,
Instructs us with a smile,
    And never fails to please.
      Bright Sandy greatly sings
      Of heroes, gods, and kings:
      He well deserves the bays,
      And ev'ry Briton's praise.

While thus our Homer shines;
  Young, with Horacian flame,
Corrects these false designs
    We push in love of fame.
      Blyth Gay, in pawky strains,
      Makes villains, clowns, and swains
      Reprove, with biting leer,
      Those in a higher sphere.

Swift, Sandy, Young, and Gay,
  Lang may you give delight ;
Let all the dunces bray,
    You're far above their spite !
      Such, from a malice sour,
      Write nonsense, lame and poor,
      Which never can succeed,
      For who the trash will read ?

LXXVI.

THE COMPLAINT.

Tune—"When absent from the nymph I love."

When absent from the nymph I love,
   I'd fain shake off the chains I wear ;
But whilst I try these to remove,
   More fetters I'm oblig'd to bear :
My captiv'd fancy, day and night,
   Fairer and fairer represents
Belinda, form'd for dear delight,
   But cruel cause of my complaints.

All day I wander thro' the groves,
   And, sighing, hear from every tree
The happy birds chirping their loves,
   Happy compar'd with lonely me.
When gentle sheep with balmy wings
   To rest fans ev'ry weary'd wight,
A thousand fears my fancy brings,
   That keep me watching all the night.

Sleep flies, while like the goddess fair,
   And all the graces in her train,
With melting smiles and killing air,
   Appears the cause of all my pain.
A while my mind delighted flies
   O'er all her sweets with thrilling joy,
Whilst want of worth makes doubts arise,
   That all my trembling hopes destroy.

Thus while my thoughts are fix'd on her,
   I'm all o'er transport and desire,
My pulse beats high, my cheeks appear
   All roses, and mine eyes all fire.

When to myself I turn my view,
 My veins grow chill, my cheeks look wan :
Thus whilst my fears my pains renew,
 I scarcely look or move a man.

LXXVII.

THE CARLE HE CAME O'ER THE CROFT.

THE carle he came o'er the croft,
 And his beard new shaven,
He look'd at me as he'd been daft,
 The carle trows that I wad hae him.
Howt awa! I winna hae him,
 Na forsooth I winna hae him,
For a' his beard's new shaven,
 Ne'er a bit will I hae him.

A siller broach he gae me neist,
 To fasten on my curtchea nooked ;
I wor'd a wee upon my breast,
 But soon, alake ! the tongue o't crooked ;
And sae may his : I winna hae him,
 Na forsooth I winna hae him ;
Ane twice a bairn's a lass's jest ;
 Sae ony fool for me may hae him.

The carle has nae fault but ane,
 For he has lands and dollars plenty ;
But waes me for him ! skin and bane
 Is no for a plump lass of twenty.
Howt awa ! I winna hae him,
 Na forsooth I winna hae him ;
What signifies his dirty riggs
 And cash, without a man with them ?

But should my canker'd daddy gar
   Me take him 'gainst my inclination,
I warn the fumbler to beware,
   That antlers dinna claim their station.
Howt awa! I winna hae him,
   Na forsooth I winna hae him;
I'm flee'd to crack the hally band,
   Sae Lawty says I should na hae him.

LXXVIII.

O MITHER DEAR! I 'GIN TO FEAR.

Chorus.

Up stairs, down stairs,
   Timber stairs fear me;
I'm laith to ly a' night my lane
   And Johny's bed sae near me.

O mither dear! I 'gin to fear,
   Tho' I'm baith good and bonny,
I winna keep; for in my sleep
   I start and dream of Johny.
When Johny then comes down the glen
   To woo me, dinna hinder;
But with content gi'e your consent,
   For we twa ne'er can sinder.

Better to marry than miscarry,
   For shame and skaith's the clink o't;
To thole the dool, to mount the stool,
   I downa bide to think o't:
Sae while 'tis time, I'll shun the crime,
   That gars poor Epps gae whinging,
With haiuches fow, and een sae blue,
   To a' the bedrals bindging.

Had Eppy's apron bidden down,
    The kirk had ne'er a kend it ;
But when the word's gane thro' the town,
    Alake ! how can she mend it ?
Now Tam man face the minister,
    And she man mount the pillar ;
And that's the way that they man gae,
    For poor folk has na siller.

Now ha'd ye'r tongue, my daughter young,
    Replied the kindly mither ;
Get Johny's hand in haly band,
    Syne wap ye'r wealth together.
I'm o' the mind, if he be kind,
    Ye'll do your part discreetly,
And prove a wife will gar his life
    And barrel run right sweetly.

LXXIX.

A SONG.

TUNE—" Busk ye, my bonny bride."

BUSK ye, busk ye, my bonny bride ;
    Busk ye, busk ye, my bonny marrow ;
Busk ye, busk ye, my bonny bride,
    Busk, and go to the braes of Yarrow ;
There will we sport and gather dew
    Dancing while lavrocks sing the morning ;
There learn frae turtles to prove true :
    O Bell ! ne'er vex me with thy scorning.

To westlin breezes Flora yields,
    And when the beams are kindly warming,
Blythness appears o'er all the fields,
    And nature looks mair fresh and charming.

Learn frae the burns that trace the mead,
　Tho' on their banks the roses blossom.
Yet hastily they flow to Tweed,
　And pour their sweetness in his bosom.

Haste ye, haste ye, my bonny Bell,
　Haste to my arms, and there I'll guard thee ;
With free consent my fears repel,
　I'll with my love and care reward thee.
Thus sang I saftly to my fair,
　Wha rais'd my hopes with kind relenting.
O queen of smiles ! I ask nae mair,
　Since now my bonny Bell's consenting.

———————

LXXX.

THE HIGHLAND LASSIE.

THE Lawland maids gang trig and fine,
　But aft they're sour and unco saucy ;
Sae proud they never can be kind,
　Like my good-humour'd Highland lassie.
　　O my bonny, bonny Highland lassie,
　　My hearty smiling Highland lassie,
　　May never care make thee less fair,
　　But bloom of youth still bless my lassie.

Than ony lass in borrows-town,
　Wha mak their cheeks with patches motie,
I'd tak my Katie but a gown,
　Barefooted, in her little coatie.
　　　O my bonny, &c.

Beneath the brier or brecken bush,
　Whene'er I kiss and court my dautie,
Happy and blyth as ane wad wish,
　My flighterin heart gangs pittie-pattie.
　　　O my bonny, &c.

O'er highest heathery hills I'll sten,
　　With cockit gun and ratches tenty,
To drive the deer out of their den,
　　To feast my lass on dishes dainty.
　　　　O my bonny, &c.

There's nane shall dare, by deed or word,
　　'Gainst her to wag a tongue or finger,
While I can wield my trusty sword,
　　Or frae my side whisk out a whinger.
　　　　O my bonny, &c.

The mountains clad with purple bloom,
　　And berries ripe, invite my treasure
To range with me; let great fowk gloom,
　　While wealth and pride confound their pleasure.
　　　　O my bonny, &c.

LXXXI.

THE AULD MAN'S BEST ARGUMENT.

O WHA's that at my chamber door?—
　　" Fair widow, are ye wawking?"—
Auld carle, your suit give o'er,
　　Your love lies a' in tawking!
Gi'e me the lad that's young and tight,
　　Sweet like an April meadow;
'Tis sic as he can bless the sight
　　And bosom of a widow.

" O widow! wilt thou let me in,
　　I'm pawky, wise, and thrifty,
And come of a right gentle kin;
　　I'm little mair than fifty."

Daft carle, dight your mouth,
　　What signifies how pawky
Or gentle born ye be ; but youth,
　　In love you're but a gawky.

" Then, widow, let these guineas speak,
　　That powerfully plead clinkan ;
And if they fail my mouth I'll steek,
　　And nae mair love will think on."
These court indeed, I maun confess,
　　I think they make you young, Sir,
And ten times better can express
　　Affection, than your tongue, Sir.

LXXXII.

TO MRS. A. C.

TUNE—"When beauty blazes."

WHEN beauty blazes heavenly bright,
　　The muse can no more cease to sing,
Than can the lark, with rising light,
　　Her notes neglect with drooping wing.
The morning shines, harmonious birds mount high ;
The dawning beauty smiles, and poets fly.

Young Annie's budding graces claim
　　The inspir'd thought, and softest lays,
And kindle in the breast a flame,
　　Which must be vented in her praise.
Tell us, ye gentle shepherds, have you seen
E'er one so like an angel tread the green ?

Ye youth, be watchful of your hearts,
    When she appears take the alarm ;
Love on her beauty points his darts,
    And wings an arrow from each charm.
Around her eyes and smiles the graces sport,
And to her snowy neck and breast resort.

But vain must every caution prove ;
    When such enchanting sweetness shines,
The wounded swain must yield to love,
    And wonder, tho' he hopeless pines.
Such flames the foppish butterfly should shun ;
The eagle's only fit to view the sun.

She's as the opening lily fair,
    Her lovely features are complete ;
Whilst heaven indulgent makes her share,
    With angels, all that's wise and sweet.
These virtues which divinely deck her mind,
Exalt each beauty of th' inferior kind.

Whether she love the rural scenes,
    Or sparkle in the airy town,
O ! happy he her favour gains ;
    Unhappy, if she on him frown.
The muse unwilling quits the lovely theme,
Adieu she sings, and thrice repeats her name.

LXXXIII.

I HAVE A GREEN PURSE, AND A WEE PICKLE GOWD.

I HAVE a green purse, and a wee pickle gowd,
    A bonny piece land and planting on't,
It fattens my flocks, and my bairns it has stow'd ;
    But the best thing of a's yet wanting on't ;

To grace it, and trace it,
 And gi'e me delight;
To bless me, and kiss me,
 And comfort my sight
With beauty by day, and kindness by night,
 And nae mair my lane gang saunt'ring on't.

My Christy she's charming, and good as she's fair,
 Her een and her mouth are enchanting sweet ;
She smiles me on fire, her frowns gi'e despair;
 I love while my heart gaes panting wi't.
  Thou fairest, and dearest,
   Delight of my mind,
  Whose gracious embraces
   By heaven were design'd
For happiest transports, and blisses refin'd,
 Nae langer delay thy granting sweet.

For thee, bonny Christy, my shepherds and hynds
 Shall carefully make the year's dainties thine :
Thus freed frae laigh care, while love fills our minds,
 Our days shall with pleasure and plenty shine.
  Then hear me, and cheer me
   With smiling consent,
  Believe me, and give me
   No cause to lament ;
Since I ne'er can be happy till thou say, Content,
 I'm pleas'd with my Jamie, and he shall be mine.

LXXXIV.

ON THE MARRIAGE OF LORD G. .

TUNE—"The Highland Laddie.'

BRIGANTIUS.

Now all thy virgin sweets are mine,
  And all the shining charms that grace thee ;
My fair Melinda, come recline
  Upon my breast, while I embrace thee,
And tell, without dissembling art,
  My happy raptures on thy bosom ;
Thus will I plant within thy heart
  A love that shall for ever blossom.

Chorus.

O the happy, happy, brave, and bonny !
  Sure the gods well-pleas'd behold ye ;
Their work admire, so great, so fair,
  And will in all your joys uphold ye.

MELINDA.

No more I blush, now that I'm thine,
  To own my love in transport tender,
Since that so brave a man is mine,
  To my Brigantius I surrender.
By sacred ties I'm now to move,
  As thy exalted thoughts direct me ;
And while my smiles engage thy love,
  Thy manly greatness shall protect me.

Chorus.
O the happy, &c.

BRIGANTIUS.

Saft fall thy words, like morning dew
  New life on blooming flowers bestowing :
Thus kindly yielding, makes me bow
  To heaven, with spirit grateful glowing.
My honour, courage, wealth, and wit,
  Thou dear delight, my chiefest treasure,
Shall be employ'd as thou thinks fit,
  As agents for our love and pleasure.

Chorus.
O the happy, &c.

MELINDA.

With my Brigantius I could live
  In lonely cot, beside a mountain,
And nature's easy wants relieve
  With shepherd's fare, and quaff the fountain.
What pleases thee, the rural grove,
  Or congress of the fair and witty,
Shall give me pleasure with thy love,
  In plains retir'd, or social city.

Chorus.
O the happy, &c.

BRIGANTIUS.

How sweetly canst thou charm my soul,
  O lovely sum of my desires !
Thy beauties all my cares control,
  Thy virtue all that's good inspires.
Tune every instrument of sound,
  Which all the mind divinely raises,
Till every height and dale rebound,
  Both loud and sweet, my darling's praises.

Chorus.
O the happy, &c.
c 2

MELINDA.

Thy love gives me the brightest shine,
    My happiness is now completed,
Since all that's generous, great, and fine,
    In my Brigantius is united;
For which I'll study thy delight,
    With kindly tale the time beguiling;
And round the change of day and night,
    Fix throughout life a constant smiling.

Chorus.
O the happy, &c.

LXXXV.

JENNY NETTLES.

Saw ye Jenny Nettles,
    Jenny Nettles, Jenny Nettles;
Saw ye Jenny Nettles,
    Coming frae the market;
Bag and baggage on her back,
    Her fee and bountith in her lap;
Bag and baggage on her back,
    And a baby in her oxter?

I met ayont the cairny
    Jenny Nettles, Jenny Nettles,
Singing till her bairny,
    Robin Rattle's bastard.
To uee the dool upon the stool,
    And ilka ane that mocks her,
She round about seeks Robin out,
    To stap it in his oxter.

Fy, fy ! Robin Rattle,
　　Robin Rattle, Robin Rattle ;
Fy, fy ! Robin Rattle,
　　Use Jenny Nettles kindly :
Score out the blame and shun the shame,
　　And without mair debate o't,
Take hame your wean, make Jenny fain,
　　The leel and leesome gate o't.

LXXXVI.

FOR THE SAKE OF SOMEBODY.

For the sake of somebody,
　　For the sake of somebody,
I could wake a winter night
　　For the sake of somebody !
I am gawn to seek a wife
　　I am gawn to buy a plaidy ;
I have three stane of woo,
　　Carling, is thy daughter ready ?
　　　　For the sake of, &c.

Betty, lassie, say 't thysell,
　　Tho" thy dame be ill to shoo,
First we'll buckle, then we'll tell,
　　Let her flyte and syne come too !
What signifies a mither's gloom,
　　When love and kisses come in play ?
Should we wither in our bloom,
　　And in simmer mak nae hay ?
　　　　For the sake, &c.

SHE.

Bonny lad, I carena by,
　　Tho' I try my luck with thee,

Since ye are content to tye
 The haff mark bridal band wi' me :
I'll slip hame and wash my feet,
 And steal on linens fair and clean,
Syne at the trysting-place we'll meet,
 To do but what my dame has done.
  For the sake, &c.

HE.

Now my lovely Betty gives
 Consent in sic a heartsome gate,
It me frae a' my care relieves,
 And doubts that gart me aft look blate :
Then let us gang and get the grace,
 For they that have an appetite
Should eat ; and lovers shou'd embrace ;
 If these be faults, 'tis nature's wyte.
  For the sake, &c.

LXXXVII.

THE GENEROUS GENTLEMAN.

TUNE—" The bonny lass of Branksome."

As I came in by Tiviot side,
 And by the braes of Branksome,
There first I saw my bonny bride,
 Young, smiling, sweet, and handsome :
Her skin was safter than the down,
 And white as alabaster ;
Her hair a shining wavy brown ;
 In straightness nane surpast her.

Life glow'd upon her lip and cheek,
 Her clear een were surprising,

And beautifully turn'd her neck,
　　Her little breasts just rising :
Nae silken hose with gushets fine,
　　Or shoon with glancing laces,
On her fair leg forbad to shine,
　　Well shapen native graces.

Ae little coat, and bodice white,
　　Was sum of a' her claithing ;—
Even these o'er mickle ;—mair delyte
　　She'd given cled wi' naithing.
She lean'd upon a flow'ry brae,
　　By which a burnie trotted ;
On her I glowr'd my saul away,
　　While on her sweets I doated.

A thousand beauties of desert
　　Before had scarce alarm'd me,
Till this dear artless struck my heart,
　　And but designing, charm'd me.
Hurry'd by love, close to my breast
　　I grasp'd this fund of blisses ;
Wha smil'd, and said, without a priest,
　　Sir, hope for nought but kisses.

I had nae heart to do her harm,
　　And yet I couldna want her ;
What she demanded, ilka charm
　　Of her's pled, I should grant her.
Since heaven had dealt to me a routh,
　　Straight to the kirk I led her,
There plighted her my faith and troth,
　　And a young lady made her.

LXXXVIII.

THE COCK LAIRD.

A COCK laird fou cadgie,
  With Jenny did meet,
He haws'd her, he kiss'd her,
  And ca'd her his sweet.
Wilt thou gae alang
  Wi' me, Jenny, Jenny?
Thouse be my ane leman,
  Jo Jenny, quoth he.

If I gae alang wi' ye,
  Ye maunna fail,
To feast me with caddels
  And good hacket-kail.
The deel's in your nicety,
  Jenny, quoth he ;
Mayna bannocks of bear-meal
  Be as good for thee ?

And I maun hae pinners
  With pearling set round,
A skirt of puddy,
  And a waistcoat of brown.
Awa with sic vanities,
  Jenny, quoth he,
For kurchis and kirtles
  Are fitter for thee.

My lairdship can yield me
  As meikle a year,
As had us in pottage
  And good knockit bear :
But having nae tenants,
  O Jenny, Jenny !

To buy ought I ne'er have
  A penny, quoth he.

The borrowstoun merchants
  Will sell ye on tick,
For we maun hae braw things,
  Abeit they soud break.
When broken, frae care
  The fools are set free,
When we make them lairds
  In the Abbey, quoth she.

LXXXIX.

LET MEANER BEAUTIES USE THEIR ART.

LET meaner beauties use their art,
  And range both Indies for their dress ;
Our fair can captivate the heart,
  In native weeds, nor look the less.
More bright unborrow'd beauties shine,
  The artless sweetness of each face
Sparkles with lustres more divine,
  When freed of every foreign grace.

The tawny nymph, on scorching plains,
  May use the aid of gems and paint,
Deck with brocade and Tyrian stains,
  Features of ruder form and taint :
What Caledonian ladies wear,
  Or from the lint or woollen twine,
Adorn'd by all their sweets, appear
  Whate'er we can imagine fine.

Apparel neat becomes the fair,
  The dirty dress may lovers cool,

But clean, our maids need have no care,
    If clad in linen, silk, or wool.
T' adore Myrtilla who can cease ?
    Her active charms our praise demand,
Clad in a mantua, from the fleece
    Spun by her own delightful hand.

Who can behold Calista's eyes,
    Her breast, her cheek, and snowy arms,
And mind what artists can devise
    To rival more superior charms ?
Compar'd with those, the diamond's dull,
    Lawns, satins, and the velvets fade,
The soul with her attractions full
    Can never be by these betray'd.

Saphira, all o'er native sweets,
    Not the false glare of dress regards,
Her wit her character completes,
    Her smile her lover's sighs rewards.
When such first beauties lead the way,
    The inferior rank will follow soon ;
Then arts no longer shall decay,
    But trade encouraged be in tune.

Millions of fleeces shall be wove,
    And flax that on the vallies blooms,
Shall make the naked nations love
    And bless the labours of our looms.
We have enough, nor want from them
    But trifles hardly worth our care;
Yet for these trifles let them claim
    What food and cloth we have to spare.

How happy's Scotland in her fair !
    Her amiable daughters shall,
By acting thus with virtuous care,
    Again the golden age recall :

Enjoying them, Edina ne'er
  Shall miss a court ; but soon advance
In wealth, when thus the lov'd appear
  Around the scenes, or in the dance.

Barbarity shall yield to sense,
  And lazy pride to useful arts,
When such dear angels in defence
  Of virtue thus engage their hearts.
Blest guardians of our joys and wealth !
  True fountains of delight and love !
Long bloom your charms, fixt be your health,
  Till, tir'd with earth, you mount above.

EPISTOLARY.

EPISTOLARY.

AN EPISTLE TO ALLAN RAMSAY,

BY JOSIAH BURCHET, ESQ.

1721.

WELL fare thee, Allan, who in mother-tongue
So sweetly hath of breathless Addie sung:
His endless fame thy nat'ral genius fir'd,
And thou hast written as if he inspir'd.
Richy and Sandy, who do him survive,
Long as thy rural stanzas last, shall live ;
The grateful swains thou'st made, in tuneful verse,
Mourn sadly o'er their late, lost patron's hearse.
Nor would the Mantuan bard, if living, blame
Thy pious zeal, or think thou'st hurt his fame,
Since Addison's inimitable lays
Give him an equal title to the bays.
When he of armies sang in lofty strains,
It seem'd as if he in the hostile plains
Had present been ; his pen hath to the life
Trac'd every action in the sanguine strife.
In council now sedate the chief appears,
Then loudly thunders in Bavarian ears ;
And still pursuing the destructive theme,
He pushes them into the rapid stream :
Thus beaten out of Blenheim's neighb'ring fields,
The Gallic gen'ral to the victor yields,

Who, as Britannia's Virgil hath observ'd,
From threaten'd fate all Europe then preserv'd.

Nor dost thou, Ramsay, sightless Milton wrong,
By ought contain'd in thy melodious song ;
For none but Addie could his thoughts sublime
So well unriddle, or his mystic rhyme.
And when he deign'd to let his fancy rove
Where sun-burnt shepherds to the nymphs make love,
No one e'er told in softer notes the tales
Of rural pleasures in the spangled vales.

So much, O Allan ! I thy lines revere,
Such veneration to his mem'ry bear,
That I no longer could my thanks refrain
For what thou 'st sung of the lamented swain.

XCI.

THE ANSWER TO THE FOREGOING.

THIRSTING for fame, at the Pierian spring,
The poet takes a waught, then 'seys to sing
Nature, and with the tentiest view to hit
Her bonny side with bauldest turns of wit.
Streams slide in verse, in verse the mountains rise ;
When earth turns toom, he rummages the skies,
Mounts up beyond them, paints the fields of rest,
Doups down to visit ilka lawland ghaist.
A heartsome labour ! wordy time and pains !
That frae the best esteem and friendship gains :
Be that my luck, and let the greedy bike,
Stock-job the warld amang them as they like.

In blyth braid Scots allow me, Sir, to shaw
My gratitude, but * fleetching or a flaw.
May rowth o' pleasures light upon you lang,
Till to the blest Elysian bow'rs ye gang,
Wha've clapt my head sae brawly for my sang.
When honour'd Burchet and his maikes are pleas'd
With my corn-pipe, up to the stars I'm heez'd ;
Whence far I glowr to the fag-end of time,
And view the warld delighted wi' my rhyme :
That when the pride of sprush-new words are laid,
I, like the classic authors, shall be read.
Stand yond, proud czar, I wadna niffer fame
With thee, for a' thy furs and paughty name.

If sic great ferlies, Sir, my muse can do,
As spin a three-plait praise where it is due,
Frae me there's nane deserves it mair than you.
Frae me !—frae ilka ane ; for sure a breast
Sae gen'rous is, of a' that's good possest !
Till I can serve ye mair, I'll wish ye weel,
And aft in sparkling claret drink your heal ;
Minding the mem'ry of the great and good
Sweet Addison, the wale of human blood,
Wha fell (as Horace anes said to his billy)
" Nulli flebilior quam tibi Virgili."

---

* "But" is frequently used for "without ; " *i.e.* without flattering.

XCII.

SEVEN FAMILIAR EPISTLES.

WHICH PASSED BETWEEN LIEUT. HAMILTON * AND THE AUTHOR.

1719.

EPISTLE I.

GILBERTFIELD, June 26th, 1719.

O FAM'D and celebrated Allan !
Renown'd Ramsay ! canty callan !
There's nowther Highland-man nor Lawlan,
  In poetrie,
But may as soon ding down Tamtallan †,
  As match wi' thee.

For ten times ten, and that's a hunder,
I ha'e been made to gaze and wonder,
When frae Parnassus thou didst thunder,
  Wi' wit and skill ;
Wherefore I'll soberly knock under,
  And quat my quill.

Of poetry the hail quintescence
Thou hast suck'd up, left nae excrescence
To petty poets, or sic messens,
  Tho' round thy stool
They may pick crumbs, and lear some lessons
  At Ramsay's school.

---

* For some account of this gentleman, see the Life of Ramsay prefixed.
† An old castle upon the Firth of Forth in East Lothian.

Tho' Ben * and Dryden of renown
Were yet alive in London town,
Like kings contending for a crown,
    'Twad be a pingle,
Whilk o' you three wad gar words sound
    And best to gingle.

Transform'd may I be to a rat,
Wer't in my power, but I'd create
Thee upo' sight the laureat †
    Of this our age,
Since thou may'st fairly claim to that
    As thy just wage.

Let modern poets bear the blame,
Gin they respect not Ramsay's name,
Wha soon can gar them greet for shame,
    To their great loss,
And send them a' right sneaking hame
    Be Weeping-cross.

Wha bourds wi' thee had need be wary,
And lear wi' skill thy thrust to parry,
When thou consults thy dictionary
    Of ancient words,
Which come from thy poetic quarry
    As sharp as swords.

Now tho' I should baith reel and rottle,
And be as light as Aristotle,
At Ed'nburgh we sall ha'e a bottle
    Of reaming claret,

---

* The celebrated Ben Jonson.

† Scots Ramsay press'd hard, and sturdily vaunted,
  He'd fight for the laurel before he would want it :
  But risit Apollo, and cry'd, Peace there, old stile,
  Your wit is obscure to one half of the isle.
                          B. SESS. OF POETS.

E 2

Gin that my half-pay * siller shottle
      Can safely spare it.

At crambo then we'll rack our brain,
Drown ilk dull care and aching pain,
Whilk aften does our spirits drain
      Of true content ;
Woy, woy ! but we's be wonder fain,
      When thus acquaint.

Wi' wine we'll gargarize our craig,
Then enter in a lasting league,
Free of ill aspect or intrigue ;
      And, gin you please it,
Like princes when met at the Hague,
      We'll solemnize it.

Accept of this, and look upon it
With favour, tho' poor I've done it :
Sae I conclude and end my sonnet,
      Who am most fully,
While I do wear a hat or bonnet,
      Yours,
            WANTON WILLY.

POSTSCRIPT.

By this my postscript I incline
To let you ken my hail design
Of sic a long imperfect line
      Lies in this sentence,

---

* He had held his commission honourably in Lord Hyndford's regiment.
    And may the stars who shine aboon,
      With honour notice real merit,
    Be to my friend auspicious soon,
      And cherish ay sae fine a spirit.

To cultivate my dull engine
  By your acquaintance.

Your answer therefore I expect ;
And to your friend you may direct
At Gilbertfield;* do not neglect,
  When ye have leisure,
Which I'll embrace with great respect,
  And perfect pleasure.

XCIII.

ANSWER I.

     EDINBURGH, July 10th, 1719.

SONSE fa' me, witty, Wanton Willy,
Gin blyth I was na as a filly ;
Not a fou pint, nor short-hought gilly,
  Or wine that's better,
Could please sae meikle, my dear Billy,
  As thy kind letter.

Before a lord and eik a knight,
In gossy Don's be candle-light,
There first I saw't, and ca'd it right,
  And the maist feck
Wha's seen't sinsyne, they ca'd as tight
  As that on Heck.

Ha, heh ! thought I, I canna say
But I may cock my nose the day,
When Hamilton the bauld and gay
  Lends me a heezy,
In verse that slides sae smooth away,
  Well tell'd and easy.

---

* Nigh Glasgow.

Sae roos'd by ane of well-kend mettle,
Nae sma' did my ambition pettle,
My canker'd critics it will nettle,
          And e'en sae be 't :
This month I 'm sure I winna settle,
          Sae proud I 'm wi't.

When I begoud first to cun verse,
And could your Ardry whins * rehearse,
Where Bonny Heck ran fast and fierce,
          It warm'd my breast ;
Then emulation did me pierce,
          Whilk since ne'er ceast.

May I be licket wi' a bittle,
Gin of your numbers I think little ;
Ye're never rugget, shan, nor kittle,
          But blyth and gabby,
And hit the spirit to a tittle
          Of standard Habby.†

Ye'll quat your quill !—that were ill, Willy,
Ye's sing some mair yet, nill ye will ye,
O'er meikle haining wad but spill ye,
          And gar ye sour ;
Then up and war them a' yet, Willy,
          'Tis in your pow'r.

To knit up dollars in a clout,
And then to card them round about,

---

* The last words of " Bonny Heck," of which he was the author.   It is printed
in a Choice Collection of Comic and Serious Scots Poems, by Watson, Edinburgh,
1706.

† The elegy on Habby Simpson, piper of Kilbarchan ; a finished piece of its kind,
which was printed in the same Choice Collection.

Syne to tell up, they downa lout
        To lift the gear ;
The malison lights on that rout,
        Is plain and clear.

The chiels of London, Cam, and Ox,
Ha'e rais'd up great poetic stocks
Of Rapes, of Buckets, Sarks, and Lock;
        While we neglect
To shaw their betters ; this provokes
        Me to reflect

On the learn'd days of Gawn Dunkell ; *
Our country then a tale could tell,
Europe had nane mair snack and snell
        At verse or prose :
Our kings† were poets too themsell,
        Bauld and jocose.

To Ed'nburgh, Sir, whene'er ye come,
I'll wait upon ye, there's my thumb,
Were't frae the gill-bells to the drum ‡,
        And tak' a bout,
And faith I hope we'll not sit dumb,
        Nor yet cast out.

---

* Gawn Douglas, the brother of the Earl of Angus, the bishop of Dunkell, who, besides several original poems, hath left a most exact translation of Virgil's Æneis into the Scotish language of his age : he died in 1522.

† James the First and Fifth.

‡ From half an hour before twelve at noon, when the music-bells begin to play, (frequently called the gill-bells, from people's taking a whetting dram at that time,) to the drum at ten o'clock at night, when the drum goes round to warn sober folks to call for a bill.

XCIV.

Epistle II.

GILBERTFIELD, July 24th, 1719.

DEAR RAMSAY,
WHEN I receiv'd thy kind epistle,
It made me dance, and sing, and whistle;
O sic a fike and sic a fistle
    I had about it!
That e'er was knight of the Scots thistle*
    Sae fain, I doubted.

The bonny lines therein thou sent me,
How to the Nines they did content me;
Tho', Sir, sae high to compliment me
    Ye might deferr'd,
For had ye but haff well a kent me,
    Some less wad ser'd.

With joyfu' heart beyond expression,
They're safely now in my possession:
O gin I were a winter session
    Near by thy lodging,
I'd close attend thy new profession,
    Without e'er budging.

In even down earnest, there's but few
To vie with Ramsay dare avow,
In verse, for to gi'e thee thy due,
    And without fleetching,

---

* The ancient and most noble order of knighthood, instituted by King Achaius, and renewed by James VII. The ordinary ensign, worn by the knights of the order, is a green ribband, to which is appended a thistle of gold crowned with an imperial crown, within a circle of gold, with this motto, "Nemo me impune lacesset."

Thou's better at that trade, I trow,
   Than some's at preaching.*

For my part, till I'm better lear't,
To troke with thee I'd best forbear't,
For an' the fouk of Ed'nburgh hear't,
   They'll ca' me daft;
I'm unco' iri, and dirt feart
   I mak' wrang waft.

Thy verses nice as ever nicket,
Made me as canty as a cricket;
I ergh to reply, lest I stick it;
   Syne like a coof
I look, or ane whose pouch is pickit
   As bare's my loof.

Heh winsom! how thy saft sweet style,
And bonny auld words gar me smile;
Thou's travell'd sure mony a mile
   Wi' charge and cost,
To learn them thus keep rank and file,
   And ken their post.

For I man tell thee, honest Allie,
(I use the freedom so to call thee,)
I think them a' sae braw and walie,
   And in sic order,
I wad nae care to be thy vallie,
   Or thy recorder.

Has thou with Rosicrucians † wandert,
Or thro' some doncie desart dandert?

---

* This compliment is entirely free of the fulsome hyperbole.

 † A people deeply learned in the occult sciences, who conversed with aeriel beings: gentlemanlike kind of necromancers, or so.

That with thy magic, town and landart,
          For ought I see,
Man a' come truckle to thy standart
          Of poetrie.

Do not mistake me, dearest heart,
As if I charg'd thee with black art;
'Tis thy good genius, still alert,
          That does inspire
Thee with ilk thing that's quick and smart
          To thy desire.

E'en mony a bonny nacky tale
Bra to sit o'er a pint of ale:
For fifty guineas I'll find bail
          Against a bodle,
That I wad quat ilk day a meal
          For sic a nodle.

And on condition I were as gabby
As either thee or honest Habby,
That I lin'd a' thy claes wi' tabby,
          Or velvet plush,
And then thou'd be sae far frae shabby,
          Thou'd look right sprush.

What tho' young empty airy sparks
May have their critical remarks
On thir my blyth diverting warks;
          'Tis sma presumption,
To say they're but unlearned clarks,
          And want the gumption.

Let coxcomb critics get a tether
To tye up a' their lang loose leather;
If they and I chance to forgether,
          The tane may rue it;

For an they winna had their blether,
　　　They's get a flewet.

To learn them for to peep and pry
In secret drolls 'twixt thee and I,
Pray dip thy pen in wrath, and cry,
　　　And ca' them skellums;
I'm sure thou needs set little by
　　　To bide their bellums.

Wi' writing I'm sae bleirt and doited,
That when I raise, in troth I stoited;
I thought I should turn capernoited,
　　　For wi' a gird,
Upon my bum I fairly cloited
　　　On the cald eard;
Which did oblige a little dumple
Upon my doup, close by my rumple:
But had ye seen how I did trumple,
　　　Ye'd split your side,
Wi' mony a lang and weary wimple,
　　　Like trough of Clyde.

XCV.

ANSWER II.

EDINBURGH, August 4th, 1719.

DEAR Hamilton, ye'll turn me dyver,
My muse sae bonny ye descrive her;
Ye blaw her sae, I'm fear'd ye rive her,
　　　For wi' a whid,
Gin ony higher up ye drive her,
　　　She'll rin red-wood.*

---

* Run distracted.

F 2

Said I.—" Whisht," quoth the vougy jade,
" William's a wise judicious lad,
Has havins mair than e'er ye had,
   Ill-bred bog-staker ; *
But me ye ne'er sae crouse had craw'd,
   Ye poor skull-thacker ! †

" It sets ye well indeed to gadge !‡
Ere I t' Apollo did ye cadge,
And got ye on his Honour's badge,
   Ungratefu' beast !
A Glasgow capon and a fadge§
   Ye thought a feast.

" Swith to Castalius' fountain brink,
Dad down a grouf, ‖ and tak' a drink,
Syne whisk out paper, pen, and ink,
   And do my bidding :
Be thankfou, else I'll gar ye stink
   Yet on a midding ! "

" My mistress dear, your servant humble,"
Said I, " I should be laith to drumble
Your passions or e'er gar ye grumble ;
   'Tis ne'er be me

---

* The muse, not unreasonably angry, puts me here in mind of the favours she has done, by bringing me from stalking over bogs or wild marshes, to lift my head a little brisker among the polite world, which could never have been acquired by the low movements of a mechanic.

† Thatcher of skulls.

‡ Ironically she says, It becomes me mighty well to talk haughtily, and affront my benefactress, by alleging so meanly, that it were possible to praise her out of her solidity.

§ A herring, and a coarse kind of leavened bread used by the common people.

‖ Fall flat on your belly.

Shall scandalize, or say ye bummil
        Ye'r poetrie."

Frae what I've tell'd, my friend may learn
How sadly I ha'e been forfairn,
I'd better been ayont side Cairn-
        amount,* I trow;
I've kiss'd the tawz,† like a good bairn.
        Now, Sir, to you:

Heal be your heart, gay couthy carle,
Lang may ye help to toom a barrel;
Be thy crown ay unclowr'd in quarrel,
        When thou inclines
To knoit thrawn-gabbit sumphs that snarl
        At our frank lines.

Ilk good chiel says, ye're well worth gowd,
And blythness on ye's well bestow'd,
'Mang witty Scots ye'r name's be row'd,
        Ne'er fame to tine ;
The crooked clinkers shall be cow'd,‡
        But ye shall shine.

Set out the burnt side of your shin,§
For pride in poets is nae sin ;
Glory's the prize for which they rin,
        And fame's their jo ;
And wha blaws best the horn shall win :
        And wharefore no ?

---

* A noted hill in Kincardineshire.

† Kissed the rod ; owned my fault like a good child.

‡ The scribbling rhymers, with their lame versification, shall be cowed, *i.e.* shorn off.

§ As if one would say, " Walk stately with your toes out." An expression used when we would bid a person (merrily) look brisk.

Quisquis vocabit nos vain-glorious,
Shaws scanter skill than *malos mores,*
Multi et magni men before us
       Did stamp and swagger ;
Probatum et exemplum, Horace
       Was a bauld bragger.

Then let the doofarts, fash'd wi' spleen,
Cast up the wrang side of their een,
Pegh, fry, and girn, wi' spite and teen,
       And fa' a flyting ;
Laugh, for the lively lads will screen
       Us frae back-biting.

If that the gypsies dinna spung us,
And foreign whiskers ha'e na dung us ;
Gin I can snifter thro' mundungus,
       Wi' boots and belt on,
I hope to see you at St. Mungo's,*
       Atween and Beltan.

XCVI.

EPISTLE III.

        GILBERTFIELD, August 24th, 1719.

ACCEPT my third and last essay.
Of rural rhyme, I humbly pray,
Bright Ramsay, and altho' it may
       Seem doilt and donsie,
Yet thrice of all things, I heard say,
       Was ay right sonsie.

Wharefore I scarce could sleep or slumber,
Till I made up that happy number :
The pleasure counterpois'd the cumber
       In every part,

---

* The High Church of Glasgow.

And snoovt away * like three-hand ombre,
  Sixpence a cart.

Of thy last poem, bearing date
August the fourth, I grant receipt ;
It was sae braw, gart me look blate,
   'Maist tyne my senses,
And look just like poor country Kate,
   In Lucky Spence's, †

I shaw'd it to our parish priest,
Wha was as blyth as gi'm a feast ;
He says, thou may had up thy creest,
   And craw fu' crouse,
The poets a' to thee's but jest,
   Not worth a souse.

Thy blyth and cheerfu' merry muse,
Of compliments is sae profuse,
For my good havins dis me roose
   Sae very finely,
It were ill breeding to refuse
   To thank her kindly.

What tho' sometimes, in angry mood,
When she puts on her barlichood,
Her dialect seem rough and rude,
   Let's ne'er be fleet,
But tak our bit, when it is good,
   And buffet wi't.

For gin we ettle anes to taunt her,
And dinna cawmly thole her banter,

---

* Whirl'd smoothly round. "Snooving" always expresses the action of a top or spindle, &c.

† Vide Elegy on Lucky Spence, vol. i. p. 217.

She'll tak' the flings,* verse may grow scanter ;
　　　　Syne wi' great shame
We'll rue the day that we do want her ;
　　　　Then wha's to blame ?

But let us still her kindness culzie,
And wi' her never breed a tulzie,
For we'll bring aff but little spulzie
　　　　In sic a barter ;
And she'll be fair to gar us fulzie,
　　　　And cry for quarter.

Sae little worth's my rhyming ware,
My pack I scarce dare apen mair,
'Till I tak' better wi' the lair,
　　　　My pen's sae blunted ;
And a' for fear I file the fair,†
　　　　And be affronted.

The dull draff-drink ‡ makes me sae dowff,
A' I can do's but bark and yowff ;
Yet set me in a claret howff,
　　　　Wi' fouk that's chancy,
My muse may lend me then a gowff
　　　　To clear my fancy.

Then Bacchus-like I'd bawl and bluster,
And a' the muses 'bout me muster ;
Sae merrily I'd squeeze the cluster,
　　　　And drink the grape,
'Twad gi'e my verse a brighter lustre,
　　　　And better shape.

---

* Turn sullen, restive, and kick.

† This phrase is used when one attempts to do what is handsome, and is affronted by not doing it right :—not a reasonable fear in him.

‡ Heavy malt-liquor.

The pow'rs aboon be still auspicious
To thy achievements maist delicious ;
Thy poems sweet, and nae way vicious,
   But blyth and canny,
To see I'm anxious and ambitious,
   Thy Miscellany.

A' blessings,* Ramsay, on thee row ;
Lang may thou live, and thrive, and dow,
Until thou claw an auld man's pow ;
   And thro' thy creed,
Be keeped frae the wirricow,
   After thou's dead.

XCVII.

ANSWER III.

EDINBURGH, Sept. 2, 1719.

MY TRUSTY TROJAN,

THY last oration orthodox,
Thy innocent auld farren jokes,
And sonsy saw of three, provokes
   Me anes again,
Tod lowrie like,† to loose my pocks,
   And pump my brain.

By a' your letters I ha'e read,
I eithly scan the man well-bred,
And soger that, where honour led,
   Has ventur'd bauld ;
Wha now to youngsters leaves the yed,
   To 'tend his fauld. ‡

---

* All this verse is a succinct cluster of kindly wishes, elegantly expressed, with a friendly spirit ; to which I take the liberty to add, Amen.

† Like Reynard the fox, to betake myself to some more of my wiles.

‡ Leaves the martial contention, and retires to a country life.

That bang'ster billy, Cæsar July,
Wha at Pharsalia wan the tooly,
Had better sped had he mair hooly
            Scamper'd thro' life,
And 'midst his glories sheath'd his gooly,
            And kiss'd his wife.

Had he, like you, as well he could,*
Upon burn banks the muses woo'd,
Retir'd betimes frae 'mang the crowd,
            Wha'd been aboon him,
The senate's durks, and faction loud,
            Had ne'er undone him.

Yet sometimes leave the riggs and bog,
Your howms, and braes, and shady scrog,
And helm-a-lee the claret cog,
            To clear your wit :
Be blyth, and let the world e'en shog
            As it thinks fit.

Ne'er fash about your neist year's state,
Nor with superior pow'rs debate,
Nor cantrapes cast to ken your fate ;
            There's ills anew
To cram our days, which soon grow late ;
            Let's live just now.

When northern blasts the ocean snurl,
And gars the heights and hows look gurl,
Then left about the bumper whirl,
            And toom the horn ; †
Grip fast the hours which hasty hurl,
            The morn 's the morn.

---

* It is well known he could write as well as fight.

† It is frequent, in the country, to drink beer out of horn cups made in shape of
a water-glass.

Thus to Leuconoe sang sweet Flaccus,*
Wha nane e'er thought a gillygacus ;
And why should we let whimsies bawk us,
    When joy's in season,
And thole sae aft the spleen to whauk us
    Out of our reason ?

Tho' I were laird of tenscore acres,
Nodding to jouks of hallen-shakers,†
Yet crush'd wi' humdrums, which the weaker's
    Contentment ruins,
I'd rather roost wi' causey-rakers,
    And sup cauld sowens.

I think, my friend, an fowk can get
A doll of roast beef piping het,
And wi' red wine their wyson wet,
    And cleathing clean,
And be na sick, or drown'd in debt,
    They're no too mean.

I read this verse to my ain kimmer,
Wha kens I like a leg of gimmer,
Or sic and sic good belly timmer :
    Quoth she, and leugh,
" Sicker of thae, winter and simmer,
    Ye're well enough."

My hearty goss, there is nae help,
But hand to nive we twa man skelp
Up Rhine and Thames, and o'er the Alp-
    pines and Pyrenians.

---

* Vide Book i. Ode 11 of Horace.

† A hallen is a fence (built of stone, turf, or a moveable flake of heather) at the sides of the door, in country places, to defend them from the wind. The trembling attendant about a forgetful great man's gate or levee, is also expressed in the term "hallenshaker."

The cheerfou carles do sae yelp
   To ha'e 's their minions.

Thy raffan rural rhyme sae rare,
Sic wordy, wanton, hand-wail'd ware,
Sae gash and gay, gars fowk gae gare*
   To ha'e them by them ;
Tho' gaffin they wi' sides sae sair,
   Cry, " Wae gae by him!"†

Fair fa' that soger did invent
To ease the poet's toil wi' prent :
Now, William, we man to the bent,
   And pouse our fortune,
And crack wi' lads wha're well content
   Wi' this our sporting.

Gin ony sour-mou'd girning bucky
Ca' me conceity keckling chucky,
That we, like nags whase necks are yucky,
   Ha'e us'd our teeth ;
I'll answer fine, Gae kiss ye'r Lucky,‡
   She dwells i' Leith.

I ne'er wi' lang tales fash my heid,
But when I speak, I speak indeed :
Wha ca's me droll, but ony feed,
   I'll own I'm sae ;
And while my champers can chew bread,
   Yours,
     —ALLAN RAMSAY.

---

* Make people very earnest.

† It is usual for many, after a full laugh, to complain of sore sides, and to bestow a kindly curse on the author of the jest : but the folks of more tender consciences have turned expletives to friendly wishes, such as this, or "sonse fa' ye," and the like.

‡ Is a cant phrase, from what rise I know not ; but it is made use of when one thinks it is not worth while to give a direct answer, or think themselves foolishly accused.

XCVIII.

AN EPISTLE TO LIEUTENANT HAMILTON,

ON RECEIVING THE COMPLIMENT OF A BARREL OF LOCHFYNE HERRINGS FROM HIM.

YOUR herrings, Sir, came hale and feer,*
 In healsome brine a' soumin,
Fu' fat they are, and gusty gear,
 As e'er I laid my thumb on ;
  Braw sappy fish
  As ane could wish
 To clap on fadge or scone ;
  They relish fine
  Good claret wine,
That gars our cares stand yon.

Right mony gabs wi' them shall gang
 About Auld Reekie's ingle,
When kedgy carles think nae lang,
 When stoups and trunchers gingle :
  Then my friend leal,
  We toss ye'r heal,
 And with bald brag advance,
  What 's hoorded in
  Lochs Broom and Fin †
Might ding the stocks of France.

A jelly sum to carry on
 A fishery's designed,‡
Twa million good of sterling pounds,
 By men of money's signed.

---

* Whole, without the least fault or want.
† Two lochs on the western seas, where plenty of herrings are taken.
‡ The royal fishery ; success to which is the wish and hope of every good man.

Had ye but seen
How unco keen
And thrang they were about it,
That we are bald,
Right rich, and ald-
farran, ye ne'er wad doubted.

Now, now, I hope, we'll ding the Dutch,
As fine as a round-robin,
Gin greediness to grow soon rich
Invites not to stock jobbing :
That poor boss shade
Of sinking trade,
And weather-glass politic,
Which heaves and sets
As public gets
A heezy, or a wee kick.

Fy, fy !—but yet I hope 'tis daft
To fear that trick come hither ;
Na, we're aboon that dirty craft
Of biting ane anither.
The subject rich
Will g' a hitch
T' increase the public gear,
When on our seas,
Like bisy bees,
Ten thousand fishers steer.

Could we catch th' united shoals
That crowd the western ocean,
The Indies would prove hungry holes,
Compar'd to this our Goshen :
Then let's to wark
With net and bark,

Them fish and faithfu' cure up ;
　　Gin sae we join,
　　We'll cleek in coin
Frae a' the ports of Europe.

Thanks t' ye, Captain, for this swatch
　　Of our store, and your favour;
Gin I be spar'd your love to match
　　Shall still be my endeavour.
　　　　Next unto you,
　　　　My service due
　　Please gi'e to Matthew Cumin,*
　　　　Wha with fair heart
　　　　Has play'd his part,
And sent them true and trim in.

XCIX.

TO THE MUSIC CLUB.

1721.

ERE on old Shinar's plain the fortress rose,
Rear'd by those giants who durst heav'n oppose,
An universal language mankind us'd,
Till daring crimes brought accents more confus'd ;
Discord and jar for punishment were hurl'd
On hearts and tongues of the rebellious world.

　The primar speech with notes harmonious clear,
(Transporting thought !) gave pleasure to the ear :
Then music in its full perfection shin'd,
When man to man melodious spoke his mind.

---

* Merchant in Glasgow, and one of the late magistrates of that city.

As when a richly-fraughted fleet is lost
In rolling deeps, far from the ebbing coast,
Down many fathoms of the liquid mass,
The artist dives in ark of oak or brass ;
Snatches some ingots of Peruvian ore,
And with his prize rejoicing makes the shore :
Oft this attempt is made, and much they find ;
They swell in wealth, tho' much is left behind.

Amphion's sons, with minds elate and bright,
Thus plunge th' unbounded ocean of delight,
And daily gain new stores of pleasing sounds,
To glad the earth, fixing to spleen its bounds ;
While vocal tubes and comfort strings engage
To speak the dialect of the golden age.
Then you, whose symphony of souls proclaim
Your kin to heav'n, add to your country's fame,
And show that music may have as good fate
In Albion's glens, as Umbria's green retreat ;
And with Correlli's soft Italian song
Mix " Cowdenknows," and " Winter nights are long : "
Nor should the martial " Pibroch " be despis'd ;
Own'd and refin'd by you, these shall the more be priz'd.

Each ravish'd ear extols your heav'nly art,
Which soothes our care, and elevates the heart ;
Whilst hoarser sounds the martial ardours move,
And liquid notes invite to shades and love.

Hail ! safe restorer of distemper'd minds,
That with delight the raging passions binds ;
Ecstatic concord, only banish'd hell,
Most perfect where the perfect beings dwell.
Long may our youth attend thy charming rites,
Long may they relish thy transported sweets.

C.

AN EPISTLE TO MR. JAMES ARBUCKLE;

DESCRIBING THE AUTHOR.

EDINBURGH, January, 1719.

As errant knight, with sword and pistol,
Bestrides his steed with mighty fistle;
Then stands some time in jumbled swither,
To ride in this road, or that ither;
At last spurs on, and disna care for
A how, a what way, or a wherefore.

    Or like extemporary quaker,
Wasting his lungs, t' enlighten weaker
Lanthorns of clay, where light is wanting,
With formless phrase, and formal canting;
While Jacob Bœhmen's* salt does season,
And saves his thought frae corrupt reason,
Gowling aloud with motions queerest,
Yerking those words out which lye nearest.

    Thus I (no longer to illustrate
With similes, lest I should frustrate
Design laconic of a letter,
With heap of language, and no matter,)
Bang'd up my blyth auld-fashion'd whistle,
To sowf ye o'er a short epistle,
Without rule, compasses, or charcoal,
Or serious study in a dark hole.
Three times I ga'e the muse a rug,
Then bit my nails, and claw'd my lug;

---

* The Teutonic philosopher, who wrote volumes of unintelligible enthusiastic bombast.

Still heavy—at the last my nose
I prim'd with an inspiring dose,*
Then did ideas dance (dear safe us !)
As they'd been daft.—Here ends the preface.

Good Mr. James Arbuckle, Sir,
(That's merchants' style as clean as fir,)
Ye're welcome back to Caledonie,†
Lang life and thriving light upon ye,
Harvest, winter, spring, and summer,
And ay keep up your heartsome humour,
That ye may thro' your lucky task go,
Of brushing up our sister Glasgow ;
Where lads are dext'rous at improving,
And docile lassies fair and loving :
But never tent these fellows' girning,
Wha wear their faces ay in mourning,
And frae pure dulness are malicious,
Terming ilk turn that's witty, vicious.

Now, Jamie, in neist place, *secundo*,
To give you what's your due *in mundo ;*
That is to say in hame-o'er phrases,
To tell ye, men of mettle praises
Ilk verse of yours, when they can light on't,
And trouth I think they're in the right on't ;
For there's ay something sae auld-farran,
Sae slid, sae unconstrain'd, and darin,
In ilka sample we have seen yet,
That little better here has been yet :
Sae much for that.—My friend Arbuckle,
I ne'er afore roos'd ane so muckle :

---

* Vide Mr. Arbuckle's Poem on Snuff.
† Having been in his native Ireland, visiting his friends.

Fause flatt'ry nane but fools will tickle,
That gars me hate it like auld Nicol :
But when ane's of his merit conscious,
He's in the wrang, when prais'd, that glunshes.

Thirdly, not tether'd to connection,
But rattling by inspir'd direction,
Whenever fame, with voice like thunder,
Sets up a chield a warld's wonder,
Either for slashing fowk to dead,
Or having wind-mills in his head,
Or poet, or an airy beau,
Or ony twa-legg'd rary-show,
They wha have never seen't are bissy
To speer what like a carlie is he.

Imprimis then, for tallness, I
Am five foot and four inches high ;
A black-a-vic'd snod dapper fallow,
Nor lean, nor over-laid wi' tallow ;
With phiz of a Morocco cut,
Resembling a late man of wit,
Auld gabbet Spec,* wha was sae cunning
To be a dummie ten years' running.

Then for the fabric of my mind,
'Tis mair to mirth than grief inclin'd ;
I rather choose to laugh at folly,
Than show dislike by melancholy :
Well judging a sour heavy face
Is not the truest mark of grace.

I hate a drunkard or a glutton,
Yet I'm nae fae to wine and mutton :

---

* *The Spectator*, who gives us a fictitious description of his short face and taci-
turnity, that he had been esteemed a dumb man for ten years.

Great tables ne'er engag'd my wishes,
When crowded with o'er mony dishes ;
A healthfu' stomach sharply set,
Prefers a back-sey piping het.

I never could imagine 't vicious
Of a fair fame to be ambitious :
Proud to be thought a comic poet,
And let a judge of numbers know it,
I court occasion thus to shew it.

Second of thirdly, pray take heed,
Ye's get a short swatch of my creed.
To follow method negatively,
Ye ken, takes place of positively :
Well then, I'm nowther Whig nor Tory,*
Nor credit give to Purgatory ;
Transub., Loretta-house and mae tricks,
As prayers to Saints Katties and Patricks,
Nor Asgilite,† nor Bess Clarksonian,‡
Nor Mountaineer,§ nor Mugletonian ; ‖

---

* Ramsay was a zealous Tory from principle. But he was much caressed by Baron Clerk and other gentlemen of opposite principles, which made him outwardly affect neutrality. His " Vision," and " Tale of Three Bonnets," are sufficient proofs of his zeal as an old Jacobite : but, wishing to disguise himself, he published this, and the " Eagle and Redbreast," as ancient poems, and with the fictitious signature of " A. R. Scot ;" whence they are generally attributed to an old poet, Alexander Scot, of whose composition there are several pieces in the collection published by RAMSAY, called " The Evergreen."

† Mr. Asgil, a late Member of Parliament, advanced (whether in jest or earnest I know not) some very whimsical opinions ; particularly, that people need not die if they pleased, but be translated alive to heaven like Enoch and Elijah.

‡ Bessy Clarkson, a Lanarkshire woman. Vide the history of her life and principles.

§ Our wild folks, who always prefer a hill side to a church under any civil authority.

‖ A kind of Quakers, so called from one Mugleton. See Leslie's " Snake in the Grass.'

Nor can believe, ant's hae great ferly,
In Cotmoor fowk and Andrew Harlay.*

Neist, Anti-Toland, Blunt, and Whiston,
Know positively I'm a Christian,
Believing truths and thinking free,
Wishing thrawn parties wad agree.

Say, wad ye ken my gate of fending,
My income, management, and spending?
Born to nae lairdship, (mair 's the pity!)
Yet denison of this fair city;
I make what honest shift I can,
And in my ain house am good-man,
Which stands on Edinburgh's street, the sun-side:
I theck the out, and line the inside
Of mony a douce and witty pash,
And baith ways gather in the cash;
Thus heartily I graze and beau it,
And keep my wife ay great wi' poet:
Contented I have sic a skair,
As does my business to a hair;
And fain wad prove to ilka Scot,
That poortith 's no the poet's lot.

Fourthly and lastly baith togither,
Pray let us ken when ye come hither;
There's mony a canty carle and me
Wad be much comforted to see ye:
And if your outward be refractory,
Send us your inward manufactory,
That when we're kedgy o'er our claret,
We correspond may with your spirit.

---

* A family or two who had a particular religion of their own, valued themselves
on using vain repetitions in prayers of six or seven hours long: were pleased
with ministers of no kind. Andrew Harlaw, a dull fellow of no education, was
head of the party.

Accept of my kind wishes, with
The same to Dons Butler, and Smith ;
Health, wit, and joy, sauls large and free,
Be a' your fates :—sae God be wi' ye.

CI.

TO THE EARL OF DALHOUSIE.

1721.

DALHOUSIE of an auld descent,
My chief, my stoup, and ornament,
For entertainment a wee while,
Accept this sonnet with a smile.
Setting great Horace in my view,
He to Mæcenas, I to you ;
But that my muse may sing with ease,
I'll keep or drap him as I please.

How differently are fowk inclin'd,
There's hardly twa of the same mind !
Some like to study, some to play,
Some on the Links to win the day,
And gar the courser rin like wood,
A' drappin down with sweat and blood:
The winner syne assumes a look
Might gain a monarch or a duke.
Neist view the man with pawky face
Has mounted to a fashious place,
Inclin'd by an o'er-ruling fate,
He's pleas'd with his uneasy state;
Glowr'd at a while, he gangs fou braw,
Till frae his kittle post he fa'.

The Lothian farmer he likes best
To be of good faugh riggs possest,
And fen upon a frugal stock,
Where his forbears had us'd the yoke ;
Nor is he fond to leave his wark,
And venture in a rotten bark,
Syne unto far aff countries steer,
On tumbling waves to gather gear.

The merchant wreck'd upon the main,
Swears he'll ne'er venture on't again ;
That he had rather live on cakes,
And shyrest swats, with landart maiks,
As rin the risk by storms to have,
When he is dead, a living grave.
But seas turn smooth, and he grows fain,
And fairly takes his word again,
Tho' he should to the bottom sink,
Of poverty he downa think.

Some like to laugh their time away,
To dance while pipes or fiddles play ;
And have nae sense of ony want,
As lang as they can drink and rant.

The rattling drum and trumpet's tout
Delight young swankies that are stout ;
What his kind frighted mother ugs,
Is music to the soger's lugs.

The hunter with his hounds and hawks
Bangs up before his wife awakes ;
Nor speers gin she has ought to say,
But scours o'er heighs and hows a' day,
Thro' moss and moor, nor does he care
Whether the day be foul or fair,
If he his trusty hounds can cheer
To hunt the tod or drive the deer.

May I be happy in my lays,
And won a lasting wreath of bays,
Is a' my wish ; well-pleas'd to sing
Beneath a tree, or by a spring,
While lads and lasses on the mead
Attend my Caledonian reed,
And with the sweetest notes rehearse
My thoughts, and reese me for my verse.

If you, my Lord, class me amang
Those who have sung baith saft and strang,
Of smiling love, or doughty deed,
To starns sublime I'll lift my head.

CII.

TO MR. AIKMAN.

1721.

'TIS granted, Sir, pains may be spar'd
    Your merit to set forth,
When there's sae few wha claim regard,
    That disna ken your worth.

Yet poets give immortal fame
    To mortals that excel,
Which if neglected they're to blame ;
    But you've done that yoursell.

While frae originals of yours
    Fair copies shall be ta'en,
And fix'd on brass to busk our bow'rs,
    Your mem'ry shall remain.

To your ain deeds the maist deny'd,
Or of a taste o'er fine,
May be ye're but o'er right, afraid
To sink in verse like mine.

The last can ne'er the reason prove,
Else wherefore with good will
Do ye my nat'ral lays approve,
And help me up the hill?

By your assistance unconstrain'd,
To courts I can repair,
And by your art my way I've gain'd
To closets of the fair.

Had I a muse like lofty Pope,
For tow'ring numbers fit,
Then I th' ingenious mind might hope
In truest light to hit.

But comic tale, and sonnet slee,
Are casten for my share,
And if in these I bear the gree,
I'll think it very fair.

CIII.

TO SIR WILLIAM BENNET.

1721.

WHILE now in discord giddy changes reel,
And some are rack'd about on fortune's wheel,
You, with undaunted stalk and brow serene,
May trace your groves, and press the dewy green;
No guilty twangs your manly joys to wound,
Or horrid dreams to make your sleep unsound.

To such as you who can mean care despise,
Nature's all beautiful 'twixt earth and skies.
Not hurried with the thirst of unjust gain,
You can delight yourself on hill or plain,
Observing when those tender sprouts appear,
Which crowd with fragrant sweets the youthful year.
Your lovely scenes of Marlefield abound
With as much choice as is in Britain found :
Here fairest plants from Nature's bosom start
From soil prolific, serv'd with curious art;
Here oft the heedful gazer is beguil'd,
And wanders thro' an artificial wild,
While native flow'ry green, and crystal strands,
Appear the labours of ingenious hands.

Most happy he who can these sweets enjoy
With taste refin'd, which does not easy cloy.
Not so plebeian souls, whom sporting fate
Thrusts into life upon a large estate,
While spleen their weak imagination sours,
They're at a loss how to employ their hours :
The sweetest plants which fairest gardens show
Are lost to them, for them unheeded grow :
Such purblind eyes ne'er view the son'rous page,
Where shine the raptures of poetic rage ;
Nor thro' the microscope can take delight
T' observe the tusks and bristles of a mite ;
Nor by the lengthen'd tube learn to descry
Those shining worlds which roll around the sky.
Bid such read hist'ry to improve their skill,
Polite excuse ! their memories are ill :
Moll's maps may in their dining-rooms make show,
But their contents they're not oblig'd to know ;
And gen'rous friendship's out of sight too fine,
They think it only means a glass of wine.

But he whose cheerful mind hath higher flown,
And adds learn'd thoughts of others to his own ;

Has seen the world, and read the volume Man,
And can the springs and ends of action scan ;
Has fronted death in service of his king,
And drunken deep of the Castalian spring ;
This man can live, and happiest life's his due ;
Can be a friend—a virtue known to few ;
Yet all such virtues strongly shine in you.

CIV.

TO A FRIEND AT FLORENCE.*

1721.

YOUR steady impulse foreign climes to view,
To study nature, and what art can shew,
I now approve, while my warm fancy walks
O'er Italy, and with your genius talks ;
We trace, with glowing breast and piercing look,
The curious gall'ry of th' illustrious duke,
Where all those masters of the arts divine,
With pencils, pens, and chisels greatly shine,
Immortalizing the Augustan age,
On medals, canvas, stone, or written page.
Profiles and busts originals express,
And antique scrolls, old ere we knew the press.
For's love to science, and each virtuous Scot,
May days unnumber'd be great Cosmus' lot!

The sweet Hesperian fields you'll next explore,
'Twixt Arno's banks and Tiber's fertile shore.
Now, now I wish my organs could keep pace,
With my fond muse and you these plains to trace ;

---

* Mr. Smibert, a painter. Mr. Walpole, in his " Anecdotes of Painting," characterises him as an ingenious artist, and a modest worthy man. He died at Boston, in New England, in 1751. ALLAN RAMSAY, the painter, was a scholar of Smibert's.

I 2

We'd enter Rome with an uncommon taste,
And feed our minds on every famous waste;
Amphitheatres, columns, royal tombs,
Triumphal arches, ruins of vast domes,
Old aerial aqueducts, and strong-pav'd roads,
Which seem to've been not wrought by men but gods.

These view'd, we'd then survey with utmost care
What modern Rome produces fine or rare;
Where buildings rise with all the strength of art,
Proclaiming their great architect's desert.
Which citron shades surround and jessamin,
And all the soul of Raphael shines within.
Then we'd regale our ears with sounding notes
Which warble tuneful thro' the beardless throats,
Join'd with the vibrating harmonious strings,
And breathing tubes, while the soft eunuch sings.

Of all those dainties take a hearty meal;
But let your resolution still prevail:
Return, before your pleasure grow a toil,
To longing friends, and your own native soil:
Preserve your health, your virtue still improve,
Hence you'll invite protection from above.

CV.

TO R. H. B.

1721.

O B—— ! could these fields of thine
Bear, as in Gaul, the juicy vine
How sweet the bonny grape would shine
        On waw's where now,
Your apricots and peaches fine
        Their branches bow.

Since human life is but a blink,
Why should we then its short joys sink ?
He disna live that canna link
        The glass about,
When warm'd with wine, like men we think,
        And grow mair stout.

The cauldrife carlies clog'd wi' care,
Wha gathering gear gang hyt and gare,
If ram'd wi' red, they rant and rair,
        Like mirthfu' men,
It soothly shaws them they can spare
        A rowth to spend.

What soger, when with wine he's bung,
Did e'er complain he had been dung,
Or of his toil, or empty spung?
        Na, o'er his glass,
Nought but braw deeds employ his tongue,
        Or some sweet lass.

Yet trouth 'tis proper we should stint
Oursells to a fresh mod'rate pint,
Why should we the blyth blessing mint
        To waste or spill,
Since aften when our reason's tint,
        We may do ill ?

Let's set these hair-brain'd fowk in view,
That when they're stupid, mad, and fou,
Do brutal deeds, which aft they rue
        For a' their days,
Which frequently prove very few
        To such as these.

Then let us grip our bliss mair sicker,
And tap our heal and sprightly liquor,

Which sober tane, makes wit the quicker,
And sense mair keen,
While graver heads that's muckle thicker
Grane wi' the spleen.

May ne'er sic wicked fumes arise
In me, shall break a' sacred ties,
And gar me like a fool despise,
With stiffness rude,
Whatever my best friends advise,
Tho' ne'er so gude.

'Tis best then to evite the sin
Of bending till our sauls gae blin,
Lest, like our glass, our breasts grow thin,
And let fowk peep
At ilka secret hid within,
That we should keep.

CVI.

TO MR. JOSEPH MITCHELL,

ON THE SUCCESSFUL REPRESENTATION OF A TRAGEDY. *

1721.

BUT jealousy, dear Jos., which aft gives pain
To scrimpit sauls, I own myself right vain
To see a native trusty friend of mine
Sae brawly 'mang our bleezing billies shine.

---

* The piece here alluded to was "Fatal Extravagance," a Tragedy, 1721; which Mitchell himself afterwards avowed to have been written by Aaron Hill, Esq., who, with a generosity peculiar to himself, allowed this author, who was himself a tolerable poet, both the reputation and the profits of this piece, to extricate him from some pecuniary embarrassments brought on by his own extravagance: thus in the very title of the piece conveying a gentle reproof, while he generously relieved him. Mitchell was the author of two volumes of miscellaneous poems; "Fatal Extravagance," a Tragedy, 8vo, 1721; the "Fatal Extravagance," enlarged, 12mo, 1725; "The Highland Fair," a ballad opera, 8vo, 1731. Mitchell died in 1738.

Yes, wherefore no, shaw them the frozen north
Can tow'ring minds with heav'nly heat bring forth :
Minds that can mount with an uncommon wing,
And frae black heath'ry-headed mountains sing,
As saft as he that haughs Hesperian treads,
Or leans beneath the aromatic shades ;
Bred to the love of lit'rature and arms,
Still something great a Scotish bosom warms ;
Tho' nurs'd on ice, and educate in snaw,
Honour and liberty eggs him up to draw
A hero's sword, or an heroic quill,
The monstrous faes of right and wit to kill.

Well may ye further in your leal design
To thwart the gowks, and gar the brethren tine
The wrang opinion which they lang have had,
That a' which mounts the stage is surely bad.
Stupidly dull !—but fools ay fools will be,
And nane's sae blind as them that winna see.
Where's vice and virtue set in juster light ?
Where can a glancing genius shine mair bright ?
Where can we human life review mair plain,
Than in the happy plot and curious scene ?

If in themsells sic fair designs were ill,
We ne'er had priev'd the sweet dramatic skill,
Of Congreve, Addison, Steele, Rowe, and Hill ;
Hill, wha the highest road to fame doth chuse,
And has some upper seraph for his muse ;
It maun be sae, else how could he display,
With so just strength the great tremendous day ?

Sic patterns, Joseph, always keep in view,
Ne'er fash if ye can please the thinking few,
Then, spite of malice, worth shall have its due.

TO ROBERT YARDE OF DEVONSHIRE.

FRAE northern mountains clad with snaw,
Where whistling winds incessant blaw,
In time now when the curling-stane
Slides murm'ring o'er the icy plain,
What sprightly tale in verse can Yarde
Expect frae a cauld Scotish bard,
With brose and bannocks poorly fed,
In hoden grey right hashly clad,
Skelping o'er frozen hags with pingle,
Picking up peets to beet his ingle,
While sleet that freezes as it fa's,
Thecks as with glass the divot waws
Of a laigh hut, where sax thegither
Ly heads and thraws on craps of heather?

Thus, Sir, of us the story gaes,
By our mair dull and scornfu' faes :
But let them tauk, and gowks believe,
While we laugh at them in our sleeve :
For we, nor barbarous nor rude,
Ne'er want good wine to warm our blood ;
Have tables crown'd, and heartsome beils,
And can in Cumin's, Don's, or Steil's,
Be serv'd as plenteously and civil
As you in London at the "Devil."
You, Sir, yourself, wha came and saw,
Own'd that we wanted nought at a'
To make us as content a nation
As any is in the creation.

This point premis'd, my canty muse
Cocks up her crest without excuse,
And scorns to screen her natural flaws
With ifs, and buts, and dull because ;

She pukes her pens, and aims a flight
Thro' regions of internal light,
Frae fancy's field these truths to bring,
That you should hear, and she should sing.

Langsyne, when love and innocence
Were human nature's best defence,
Ere party jars made lawtith less,
By cleathing 't in a monkish dress ;
Then poets shaw'd these evenly roads
That lead to dwellings of the gods.
In these dear days, well kend of fame,
Divini vates was their name.
It was, and is, and shall be ay,
While they move in fair Virtue's way ;
Tho' rarely we to stipends reach,
Yet nane dare hinder us to preach.

Believe me, Sir, the nearest way
To happiness is to be gay ;
For spleen indulg'd will banish rest
Far frae the bosoms of the best ;
Thousands a year's no worth a prin,
Whene'er this fashious guest gets in :
But a fair competent estate
Can keep a man frae looking blate ;
Sae eithly it lays to his hand
What his just appetites demand.
Wha has, and can enjoy, O wow !
How smoothly may his minutes flow !
A youth thus blest with manly frame,
Enliven'd with a lively flame,
Will ne'er with sordid pinch control
The satisfaction of his soul.
Poor is that mind, ay discontent,
That canna use what God has lent,
But envious girns at a' he sees,
That are a crown richer than he's ;

Which gars him pitifully hane,
And hell's ase-middins rake for gain ;
Yet never kens a blythsome hour,
Is ever wanting, ever sour.

Yet ae extreme should never make
A man the gowden mean forsake,
It shaws as much a shallow mind,
And ane extravagantly blind,
If careless of his future fate,
He daftly wastes a good estate,
And never thinks till thoughts are vain,
And can afford him nought but pain.
Thus will a joiner's shavings' bleeze
Their low will for some seconds please,
But soon the glarin' gleam is past,
And cauldrife darkness follows fast ;
While slaw the faggots large expire,
And warm us with a lasting fire.
Then neither, as I ken ye will,
With idle fears your pleasures spill ;
Nor with neglecting prudent care,
Do skaith to your succeeding heir :
Thus steering cannily thro' life,
Your joys shall lasting be and rife.
Give a' your passions room to reel,
As lang as reason guides the wheel :
Desires, tho' ardent, are nae crime,
When they harmoniously keep time ;
But when they spang o'er reason's fence,
We smart for't at our ain expence.
To recreate us we're allow'd,
But gaming deep boils up the blood,
And gars ane at groom-porter's ban
The Being that made him a man,
When his fair gardens, house, and lands,
Are fa'n amongst the sharpers' hands.

A cheerfu' bottle soothes the mind,
Gars carles grow canty, free, and kind,
Defeats our care, and heals our strife,
And brawly oils the wheels of life;
But when just quantums we transgress,
Our blessing turns the quite reverse.

To love the bonny smiling fair,
Nane can their passions better ware;
Yet love is kittle and unruly,
And should move tentily and hooly;
For if it get o'er meikle head,
'Tis fair to gallop ane to dead:
O'er ilka hedge it wildly bounds,
And grazes on forbidden grounds,
Where constantly like furies range
Poortith, diseases, death, revenge:
To toom anes poutch to daunty clever,
Or have wrang'd husband probe ane's liver,
Or void ane's saul out thro' a shanker,
In faith 'twad any mortal canker.

Then wale a virgin worthy you,
Worthy your love and nuptial vow;
Syne frankly range o'er a' her charms,
Drink deep of joy within her arms;
Be still delighted with her breast,
And on her love with rapture feast.

May she be blooming, saft, and young,
With graces melting from her tongue;
Prudent and yielding to maintain
Your love, as well as you her ain.

Thus with your leave, Sir, I've made free
To give advice to ane can gi'e

As good again:—but as mass John
Said, when the sand tald time was done,
" Ha'e patience, my dear friends, a wee,
And take ae ither glass frae me ;
And if ye think there's doublets due,
I shanna bauk the like frae you."

CVIII.

AN EPISTLE FROM MR. WILLIAM STARRAT.

AE windy day last owk, I'll ne'er forget,
I think I hear the hailstanes rattling yet ;
On Crochan-buss my hirdsell took the lee
As ane wad wish, just a' beneath my ee :
I in the bield of yon auld birk-tree side,
Poor cauldrife Coly whing'd aneath my plaid.
Right cozylie was set to ease my stumps,
Well hap'd with bountith hose and twa-sol'd pumps ;
Syne on my four-hours' luncheon chew'd my cood,
Sic kilter pat me in a merry mood ;
My whistle frae my blanket nook I drew,
And lilted owre thir twa three lines to you.

Blaw up my heart-strings, ye Pierian quines,
That gae the Grecian bards their bonny rhymes,
And learn'd the Latin lowns sic springs to play
As gars the world gang dancing to this day.

In vain I seek your help,—'tis bootless toil
With sic dead ase to muck a moorland soil ;
Give me the muse that calls past ages back,
And shaws proud southern sangsters their mistak,
That frae their Thames can fetch the laurel north,
And big Parnassus on the Firth of Forth.

Thy breast alane this gladsome guest does fill
With strains that warm our hearts like cannel gill,
And learns thee, in thy umquhile gutcher's tongue,
The blythest lilts that e'er my lugs heard sung.
Ramsay ! for ever live ; for wha like you,
In deathless sang, sic life-like pictures drew ?
Not he wha whilome with his harp could ca'
The dancing stanes to big the Theban wa' ;
Nor he (shame fa's fool head !) as stories tell,
Could whistle back an auld dead wife frae hell ;
Nor e'en the loyal brooker of Belltrees,
Wha sang with hungry wame his want of fees ;
Nor Habby's drone, could with thy windpipe please,
When, in his well-ken'd clink, thou manes the death
Of Lucky Wood and Spence, (a matchless skaith
To Canigate,) sae gash thy gab-trees gang,
The carlines live for ever in thy sang.

Or when thy country bridal thou pursues,
To red the regal tulzie sets thy muse,
Thy soothing sangs bring canker'd carles to ease,
Some loups to Lutter's pipe, some birls bawbees.

But gin to graver notes thou tunes thy breath,
And sings poor Sandy's grief for Adie's death,
Or Matthew's loss, the lambs in concert mae,
And lanesome Ringwood yowls upon the brae.

Good God ! what tuneless heart-strings wadna twang,
When love and beauty animate the sang ?
Skies echo back, when thou blaws up thy reed
In Burchet's praise for clapping of thy head :
And when thou bids the paughty Czar stand yon,
The wandought seems beneath thee on his throne.
Now, be my saul, and I have nought behin,
And well I wat fause swearing is a sin,
I'd rather have thy pipe and twa three sheep,
Than a' the gowd the monarch's coffers keep.

Coly, look out, the few we have 's gane wrang,
This se'enteen owks I have not play'd sae lang ;
Ha ! Crummy, ha ! trowth I man quat my sang ;
But, lad, neist mirk we'll to the haining drive,
When in fresh lizar they get spleet and rive :
The royts will rest, and gin ye like my play,
I'll whistle to thee all the live-lang day.

TO MR. WILLIAM STARRAT,

ON RECEIVING THE FOREGOING.

FRAE fertile fields where nae curs'd ethers creep,
To stang the herds that in rash busses sleep ;
Frae where Saint Patrick's blessing freed the bogs
Frae taids, and asks, and ugly creeping frogs ;
Welcome to me the sound of Starrat's pipe,
Welcome as westlan winds or berries ripe,
When speeling up the hill, the dog-days' heat
Gars a young thirsty shepherd pant and sweet :
Thus while I climb the muses' mount with care,
Sic friendly praises give refreshing air.
O ! may the lasses loo thee for thy pains,
And may thou lang breathe healsome o'er the plains :
Lang mayst thou teach, with round and nooked lines,
Substantial skill, that's worth rich siller mines ;
To shaw how wheels can gang with greatest ease,
And what kind barks sail smoothest o'er the seas ;
How wind-mills should be made ; and how they work
The thumper that tells hours upon the kirk ;
How wedges rive the aik ; how pullisees
Can lift on highest roofs the greatest trees,
Rug frae its roots the craig of Edinburgh castle,
As easily as I could break my whistle ;

What pleugh fits a wet soil, and whilk the dry ;
And mony a thousand useful things forby.

  I own 'tis cauld encouragement to sing,
When round ane's lugs the blatran hail-stanes ring ;
But feckfu' folks can front the baldest wind,
And slunk thro' moors, and never fash their mind.
Aft have I wid thro' glens with chorking feet,
When neither plaid nor kelt could fend the weet ;
Yet blythly wald I bang out o'er the brae,
And stend o'er burns as light as ony rae,
Hoping the morn might prove a better day.
Then let 's to lairds and ladies leave the spleen,
While we can dance and whistle o'er the green.
Mankind's account of good and ill's a jest,
Fancy's the rudder, and content's a feast.

  Dear friend of mine ! ye but o'er meikle reese
The lawly mints of my poor moorland muse,
Wha looks but blate, when even'd to ither twa,
That lull'd the deel, or bigg'd the Theban wa' ;
But trowth 'tis natural for us a' to wink
At our ain fauts, and praises frankly drink.
Fair fa' ye then, and may your flocks grow rife,
And may nae elf twin crummy of her life.

  The sun shines sweetly, a' the lift looks blue,
O'er glens hing hov'ring clouds of rising dew.
Maggy, the bonniest lass of a' our town,
Brent is her brow, her hair a curly brown,
I have a tryst with her and man away,
Till ye'll excuse me till anither day
When I've mair time, for shortly I'm to sing
Some dainty sangs, that sall round Crochan ring.

CX.

TO MR. GAY,

ON HEARING THE DUCHESS OF QUEENSBURY COMMEND SOME OF HIS
POEMS.*

DEAR lad, wha linkan o'er the lee,
Sang Blowzalind and Bowzybee,
And, like the lavrock, merrily
    Wak'd up the morn,
When thou didst tune, with heartsome glee,
    Thy bog-teed horn.

To thee frae edge of Pentland height,
Where fawns and fairies take delight,
And revel a' the live-lang night
    O'er glens and braes,
A bard that has the second sight
    Thy fortune spaes.

Now lend thy lug and tent me, Gay,
Thy fate appears like flow'rs in May,
Fresh, flourishing, and lasting ay
    Firm as the aik,
Which envious winds, when critics bray,
    Shall never shake.

Come, shaw your loof;—ay, there's the line
Foretells thy verse shall ever shine,
Dawted whilst living by the nine,
    And a' the best,
And be, when past the mortal line,
    Of fame possest.

---

* Gay was a great admirer of the Poems of Ramsay, particularly of his "Gentle
Shepherd;" and they afterwards became personally acquainted, when Gay
visited Scotland with the Duke and Duchess of Queensbury.

Immortal Pope, and skilfu' John,[*]
The learned Leach frae Callidon,
With mony a witty dame and don,
    O'er lang to name,
Are of your roundels very fon,
    And sound your fame.

And sae do I, wha reese but few,
Which nae sma' favour is to you;
For to my friends I stand right true,
    With shanks a-spar;
And my good word (ne'er gi'en but due)
    Gangs unko far.

Here mettled men my muse maintain,
And ilka beauty is my friend;
Which keeps me canty, brisk, and bein,
    Ilk wheeling hour,
And a sworn fae to hatefu' spleen
    And a' that's sour.

But bide ye, boy, the main's to say;
Clarinda, bright as rising day,
Divinely bonny, great, and gay,
    Of thinking even,
Whase words, and looks, and smiles, display
    Full views of heaven.

To rummage Nature for what's braw,
Like lilies, roses, gems, and snaw,
Compar'd with hers, their lustre fa'
    And bauchly tell
Her beauties,—she excels them a'
    And's like hersell;

---

[*] Dr. John Arbuthnot.

As fair a form as e'er was blest
To have an angel for a guest ;
Happy the prince who is possest
　　　Of sic a prize,
Whose virtues place her with the best
　　　Beneath the skies.

O sonsy Gay ! this heavenly born,
Whom ev'ry grace strives to adorn,
Looks not upon thy lays with scorn ;
　　　Then bend thy knees,
And bless the day that ye was born
　　　With arts to please.

She says thy sonnet smoothly sings,
Sae ye may craw and clap your wings,
And smile at ethercapit stings
　　　With careless pride,
When sae much wit and beauty brings
　　　Strength to your side.

Lift up your pipes, and rise aboon
Your Trivia and your Moorland tune,
And sing Clarinda late and soon,
　　　In tow'ring strains,
Till gratefu' gods cry out—"Well done,"
　　　And praise the pains.

Exalt thy voice, that all around
May echo back the lovely sound,
Frae Dover cliffs with samphire crown'd
　　　To Thule's shore,
Where northward no more Britain's found,
　　　But seas that rore.

Thus sing :—Whilst I frae Arthur's height,
O'er Chiviot glow'r with tired sight,

And langing wish, like raving wight,
        To be set down,
Frae coach and sax, baith trim and tight,
        In London town.

But lang I'll gove and bleer my ee,
Before, alake ! that sight I see ;
Then (best relief) I'll strive to be
        Quiet and content,
And streek my limbs down easylie
        Upon the bent.

There sing the gowans, broom, and trees,
The crystal burn and westlin breeze,
The bleeting flocks and bisy bees,
        And blythsome swains,
Wha rant and dance, with kiltit dees,
        O'er mossy plains.

Farewell.   But ere we part, let's pray
God save Clarinda night and day,
And grant her a' she'd wish to ha'e,
        Withoutten end.—
Nae mair at present I've to say,
        But am your friend.

AN EPISTLE TO JOSIAH BURCHET,

ON HIS BEING CHOSEN MEMBER OF PARLIAMENT.

My Burchet's name well pleas'd I saw
        Amang the chosen leet
Wha are to give Britannia law,
        And keep her rights complete.

O may the rest wha fill the house
    Be of a mind with thee,
And British liberty espouse ;
    We glorious days may see.

The name of patriot is mair great
    Than heaps of ill-won gear ;
What boots an opulent estate
    Without a conscience clear ?

While sneaking sauls for cash wad trock
    Their country, God, and king,
With pleasure we the villain mock
    And hate the worthless thing.

With a' your pith,—the like of you
    Superior to what's mean,—
Should gar the trockling rogues look blue,
    And cow them laigh and clean.

Down with them,—down with a' that dare
    Oppose the nation's right ;
Sae may your fame, like a fair star,
    Through future times shine bright.

Sae may kind heaven propitious prove,
    And grant whate'er ye crave ;
And him a corner in your love
    Wha is your humble slave.

CXII.

TO MR. DAVID MALLOCH,

ON HIS DEPARTURE FROM SCOTLAND.

SINCE fate, with honour, bids thee leave
 Thy country for a while,
It is nae friendly part to grieve
 When powers propitious smile.

The task assign'd thee's great and good,—
 To cultivate two Grahams,
Wha from bauld heroes draw their blood,
 Of brave immortal names.

Like wax, the dawning genius takes
 Impressions thrawn or even ;
Then he wha fair the moulding makes
 Does journey-work for heaven.

The sour weak pedants spoil the mind
 Of those beneath their care,
Who think instruction is confin'd
 To poor grammatic ware.

But better kens my friend, and can
 Far nobler plans design
To lead the boy up to a man
 That's fit in courts to shine.

Frae Grampian heights (some may object)
 Can you sic knowledge bring ?
But those laigh tinkers ne'er reflect
 Some sauls ken ilka thing,

With vaster ease, at the first glance,
 Than misty minds that plod
And thresh for thought, but ne'er advance
 Their stawk aboon their clod.

But he that could, in tender strains,
 Raise Margaret's plaining shade,*
And paint distress that chills the veins
 While William's crimes are red ;

Shaws to the world, could they observe,
 A clear deserving flame :—
Thus I can reese without reserve
 When truth supports my theme.

Gae, lad, and win a nation's love
 By making those in trust,
Like Wallace's Achates,† prove
 Wise, generous, brave, and just.

Sae may his Grace th' illustrious sire
 With joy paternal see
Their rising blaze of manly fire,
 And pay his thanks to thee.

CXIII.

TO WILLIAM SOMERVILLE OF WARWICKSHIRE.

1728.

SIR, I have read, and much admire
 Your muse's gay and easy flow,
Warm'd with that true Idalian fire
 That gives the bright and cheerful glow.

---

* "William and Margaret," a ballad in imitation of the old manner, wherein the strength of thought and passion is more observed than a rant of unmeaning words.

† The heroic Sir John Graham, the glory of his name, the dearest friend of the renowned Sir William Wallace, and the ancestor of his Grace the Duke of Montrose.

I con'd each line with joyous care,
 As I can such from sun to sun ;
And, like the glutton o'er his fare,
 Delicious, thought them too soon done.

The witty smile, nature and art,
 In all your numbers so combine
As to complete their just desert,
 And grace them with uncommon shine.

Delighted we your muse regard
 When she, like Pindar's, spreads her wings,
And virtue, being its own reward,
 Expresses by " The Sister Springs."

Emotions tender crowd the mind
 When with the royal bard you go,
To sigh in notes divinely kind,
 " The Mighty fall'n on Mount Gilbo."

Much surely was the virgin's joy
 Who with the Iliad had your lays,
For, ere and since the siege of Troy,
 We all delight in love and praise.

These heaven-born passions, such desire,
 I never yet could think a crime,
But first-rate virtues, which inspire
 The soul to reach at the sublime.

But often men mistake the way
 And pump for fame by empty boast,
Like your " Gilt Ass," who stood to bray
 Till in a flame his tail he lost.

Him th' incurious bencher hits
 With his own tale, so tight and clean,
That while I read, streams gush by fits
 Of hearty laughter from my een.

Old Chaucer, bard of vast ingine,—
    Fontaine and Prior, who have sung
Blyth tales the best,—had they heard thine
    On Lob, they'd own themselves outdone.

The plot's pursu'd with so much glee,
    The too officious dog and priest,
The squire oppress'd, I own for me
    I never heard a better jest.

Pope well describ'd an ombre game,
    And king revenging captive queen ;
He merits, but had won more fame,
    If author of your " Bowling-green."

You paint your parties, play each bowl,
    So natural, just, and with such ease,
That while I read, upon my soul,
    I wonder how I chance to please.

Yet I have pleas'd, and please the best ;
    And sure to me laurels belong,
Since British fair, and 'mong the best,
    Somerville's consort likes my song.

Ravish'd I heard th' harmonious fair
    Sing, like a dweller of the sky,
My verses with a Scotian air ;
    Then saints were not so blest as I.

In her the valu'd charms unite,
    She really is what all would seem,
Gracefully handsome, wise, and sweet ;
    'Tis merit to have her esteem.

Your noble kinsman, her lov'd mate,
    Whose worth claims all the world's respect,

Met in her love a smiling fate,
　　Which has, and must have good effect.

You both from one great lineage spring,
　　Both from de Somerville, who came
With William, England's conquering king,
　　To win fair plains and lasting fame :

Whichnour, he left to 's eldest son,
　　That first-born chief you represent ;
His second came to Caledon,
　　From whom our Somer'le takes descent.

On him and you may Fate bestow
　　Sweet balmy health and cheerful fire,
As long 's ye'd wish to live below,
　　Still blest with all you would desire.

O Sir ! oblige the world, and spread
　　In print * those and your other lays ;
This shall be better'd while they read,
　　And after-ages sound your praise.

I could enlarge ;—but if I should
　　On what you've wrote, my ode would run
Too great a length ; your thoughts so crowd,
　　To note them all I'd ne'er have done.

Accept this offering of a muse,
　　Who on her Pictland hills ne'er tires ;
Nor should, when worth invites, refuse
　　To sing the person she admires.

---

* Since the writing of this Ode, Mr. Somerville's Poems are printed by Mr.
Lintot in an 8vo. volume.—Somerville died in 1742. This *superior* to Pope is
allowed by Johnson " to write well for a gentleman."

CXIV.

AN EPISTLE FROM MR. SOMERVILLE.

NEAR fair Avona's silver tide,
Whose waves in soft meanders glide,
I read to the delighted swains
Your jocund songs and rural strains.
Smooth as her streams your numbers flow,
Your thoughts in vary'd beauties show,
Like flow'rs that on her borders grow.
While I survey, with ravish'd eyes,
This friendly gift,* my valu'd prize,
Where sister arts, with charms divine,
In their full bloom and beauty shine,
Alternately my soul is blest :
Now I behold my welcome guest,
That graceful, that engaging air,
So dear to all the brave and fair.
Nor has th' ingenious artist shown
His outward lineaments alone,
But in th' expressive draught design'd
The nobler beauties of his mind ;
True friendship, love, benevolence,
Unstudied wit and manly sense.
Then as your book I wander o'er,
And feast on the delicious store,
(Like the laborious busy bee,
Pleas'd with the sweet variety,)
With equal wonder and surprise,
I see resembling portraits rise.

---

* Lord Somerville was pleased to send me his own picture and Mr. RAMSAY's
Works. In 1730, Somerville concluded a bargain with James, Lord Somerville, for
the reversion of his estate at his death. His connection with Lord Somerville
probably occasioned his poetical correspondence with RAMSAY, who was patronized
by that nobleman.

Brave archers march in bright array,
In troops the vulgar line the way:
Here the droll figures slyly sneer,
Or coxcombs at full length appear:
There woods and lawns, a rural scene,
And swains that gambol on the green.
Your pen can act the pencil's part,
With greater genius, fire, and art.

Believe me, bard, no hunted hind
That pants against the southern wind,
And seeks the streams thro' unknown ways;
No matron in her teeming days,
E'er felt such longings, such desires,
As I to view those lofty spires,
Those domes where fair Edina shrouds
Her tow'ring head amid the clouds.
But oh! what dangers interpose!
Vales deep with dirt and hills with snows,
Proud winter-floods, with rapid force,
Forbid the pleasing intercourse.
But sure we bards, whose purer clay
Nature has mixt with less allay,
Might soon find out an easier way.
Do not sage matrons mount on high
And switch their broomsticks thro' the sky,
Ride post o'er hills, and woods, and seas,
From Thule to the Hesperides?*
And yet the men of Gresham own
That this, and stranger feats, are done
By a warm fancy's power alone.
This granted, why can't you and I
Stretch forth our wings and cleave the sky?
Since our poetic brains, you know,
Than theirs must more intensely glow.

---

* The Scilly Islands were so called by the ancients, as Mr. Camden observes.

Did not the Theban swan take wing,
Sublimely soar, and sweetly sing ?
And do not we, of humbler vein,
Sometimes attempt a loftier strain,
Mount sheer out of the reader's sight,
Obscurely lost in clouds and night ?

Then climb your Pegasus with speed,
I'll meet thee on the banks of Tweed ;
Not as our fathers did of yore,
To swell the flood with crimson gore,—
Like the Cadmean murd'ring brood,
Each thirsting for his brother's blood,—
For now all hostile rage shall cease,
Lull'd in the downy arms of peace ;
Our honest hands and hearts shall join
O'er jovial banquets, sparkling wine.
Let Peggy at thy elbow wait,
And I shall bring my bonny Kate.
But hold :—oh ! take a special care
T' admit no prying kirkman there ;
I dread the penitential chair.
What a strange figure should I make,—
A poor abandon'd English rake,
A squire well born, and six foot high,—
Perch'd in that sacred pillory !
Let spleen and zeal be banish'd thence,
And troublesome impertinence,
That tells his story o'er again ;
Ill-manners and his saucy train,
And self-conceit, and stiff-rumpt pride,
That grin at all the world beside ;
Foul scandal, with a load of lies,
Intrigues, rencounters, prodigies,
Fame's busy hawker, light as air,
That feeds on frailties of the fair ;
Envy, hypocrisy, deceit,

Fierce party rage and warm debate,
And all the hell-hounds that are foes
To friendship and the world's repose.
But mirth instead, and dimpling smiles,
And wit, that gloomy care beguiles,
And joke and pun, and merry tale,
And toasts, that round the table sail ;
While laughter, bursting thro' the crowd
In vollies, tells our joys aloud.
Hark ! the shrill piper mounts on high,
The woods, the streams, the rocks reply
To his far-sounding melody.
Behold each lab'ring squeeze prepare
Supplies of modulated air.
Observe Croudero's active bow,
His head still nodding to and fro,
His eyes, his cheeks with raptures glow ;
See, see the bashful nymphs advance,
To lead the regulated dance.
Flying still, the swains pursuing,
Yet with backward glances wooing.
This, this shall be the joyous scene ;
Nor wanton elves that skim the green,
Shall be so blest, so blyth, so gay,
Or less regard what dotards say.
My rose shall then your thistle greet,
The union shall be more complete,
And in a bottle and a friend
Each national dispute shall end.

CXV.

AN ANSWER TO THE FOREGOING.

SIR, I had yours, and own my pleasure,
On the receipt, exceeded measure.
You write with so much sp'rit and glee,
Sae smooth, sae strong, correct, and free,
That any he (by you allow'd
To have some merit) may be proud.
If that's my fault, bear you the blame
Wha 've lent me sic a lift to fame.
Your ain tow'rs high, and widens far,
Bright glancing like a first-rate star,
And all the world bestow due praise
On the Collection of your lays ;
Where various arts and turns combine,
Which even in parts first poets shine :
Like Matt. and Swift ye sing with ease,
And can be Waller when you please.
Continue, Sir, and shame the crew
That's plagu'd with having nought to do ;
Whom Fortune, in a merry mood,
Has overcharg'd with gentle blood,
But has deny'd a genius fit
For action or aspiring wit.
Such kenna how t' employ their time,
And think activity a crime.
Ought they to either do or say,
Or walk, or write, or read, or pray,
When money, their factotum's able
To furnish them a numerous rabble
Who will, for daily drink and wages,
Be chairmen, chaplains, clerks, and pages ?
Could they, like you, employ their hours
In planting these delightful flowers
Which carpet the poetic fields

And lasting funds of pleasure yields,
Nae mair they'd gaunt and gove away,
Or sleep or loiter out the day,
Or waste the night, damning their sauls
In deep debauch and bawdy·brawls,
Whence pox and poverty proceed,
An early eild and spirits dead.
Reverse of you, and him you love,
Whose brighter spirit tow'rs above
The mob of thoughtless lords and beaux,
Who in his ilka action shows
" True friendship, love, benevolence,
Unstudy'd wit, and manly sense."
Allow here what you've said yoursell,
Nought can b' exprest so just and well.
To him and her, worthy his love,
And every blessing from above,
A son is given,—God save the boy,
For theirs and every Som'ril's joy.
Ye wardens ! round him take your place,
And raise him with each manly grace ;
Make his meridian virtues shine
To add fresh lustres to his line ;
And many may the mother see
Of such a lovely progeny.

Now, Sir, when Boreas nae mair thuds
Hail, snaw, and sleet, frae blacken'd clouds ;
While Caledonian hills are green,
And a' her straths delight the een ;
While ilka flower with fragrance blows,
And a' the year its beauty shows ;
Before again the winter lour,
What hinders then your northern tour ?
Be sure of welcome, nor believe
These wha an ill report would give
To Ed'nburgh and the land of cakes,

That nought what's necessary lacks.
Here Plenty's goddess, frae her horn,
Pours fish and cattle, claith and corn,
In blyth abundance. And yet mair,
Our men are•brave, our ladies fair ;
Nor will North Britain yield for fouth
Of ilka thing, and fellows couth,
To ony but her sister South.

True, rugged roads are cursed dreigh,
And speats aft roar frae mountains heigh ;
The body tires, (poor tottering clay!)
And likes with ease at hame to stay ;
While sauls stride warlds at ilka stend,
And can their widening views extend.
Mine sees you, while you cheerfu' roam
On sweet Avona's flow'ry howm,
There recollecting, with full view,
These follies which mankind pursue ;
While conscious of superior merit
You rise with a correcting spirit,
And, as an agent of the gods,
Lash them with sharp satyric rods :
Labour divine !—Next, for a change,
O'er hill and dale I see you range
After the fox or whidding hare,
Confirming health in purest air ;
While joy frae heights and dales resounds,
Rais'd by the holla, horn and hounds.
Fatigu'd, yet pleas'd, the chase outrun,
I see the friend and setting sun
Invite you to the temp'rate bicker,
Which makes the blood and wit flow quicker.
The clock strikes twelve, to rest you bound
To save your health by sleeping sound.
Thus, with cool head and healsome breast,
You see new day stream frae the east ;

Then all the muses round you shine,
Inspiring ev'ry thought divine.
Be long their aid.   Your years and blisses,
Your servant ALLAN RAMSAY wishes.

CXVI.

AN EPISTLE FROM W. SOMERVILLE TO ALLAN RAMSAY,

ON PUBLISHING HIS SECOND VOLUME OF POEMS.

HAIL ! Caledonian bard ! whose rural strains
Delight the list'ning hills, and cheer the plains ;
Already polish'd by some hand divine,
Thy purer ore what furnace can refine ?
Careless of censure, like the sun shine forth
In native lustre and intrinsic worth.
To follow Nature, is by rules to write ;
She led the way and taught the Stagyrite,
From her the critic's taste, the poet's fire,
Both drudge in vain till she from heav'n inspire.
By the same guide instructed how to soar,
ALLAN is now what Homer was before.

Ye chosen youths wha dare like him aspire,
And touch with bolder hand the golden lyre,
Keep Nature still in view ; on her intent,
Climb by her aid the dang'rous steep ascent
To lasting fame.   Perhaps a little art
Is needful to plane o'er some rugged part ;
But the most labour'd elegance and care,
T' arrive at full perfection, must despair.
Alter, blot out, and write all o'er again,
Alas ! some venial sins will yet remain.
Indulgence is to human frailty due,
E'en Pope has faults, and Addison a few;

But those, like mists that cloud the morning ray,
Are lost and vanish in the blaze of day.
Tho' some intruding pimple find a place
Amid the glories of Clarinda's face,
We still love on, with equal zeal adore,
Nor think her less a goddess than before.
Slight wounds in no disgraceful scars shall end,
Heal'd by the balm of some good-natur'd friend.
In vain shall canker'd Zoilus assail,
While Spence* presides, and Candor holds the scale.
His gen'rous breast nor envy sow'rs, nor spite ;
Taught by his founder's motto † how to write,
Good manners guides his pen,—learn'd without pride,
In dubious points not forward to decide.
If here and there uncommon beauties rise,
From flow'r to flow'r he roves with glad surprise.
In failings no malignant pleasure takes,
Nor rudely triumphs over small mistakes ;
No nauseous praise, no biting taunts offend,
We expect a censor, and we find a friend.
Poets, improv'd by his correcting care,
Shall face their foes with more undaunted air
Strip'd of their rags, shall like Ulysses shine †
With more heroic port and grace divine.
No pomp of learning, and no fund of sense,
Can e'er atone for lost benevolence.
May Wickham's sons,—who in each art excel,
And rival ancient bards in writing well,
While, from their bright examples taught, they sing
And emulate their flights with bolder wing,—
From their own frailties learn the humbler part,
Mildly to judge in gentleness of heart.

---

* Mr. Spence, Poetry Professor in Oxford and Fellow of New College.

† William of Wickham, Founder of New College in Oxford and of Winchester College.   His motto is—" Manners maketh man."

‡ Vide Hom. Od., lib. xxiv.

Such critics, Ramsay, jealous for our fame,
Will not with malice insolently blame ;
But, lur'd by praise, the haggard muse reclaim,
Retouch each line till all is just and neat,
A whole of proper parts, a work almost complete.

So when some beauteous dame,—a reigning toast,
The flow'r of Forth, and proud Edina's boast,—
Stands at her toilet in her tartan plaid,
And all her richest headgear, trimly clad,
The curious handmaid, with observant eye,
Corrects the swelling hoop that stands awry ;
Thro' ev'ry plait her busy fingers rove,
And now she plys below, and then above ;
With pleasing tattle entertains the fair,
Each ribbon smooths, adjusts each rambling hair,
Till the gay nymph in her full lustre shine,
And Homer's Juno was not half so fine.*

CXVII.

RAMSAY'S ANSWER TO THE FOREGOING.

1729.

AGAIN, like the return of day,
From Avon's banks the cheering lay
Warms up a muse was well-nigh lost
In depths of snow and chilling frost ;
But, generous praise the soul inspires
More than rich wines and blazing fires.

---

* Vide Hom. Il., lib. xiv.

Tho' on the Grampians I were chain'd,
And all the winter on me rain'd,
Altho' half starv'd, my sp'rit would spring
Up to new life to hear you sing.

I take even criticism kind,
That sparkles from so clear a mind.
Friends ought and may point out a spot,
But enemies make all a blot ;
Friends sip the honey from the flow'r,—
All's verjuice to the waspish sour.

With more of Nature than of art,
From stated rules I often start,—
Rules never studied yet by me.
My muse is British, bold and free,
And loves at large to frisk and bound,
Unmankl'd, o'er poetic ground.

I love the garden, wild and wide,
Where oaks have plum-trees by their side,—
Where woodbines and the twisting vine
Clip round the pear-tree and the pine,—
Where mixt jonckeels and gowans grow,
And roses 'midst rank clover blow
Upon a bank of a clear strand,
Its wimplings led by Nature's hand.
Tho' docks and bramble here and there
May sometimes cheat the gard'ner's care,
Yet this to me's a paradise
Compar'd with prime cut plots and nice,
Where Nature has to Art resign'd
Till all looks mean, stiff, and confin'd.

May still my notes of rustic turn
Gain more of your respect than scorn,
I'll hug my fate, and tell sour fools
I'm more oblig'd to heav'n than schools.

Heaven Homer taught ; the critic draws
Only from him, and such, their laws.
The native bards first plunge the deep
Before the artful dare to leap ;
I've seen myself right many a time
Copy'd in diction, mode, and rhyme.

Now, Sir, again let me express
My wishing thoughts in fond address ;
That for your health and love you bear
To two of my chief patrons * here,
You'd,—when the lavrocks rouse the day,
When beams and dews make blythsome May,
When blooming fragrance glads our isle
And hills with purple heather smile,—
Drop fancy'd ails, with courage stout,
Ward off the spleen, the stone, and gout.
May ne'er such foes disturb your nights,
Or elbow out your day delights.
Here you will meet the jovial train
Whose clangours echo o'er the plain,
While hounds with gowls both loud and clear,
Well tun'd, delight the hunter's ear,
As they on coursers, fleet as wind,
Pursue the fox, hart, hare, or hind.
Delightful game ! where friendly ties
Are closer drawn, and health the prize.

We long for, and we wish you here,
Where friends are kind and claret clear.
The lovely hope of Som'ril's race
Who smiles with a seraphic grace,
And the fair sisters of the boy,
Will have, and add much to your joy.

---

* Lord and Lady Somerville.

Give warning to your noble friend.
Your humble servant shall attend
A willing Sancho and your slave,
With the best humour that I have,
To meet you on that river's shore
That Britons now divides no more.

ALLAN RAMSAY.

CXVIII.

TO DONALD M'EWEN, JEWELLER, AT ST. PETERSBURG.

How far frae hame my friend seeks fame !
    And yet I canna wyte ye
T' employ your fire, and still aspire
    By virtues that delyte ye.

Should fortune lour, 'tis in your power
    (If heaven grant balmy health)
T' enjoy ilk hour a saul unsow'r,—
    Content's nae bairn of wealth.

It is the mind that's not confin'd
    To passions mean and vile
That's never pin'd, while thoughts refin'd
    Can gloomy cares beguile.

Then Donald may be e'en as gay
    On Russia's distant shore
As on the Tay, where usquebae
    He us'd to drink before.

But, howsoe'er, haste, gather gear,
    And syne pack up your treasure ;
Then to Auld Reekie come and beek ye,
    And close your days with pleasure.

CXIX.

TO THE SAME,

ON RECEIVING A PRESENT OF A GOLD SEAL, WITH HOMER'S HEAD.

THANKS to my frank, ingenious friend.
Your present's most genteel and kind,
Baith rich and shining as your mind ;
    And that immortal laurell'd pow
Upon the gem, sae well design'd
    And execute, sets me on low.

The heavenly fire inflames my breast,
Whilst I unweary'd am in quest
Of fame ; and hope that ages neist
    Will do their Highland bard the grace
Upon their seals to cut his crest,
    And blythest strakes of his short face.

Far less great Homer ever thought
(When he, harmonious beggar ! sought
His bread thro' Greece) he should be brought
    Frae Russia's shore by Captain Hugh *
To Pictland plains, sae finely wrought
    On precious stone, and set by you.

---

* Captain Hugh Eccles, master of a fine merchant-ship, which he lost in the
unhappy fire at St. Petersburg.

CXX.

TO HIS FRIENDS IN IRELAND,

WHO, ON A REPORT OF HIS DEATH, MADE AND PUBLISHED
SEVERAL ELEGIES, ETC.

1728.

SIGHING shepherds of Hibernia,
Thank ye for your kind concern a',
When a fause report beguiling
Prov'd a drawback on your smiling.
Dight your een, and cease your grieving,
Allan's hale, and well, and living,—
Singing, laughing, sleeping soundly,
Cowing beef, and drinking roundly,—
Drinking roundly rum and claret,
Ale and usquæ, bumpers fair out,
Supernaculum but spilling,
The least diamond* drawing, filling,—
Sowsing sonnets on the lasses,
Hounding satires at the asses,
Smiling at the surly critics
And the pack-horse of politics,—
Painting meadows, shaws, and mountains,
Crooking burns and flowing fountains,
Flowing fountains where ilk gowan
Grows about the borders glowan,
Swelling sweetly, and inviting
Poets' lays and lovers meeting,
Meeting kind to niffer kisses,
Bargaining for better blisses.

Hills in dreary dumps now lying,
And ye zephyrs swiftly flying,
And ye rivers gently turning,
And ye Philomelas mourning,

---

* See the Note ‡ on p. 162, Vol. I.

And ye double-sighing echoes,—
Cease your sobbing, tears, and hey-ho's !
Banish a' your care and grieving,
Allan's hale, and well, and living.
Early up on mornings shining,
Ilka fancy warm refining ;
Giving ilka verse a burnish
That man second volume furnish,
To bring in frae lord and lady
Meikle fame, and part of ready.
Splendid thing of constant motion
Fish'd for in the southern ocean,
Prop of gentry, nerve of battles,
Prize for which the gamester rattles ;
Belzie's banes—deceitfu'—kittle,
Risking a' to gain a little.

Pleasing Philip's tunefu' tickle,
Philomel, and kind Arbuckle ;
Singers sweet, baith lads and lasses,
Tuning pipes on hill Parnassus,
Allan kindly to you wishes
Lasting life and rowth of blisses ;
And that he may, when ye surrender
Sauls to heaven, in numbers tender
Give a' your fames a happy heezy,
And gratefully immortalise ye.

CXXI.

AN EPISTLE FROM A GENTLEMAN IN THE COUNTRY TO HIS FRIEND IN EDINBURGH.

O FRIEND! to smoke and din confin'd,—
Which fouls your claiths and frets your mind,
And makes you rusty look and crabbed,
As if you were bep—'d or scabbed,
Or had been going thro' a dose
Of mercury to save your nose,—
Let me advise you, out of pity,
To leave the chatt'ring, stinking city,
Where pride and emptiness take place
Of plain integrity and grace ;
Where hideous screams wad kill a cat
Of wha buys this ? or why buys that ?
And thro' the day, frae break o' morning
The buzz of bills, protests, and horning,
Besides the everlasting squabble
Among the great and little rabble,
Wha tear their lungs and deave your ears,
With all their party hopes and fears,
While rattling o'er their silly cant
Learn'd frae the *Mercury* and *Courant*
About the aid that comes frae Russia,
And the neutrality of Prussia ;
Of France's tyranny and slavery,
Their faithless fickleness and knavery ;
Of Spain, the best-beloved son
Of the old whore of Babylon,—
The warden of her whips and faggots,
And all her superstitious maggots ;
Of all our gambols on the green
To aid the bauld Imperial Queen,
When the Most Christian shoars to strike,
And fasheous Frederic gars her fike ;

Of Genoa, and the resistance
Of Corsica without assistance;
Of wading var-freging Savona,
And breaking fiddles at Cremona;
What jaws of blood and gore it cost
Before a town is won or lost,—
How much the allied armies have been a'
Propp'd by the monarch of Sardinia;
Of popes, stadtholders, faith's defenders,
Generals, marshals, and pretenders;
Of treaties, ministers, and kings,
And of a thousand other things,—
Of all which their conceptions dull
Suits with the thickness of the skull.
Yet with such stuff ane man be worried,
That's thro' your city's gauntlet hurried.
But ah! (ye cry) ridotts and dances,
With lasses trig that please your fancies,
For five or six gay hours complete,
In circles of th' assembly sweet;
Wha can forsake so fair a field,
Where all to conquering beauty yield?
No doubt, while in this am'rous fit,
Your next plea's boxes and the pit;
Where wit and humour of the age
Flow entertaining from the stage;
Where, if the drama's right conducted,
Ane's baith diverted and instructed.—
Well, I shall grant it 'grees wi' reason,
These have their charms in proper season;
But must not be indulg'd too much,
Lest they the saften'd saul bewitch,
And faculties in fetters bind,
That are for greater ends design'd.
Then rouse ye frae these dozing dreams,
And view with me the golden beams

Which Phœbus ilka morning pours
Upon our plains adorn'd with flow'rs;
With me thro' howms and meadows stray,
Where wimpling waters make their way;
Here, frae the aiks and elms around,
You'll hear the saft melodious sound
Of a' the quiristers on high,
Whase notes re-echo thro' the sky,
Better than concerts in your town,
Yet do not cost you half a crown:
Here blackbirds, mavises, and linnets,
Excel your fiddles, flutes, and spinnets;
Our jetty rooks e'en far excels
Your strim-strams and your jingling bells,
As do the cloven-footed tribes,
And rustics whistling o'er the glybes.
Here we with little labour gain
Firm health, with all its joyful train;
Silent repose, the cheerful smile
Which can intruding cares beguile:
Here fragrant flow'rs of tinctures bright,
Regale the smell and please the sight,
And make the springs of life to flow
Through every vein with kindly glow,
Giving the cheek a rosy tint
Excelling all the arts of paint.
If cauld or rain keep us within,
We've rooms neat, warm, and free from din;
Where, in the well-digested pages,
We can converse with by-past ages;
And oft, to set our dumps adrift,
We smile with Prior, Gay, and Swift;
Or with great Newton take a flight
Amongst the rolling orbs of light;
With Milton, Pope, and all the rest
Who smoothly copy Nature best:

From those inspir'd, we often find
What brightens and improves the mind,
And carry men a pitch beyond
Those views of which low souls are fond.
This hinders not the jocund smile
With mirth to mix the moral style ;
In conversation this being right,
As is in painting shade and light.

This is the life poets have sung,
Wish'd for, my friend, by auld and young ;
By all who would heaven's favour share :
Where least ambition, least of care
Disturbs the mind ; where virtuous ease
And temperance never fail to please.

ALLAN RAMSAY.

PENNYCUICK, May, 1748.

CXXII.

AN EPISTLE TO JAMES CLERK, ESQ. OF PENNYCUICK.

BLYTHE may he be wha o'er the haugh,
All free of care, may sing and laugh ;
Whase owsen lunges o'er a plain
Of wide extent, that's a' his ain.
No humdrum fears need break his rest,
Wha's not with debts and duns opprest ;
Wha has enough, even tho' it's little,
If it can ward frae dangers kittle,
That chiels, fated to skelp vile dubs thro',
For living are oblig'd to rub thro',
To fend by troaking, buying, selling,
The profit's aft no worth the telling.

When aft'er, in ane honest way,
We've gained by them that timely pay,
In comes a customer, looks big,
Looks generous, and scorns to prig,
Buys heartily, bids mark it down,
He'll clear before he leaves the town ;
Which, tho' they say't, they ne'er intend it ;
We're bitten sair, but canna mend it.
A year wheels round, we hing about ;
He's sleeping, or he's just gane out :
If catch'd, he glooms like ony devil,
Swears braid, and calls us damn'd uncivil :
Or aft our doited lugs abuses,
With a ratrime of cant excuses ;
And promises they stoutly ban to,
Whilk they have ne'er a mind to stand to.
As lang's their credit hads the feet o't,
They hound it round to seek the meat o't,
Till jointly we begin to gaud them,
And Edinburgh grows o'er het to had them :
Then aff they to the country scowp,
And reave us baith of cash and hope.
Syne we, the lovers of fair dealing,
Wha deem ill payment next to stealing,
Rin wud with care how we shall pay
Our bills against the destin'd day ;
For lame excuse the banker scorns,
And terrifies with caps and horns ;
Nae trader stands of trader awe,
But *nolens volens* gars him draw.

   'Tis hard to be laigh poortith's slave,
And like a man of worth behave ;
Wha creeps beneath a laid of care,
When interest points he's gleg and gare,
And will at naithing stap or stand,
That reeks him out a helping hand.

But here, dear Sir, do not mistake me,
As if grace did sae far forsake me,
As to allege that all poor fellows,
Unblest with wealth, deserv'd the gallows.
Na, God forbid that I should spell
Sae vile a fortune to mysell,
Tho' born to not ae inch of ground,
I keep my conscience white and sound;
And tho' I ne'er was a rich heaper,
To make that up I live the cheaper;
By this ae knack I've made a shift
To drive ambitious care a-drift;
And now in years and sense grown auld,
In ease I like my limbs to fauld.
Debts I abhor, and plan to be
Frae shochling trade and danger free,
That I may, loos'd frae care and strife,
With calmness view the edge of life;
And when a full ripe age shall crave,
Slide easily into my grave.
Now seventy years are o'er my head,
And thirty mae may lay me dead;
Should dreary care then stunt my muse,
And gar me aft her jogg refuse?
Sir, I have sung, and yet may sing,
Sonnets that o'er the dales may ring,
And in gash glee couch moral saw,
Reese virtue and keep vice in awe;
Make villainy look black and blue,
And give distinguish'd worth its due;
Fix its immortal fame in verse,
That men till doomsday shall rehearse.

I have it even within my pow'r,
The very kirk itself to scow'r,
And that you'll say's a brag right bauld;
But did not Lindsay this of auld?

Sir David's satyres help'd our nation
To carry on the Reformation,
And gave the scarlet whore a box
Mair snell than all the pelts of Knox.

Thus far, Sir, with no mean design,
To you I've poured out my mind,
And sketch'd you forth the toil and pain
Of them that have their bread to gain
With cares laborious, that you may,
In your blest sphere be ever gay,
Enjoying life with all that spirit
That your good sense and virtues merit.
Adieu, and ma' ye as happy be
As ever shall be wish'd by me,

Your ever obliged,
Humble servant,

ALLAN RAMSAY.

PENNYCUICK, May 9th, 1755.

CXXIII.

TO A. R. ON THE POVERTY OF THE POETS.

1728.

DEAR ALLAN, with your leave, allow me
    To ask you but one question civil ;
Why thou'rt a poet pray thee show me,
    And not as poor as any devil ?

I own your verses make me gay,
    But as right poet still I doubt ye ;
For we hear tell benorth the Tay,
    That nothing looks like want about ye.

In answer then, attempt solution,
　　Why poverty torments your gang ?
And by what fortitude and caution
　　Thou guards thee from its meagre fang ?

　　　　　　　Yours, &c.,

　　　　　　　　　W. L.

CXXIV.

THE ANSWER.

　Sir,

THAT mony a thriftless poet's poor,
　　Is what they very well deserve,
'Cause aft their muse turns common whore,
　　And flatters fools that let them starve.

Ne'er minding business, they lye,
　　Indulging sloth, in garret couches,
And gape like gorblins to the sky,
　　With hungry wames and empty pouches.

Dear billies, tak advice for anes,
　　If ye'd hope honour by the muse,
Rather to masons carry stanes,
　　Than for your patrons blockheads chuse :

For there's in nature's secret laws
　　Of sympath and antipathy,
Which is, and will be still the cause,
　　Why fools and wits can ne'er agree.

A wee thing serves a cheerfu' mind
   That is disposed to be contented,
But he nae happiness can find
   That is with pride and sloth tormented.

Still cautious to prevent a dun,
   With caps and horns on bills and bands ;
The sweets of life I quietly cun,
   And answer nature's small demands.

Lucky for me, I never sang
   Fause praises to a worthless wight,
And still took pleasure in the thrang
   Of them wha in good sense delight.

To such I owe what gave the rise
   To ought thou in my verse esteems,
And, Phœbe like, in darker skies,
   I but reflect their brighter beams.

FABLES AND TALES.

ADVERTISEMENT.

1722—1730.

SOME of the following are taken from Messieurs la Fontaine and la Motte, whom I have endeavoured to make speak Scots with as much ease as I can; at the same time aiming at the spirit of these eminent authors, without being too servile a translator. If my manner of expressing a design already invented have any particularity that is agreeable, good judges will allow such imitations to be originals formed upon the idea of another. Others, who drudge at the dull verbatim, are like timorous attendants, who dare not move one pace without their master's leave, and are never from their back but when they are not able to come up with them.

Those amongst them which are my own invention, with respect to the plot as well as the numbers, I leave the reader to find out; or if he think it worth his while to ask me, I shall tell him.

If this Collection prove acceptable, as I hope it will, I know not how far the love I have for this manner of writing may engage me to be divertingly useful. Instruction in such a dress is fitted for every palate, and strongly imprints a good moral upon the mind. When I think on the "Clock and the Dial," I am never upon the blush, although I should sit in company ten minutes without speaking. The thoughts of the "Fox and Rat" has hindered me sometimes from disobliging a person I did not much value. "The Wise Lizard" makes me content with low life. "The Judgment of Minos" gives me a disgust at avarice; and "Jupiter's Lottery" helps to keep me humble, though I own it has "e'en enough ado wi't," &c.

A man who has his mind furnished with such a stock of good sense as may be had from those excellent Fables, which have been approved of by ages, is proof against the insults of all those mistaken notions which so much harass human life: and what is life without serenity of mind?

How much of a philosopher is this same moral muse like to make of me!—"But," says one, "ay, ay, you're a canny lad! ye want to make the other penny by her!"—Positively I dare not altogether deny this, no more than if I were a clergyman or physician; and although all of us love to be serviceable to the world, even for the sake of bare naked virtue, yet approbation and encouragement make our diligence still more delightful.

FABLES AND TALES.

Important truths still let your Fables hold,
And moral mysteries with art unfold:
As veils transparent cover, but not hide;
Such metaphors appear, when right apply'd.

LD. LANSDOWNE.

CXXV.

AN EPISTLE TO DUNCAN FORBES, LORD ADVOCATE.

SHUT in a closet six foot square,
No fash'd with meikle wealth or care,
   I pass the live-lang day;
Yet some ambitious thoughts I have,
Which will attend me to my grave,
   Sic busked baits they lay.

These keep my fancy on the wing,
Something that's blyth and snack to sing,
   And smooth the runkled brow:
Thus care I happily beguile,
Hoping a plaudit and a smile
   Frae best of men, like you.

You wha in kittle casts of state,
When property demands debate,
   Can right what is done wrang;

Yet blythly can, when ye think fit,
Enjoy your friend, and judge the wit
    And slidness of a sang.

How mony, your reverse, unblest,
Whase minds gae wand'ring thro' a mist,
    Proud as the thief in hell,
Pretend, forsooth, they're gentle-fowk,
'Cause chance gi'es them of gear the yowk,
    And better chiels the shell!

I've seen a wean aft vex itsell,
And greet because it was not tall:
    Heez'd on a board, O! then,
Rejoicing in the artfu' height,
How smirky look'd the little wight,
    And thought itsell a man!

Sic bairns are some, blawn up a wee
With splendour, wealth, and quality,
    Upon these stilts grown vain,
They o'er the pows of poor folk stride,
And neither are to had nor bide,
    Thinking this height their ain.

Now should ane speer at sic a puff,
What gars thee look sae big and bluff?
    Is't an attending menzie?
Or fifty dishes on your table?
Or fifty horses in your stable?
    Or heaps of glancing cunzie?

Are these the things thou ca's thysell?
Come, vain gigantic shadow, tell!
    If thou sayest yes, I'll shaw

Thy picture ; mean's thy silly mind,
Thy wit's a croil, thy judgment blind,
    And love worth nought ava.

Accept our praise, ye nobly born,
Whom heaven takes pleasure to adorn
    With ilka manly gift ;
In courts or camps to serve your nation,
Warm'd with that generous emulation
    Which your forbears did lift.

In duty, with delight, to you
Th' inferior world do justly bow,
    While you're the maist deny'd ;
Yet shall your worth be ever priz'd,
When strutting naethings are despis'd,
    With a' their stinking pride.

This to set aff as I am able,
I'll frae a Frenchman thigg a fable,
    And busk it in a plaid ;
And tho' it be a bairn of Motte's,*
When I have taught it to speak Scots,
    I am its second dad.

---

* Mons. la Motte, who has written lately a curious Collection of Fables, from
which the following is imitated.

CXXVI.

FABLE I.

THE TWA BOOKS.

TWA books, near neighbours in a shop,
The tane a gilded Turky fop ;
The tither's face was weather-beaten,
And cauf-skin jacket sair worm-eaten.
The corky, proud of his braw suit,
Curled up his nose, and thus cry'd out :
" Ah ! place me on some fresher binks !
Figh ! how this mouldy creature stinks !
How can a gentle book like me
Endure sic scoundrel company !
What may fowk say to see me cling
Sae close to this auld ugly thing,
But that I'm of a simple spirit,
And disregard my proper merit ! "—
Quoth grey-baird, " Whist, Sir, with your din !
For a' your meritorious skin,
I doubt if you be worth within :
For as auld fashion'd as I look,
May be I am the better book. "—
" O heavens ! I canna thole the clash
Of this impertinent auld hash ;
I winna stay ae moment langer ! "—
" My lord, please to command your anger ;
Pray only let me tell you that——"
" What wad this insolent be at ?
Rot out your tongue ! pray, master Symmer,
Remove me frae this dinsome rhymer ;
If you regard your reputation,
And us of a distinguish'd station,
Hence frae this beast let me be hurried,
For with his stour and stink I'm worried."

Scarce had he shook his paughty crap,
When in a customer did pap ;

He up douse Stanza lifts, and eyes him,
Turns o'er his leaves, admires, and buys him :
" This book," said he, " is good and scarce,
The saul of sense in sweetest verse."
But reading title of gilt cleathing,
Cries, " Gods ! wha buys this bonny naithing ?
Nought duller e'er was put in print :
Wow ! what a deal of Turky's tint !"

Now, Sir, t' apply what we've invented :
You are the buyer represented ;
    And may your servant hope
My lays shall merit your regard,
I'll thank the gods for my reward,
    And smile at ilka fop.

CXXVII.

FABLE II.

THE CLOCK AND THE DIAL.

Ae day a Clock wad brag a Dial,
And put his qualities to trial,
Spake to him thus : " My neighbour, pray
Can'st tell me what's the time of day ?"
The dial said, " I dinna ken."—
" Alake ! what stand you there for then ?"—
" I wait here till the sun shines bright,
For nought I ken but by his light."—
" Wait on," quoth Clock, " I scorn his help ;
Baith night and day my lane I skelp :
Wind up my weights but anes a week,
Without him I can gang and speak ;

Nor like a useless sumph I stand,
But constantly wheel round my hand :
Hark, hark ! I strike just now the hour,
And I am right—ane, twa, three, four."

While thus the Clock was boasting loud,
The bleezing sun brak thro' a cloud :
The Dial, faithfu' to his guide,
Spake truth, and laid the thumper's pride :
" Ye see," said he, " I've dung you fair,
'Tis four hours and three quarters mair.
" My friend," he added, " count again,
And learn a wee to be less vain ;
Ne'er brag of constant clavering cant,
And that you answers never want ;
For you're not ay to be believ'd,
Wha trust to you may be deceived.
Be counsell'd to behave like me ;
For when I dinna clearly see,
I always own I dinna ken,
And that's the way of wisest men."

CXXVIII.

FABLE III.

THE RAM AND THE BUCK.

A RAM, the father of a flock,
Wha'd mony winters stood the shock
Of northern winds and driving snaw,
Leading his family in a raw,
Through wraiths that clad the laigher field,
And drave them frae the lowner bield,
To crop contented frozen fare,
With honesty on hills blown bare :

This Ram, of upright hardy spirit,
Was really a horn'd head of merit.
Unlike him was a neighbouring Goat,
A mean-saul'd, cheating, thieving sot,
That tho' possest of rocks the prime,
Crown'd with fresh herbs and rowth of thyme,
Yet, slave to pilfering, his delight
Was to break gardens ilka night,
And round him steal, and aft destroy
Even things he never could enjoy;
The pleasure of a dirty mind,
That is sae viciously inclin'd.

Upon a barrowing day, when sleet
Made twinters and hog-wedders bleet,
And quake with cauld; behind a ruck
Met honest Toop and sneaking Buck;
Frae chin tae tail clad with thick hair,
He bad defiance to thin air;
But trusty Toop his fleece had riven,
When he amang the birns was driven;
Half naked the brave leader stood,
His look compos'd, unmov'd his mood:
When thus the Goat, that had tint a'
His credit baith with great and sma',
Shun'd by them as a pest, wad fain
New friendship with this worthy gain:
" Ram, say, shall I give you a part
Of mine? I'll do't with all my heart:
'Tis yet a lang cauld month tae Beltan,
And ye've a very ragged kelt on;
Accept, I pray, what I can spare,
To clout your doublet with my hair."
" No," says the Ram, " tho' my coat's torn,
Yet ken, thou worthless, that I scorn
To be oblig'd at any price
To sic as you, whose friendship's vice!

I'd have less favour frae the best,
Clad in a hatefu' hairy vest
Bestow'd by thee, than as I now
Stand but ill drest in native woo'.
Boons frae the generous make ane smile;
From miscreants, make receivers vile."

CXXIX.

FABLE IV.

THE LOVELY LASS AND THE MIRROR.

A NYMPH with ilka beauty grac'd,
Ae morning by her toilet plac'd,
Where the leal-hearted Looking-glass
With truths addrest the lovely Lass.
" To do ye justice, heavenly fair,
Amaist in charms ye may compare
With Venus' sell; but mind amaist,
For tho' you're happily possest
Of ilka grace which claims respect,
Yet I see faults you should correct.
I own they only trifles are,
Yet of importance to the fair.
What signifies that patch o'er braid,
With which your rosy cheek's o'erlaid?
Your natural beauties you beguile,
By that too much affected smile;
Saften that look; move ay with ease,
And you can never fail to please."

Those kind advices she approv'd,
And mair her monitor she lov'd,
Till in came visitants a threave;
To entertain them she man leave

Her Looking-glass.—They fleetching praise
Her looks, her dress, and a' she says,
Be't right or wrang; she's hale complete,
And fails in nathing fair or sweet.
Sae much was said, the bonny Lass
Forgat her faithfu' Looking-glass.

Clarinda, this dear beauty's you;
    The mirror is ane good and wise,
Wha, by his counsels just, can shew
    How nobles may to greatness rise.
God bless the wark!—If you're opprest
    By parasites with fause design,
Then will sic faithfu' mirrors best
    These under-plotters countermine.

CXXX.

FABLE V.

JUPITER'S LOTTERY.

Anes Jove, by ae great act of grace,
Wad gratify his human race,
And order'd Hermes, in his name,
With tout of trumpet to proclaim
A royal lott'ry frae the skies,
Where ilka ticket was a prize.
Nor was there need for ten per cent.
To pay advance for money lent;
Nor brokers nor stock-jobbers here
Were thol'd to cheat fowk of their gear.
The first-rate benefits were health,
Pleasures, honours, empire, and wealth;
But happy he to whom wad fa'
Wisdom, the highest prize of a'.

Hopes of attaining things the best,
Made up the maist feck of the rest.
Now ilka ticket sald with ease,
At altárs, for a sacrifice :
Jove a' receiv'd, ky, gaits, and ewes,
Moor-cocks, lambs, dows, or bawbee-rows ;
Nor wad debar e'en a poor droll,
Wha nought could gi'e but his parol.
Sae kind was he no to exclude
Poor wights for want of wealth or blood ;
Even whiles the gods, as record tells,
Bought several tickets for themsells.
When fou, and lots put in the wheel,
Aft were they turn'd to mix them weel ;
Blind Chance to draw, Jove order'd syne,
That nane with reason might repine.
He drew, and Mercury was clark,
The number, prize, and name to mark.
Now hopes by millions fast came forth,
But seldom prizes of mair worth,
Sic as dominion, wealth, and state,
True friends, and lovers fortunate.
Wisdom at last, the greatest prize,
Comes up :—aloud clark Hermes cries,
" Number ten thousand ! Come, let's see
The person blest !"—Quoth Pallas, "Me !"
Then a' the gods for blythness sang,
Thro' heaven glad acclamations rang ;
While mankind, grumbling, laid the wyte
On them, and ca'd the hale a byte.
" Yes," cry'd ilk ane, with sobbing heart,
" Kind Jove has play'd a parent's part,
Wha did this prize to Pallas send,
While we're sneg'd off at the wob's end !"

Soon to their clamours Jove took tent,
To punish which to wark he went :

He straight with follies fill'd the wheel;
In Wisdom's place they did as weel;
For ilka ane wha Folly drew,
In their conceit a' sages grew.
Sae, thus contented, a' retir'd,
And ilka fool himself admir'd.

CXXXI.

FABLE VI.

THE MISER AND MINOS.

SHORT syne there was a wretched miser,
With pinching had scrap'd up a treasure;
Yet frae his hoords he doughtna take
As much would buy a mutton-stake,
Or take a glass to comfort nature,
But scrimply fed on crumbs and water:
In short, he famish'd 'midst his plenty,
Which made surviving kindred canty,
Wha scarcely for him pat on black,
And only in his loof a plack,
Which even they grudg'd. Sic is the way
Of them wha fa' upon the prey;
They'll scarce row up the wretch's feet,
Sae scrimp they make his winding-sheet,
Tho' he should leave a vast estate,
And heaps of gowd like Arthur's Seat.

Well, down the starving ghaist did sink,
Till it fell on the Stygian brink;
Where auld Van Charon stood and raught
His wither'd loof out for his fraught;
But them that wanted wherewitha',
He dang them back to stand and blaw.

The Miser lang being us'd to save,
Fand this, and wadna passage crave;
But shaw'd the ferryman a knack,
Jumpt in, swam o'er, and hain'd his plack.
Charon might damn, and sink, and roar;
But a' in vain, he gain'd the shore.
Arriv'd, the three-pow'd dog of hell
Gowl'd terrible a triple yell;
Which rous'd the snaky sisters three,
Wha furious on this wight did flee,
Wha'd play'd the smuggler on their coast,
By which Pluto his dues had lost;
Then brought him for this trick sae hainous
Afore the bench of justice Minos.

The case was new, and very kittle,
Which puzzl'd a' the court na little;
Thought after thought with unco' speed
Flew round within the judge's head,
To find what punishment was due
For sic a daring crime, and new.
Should he the plague of Tantal feel?
Or stented be on Ixion's wheel?
Or stung wi' bauld Prometheus' pain?
Or help Sysiph to row his stane?
Or sent amang the wicked route,
To fill the tub that ay rins out?—
" No, no," continues Minos, "no!
Weak are our punishments below
For sic a crime; he man be hurl'd
Straight back again into the world.
I sentence him to see and hear
What use his friends make of his gear."

CXXXII.

FABLE VII.

THE APE AND THE LEOPARD.

The Ape and Leopard, beasts for show,
The first a wit, the last a beau,
To make a penny at a fair,
Advertis'd a' their parts sae rare.
The tane gae out with meikle wind,
His beauty 'boon the brutal kind:
Said he, " I'm kend baith far and near,
Even kings are pleas'd when I appear ;
And when I yield my vital puff,
Queens of my skin will make a muff;
My fur sae delicate and fine,
With various spots does sleekly shine."

Now lads and lasses fast did rin
To see the beast with bonny skin.
His keeper shaw'd him round about ;
They saw him soon, and soon came out.

But master Monkey, with an air,
Hapt out, and thus harangu'd the fair:
" Come, gentlemen, and ladies bonny,
I'll give ye pastime for your money !
I can perform, to raise your wonder,
Of pawky tricks mae than a hunder.
My cousin Spotty, true he's braw,
He has a curious suit to shaw,
And naithing mair.—But frae my mind
Ye shall blyth satisfaction find :
Sometimes I'll act a chiel that 's dull,
Look thoughtfu', grave, and wag my scull ;
Then mimic a light-headed rake,
When on a tow my houghs I shake ;
Sometimes, like modern monks, I'll seem
To make a speech, and naithing mean.

R 2

But come away, ye needna speer
What ye're to pay, I'se no be dear ;
And if ye grudge for want of sport,
I'll give it back t' ye at the port."
The Ape succeeded ; in fowk went ;
Stay'd long, and came out well content.
Sae much will wit and spirit please,
Beyond our shape, and brawest claiths.
How mony, ah ! of our fine gallants
Are only Leopards in their talents !

CXXXIII.

FABLE VIII.

THE ASS AND THE BROCK.

Upon a time a solemn Ass
Was dand'ring thro a narrow pass,
Where he forgather'd with a Brock,
Wha him saluted frae a rock,—
Speer'd how he did ? how markets gade ?
What's a ye'r news ? and how is trade ?
How does Jock Stot and Lucky Yad,
Tam Tup, and Bucky, honest lad ?—
Replied the Ass, and made a heel,
" E'en a' the better that ye're weel :
But Jackanapes and snarling Fitty
Are grown sae wicked, (some ca's 't witty,)
That we wha solid are and grave,
Nae peace on our ain howms can have.
While we are bisy gathering gear,
Upon a brae they'll sit and sneer.
If ane should chance to breathe behin',
Or ha'e some slaver at his chin,
Or 'gainst a tree should rub his arse,
That's subject for a winsome farce.

There draw they me, as void of thinking :
And you, my dear, famous for stinking ;
And the bauld birsy bair, your frien',
A glutton, dirty to the een,
By laughing dogs and apes abus'd,
Wha is't can thole to be sae us'd ! "

" Dear me ! heh ! wow ! and say ye sae ? "
Return'd the Brock :—" I'm unko wae,
To see this flood of wit break in !
O scour about, and ca't a sin ;
Stout are your lungs, your voice is loud,
And ought will pass upon the crowd."

The Ass thought this advice was right,
And bang'd away with a' his might :
Stood on a knowe among the cattle,
And furiously 'gainst wit did rattle ;
Pour'd out a deluge of dull phrases ;
While dogs and apes leugh and made faces.
Thus a' the angry Ass held forth
Serv'd only to augment their mirth.

CXXXIV.

FABLE IX.

THE FOX AND THE RAT.

THE lion and the tyger lang maintain'd
A bloody weir ; at last the lion gain'd.
The royal victor strak the earth with awe,
And the four-footed world obey'd his law.
Frae ilka species deputies were sent,
To pay their homage due, and compliment
Their sov'reign liege, wha'd gar the rebels cour
And own his royal right and princely power.

After dispute, the moniest votes agree
That Reynard should address his majesty,
Ulysses-like, in name of a' the lave ;
Wha thus went on :—"O prince ! allow thy slave
To reese thy brave achievements and renown,
Nane but thy daring front should wear the crown,
Wha art like Jove, whase thunderbolt can make
The heavens be hush, and a' the earth to shake ;
Whase very gloom, if he but angry nods,
Commands a peace, and flegs th' inferior gods.
Thus thou, great king, hast by thy conqu'ring paw
Gi'en earth a shog, and made thy will a law :
Thee a' the animals with fear adore,
And tremble if thou with displeasure roar ;
O'er a' thou canst us eith thy sceptre sway,
As badrans can with cheeping rottans play."

    This sentence vex'd the envoy Rottan sair ;
He threw his gab, and girn'd ; but durst nae mair ;
The monarch pleas'd with Lowry, wha durst gloom ?
A warrant's ordered for a good round sum,
Which Dragon, lord-chief-treasurer, must pay
To sly-tongu'd Fleechy on a certain day ;
Which secretary Ape in form wrote down,
Sign'd, Lion, and a wee beneath, Baboon.—
'Tis given the Fox.—Now Bobtail, tap o' kin,
Made rich at anes, is nor to had nor bin !
He dreams of nought but pleasure, joy, and peace,
Now blest with wealth to purchase hens and geese.
Yet in his loof he hadna tell'd the gowd,
And yet the Rottan's breast with anger glow'd ;
He vow'd revenge, and watch'd it night and day ;
He took the tid when Lowry was away,
And thro' a hole into his closet slips,
There chews the warrant a' in little nips.
Thus what the Fox had for his flatt'ry gotten,
E'en frae a Lion, was made nought by an offended Rottan.

FABLE X.

THE CATERPILLAR AND THE ANT.

A PENSY Ant, right trig and clean,
Came ae day whidding o'er the green;
Where, to advance her pride, she saw
A Caterpillar moving slaw.
" Good ev'n 't ye, mistress Ant," said he;
" How's a' at hame? I'm blyth to s' ye!"
The saucy Ant view'd him with scorn,
Nor wad civilities return;
But gecking up her head, quoth she,
" Poor animal! I pity thee;
Wha scarce can claim to be a creature,
But some experiment of Nature,
Whase silly shape displeas'd her eye,
And thus unfinish'd was flung bye.
For me, I'm made with better grace,
With active limbs, and lively face;
And cleverly can move with ease
Frae place to place where'er I please;
Can foot a minuet or a jig,
And snoov't like ony whirly-gig;
Which gars my jo aft grip my hand,
Till his heart pitty-pattys, and——
But laigh my qualities I bring,
To stand up clashing with a thing,
A creeping thing the like of thee,
Not worthy of a farewell t' ye."
The airy Ant syne turned awa,
And left him with a proud gaffa.
The Caterpillar was struck dumb,
And never answer'd her a mum :
The humble reptile fand some pain,
Thus to be banter'd with disdain.

But tent neist time the Ant came by,
The worm was grown a Butterfly ;
Transparent were his wings and fair,
Which bare him flight'ring through the air.
Upon a flower he stapt his flight,
And thinking on his former slight,
Thus to the Ant himself addrest :
" Pray, Madam, will ye please to rest ?
And notice what I now advise :
Inferiors ne'er too much despise,
For fortune may gi'e sic a turn,
To raise aboon ye what ye scorn :
For instance, now I spread my wing
In air, while you're a creeping thing."

CXXXVI.

FABLE XI.

THE TWA CATS AND THE CHEESE.

Twa Cats anes on a cheese did light,
To which baith had an equal right ;
But disputes, sic as aft arise,
Fell out a sharing of the prize.
" Fair play," said ane, " ye bite o'er thick,
Thae teeth of yours gang wonder quick !
Let's part it, else lang or the moon
Be chang'd, the kebuck will be doon."
But wha's to do't ? They're parties baith,
And ane may do the other skaith.
Sae with consent away they trudge,
And laid the cheese before a judge :
A monkey with a campsho face,
Clerk to a justice of the peace.
A judge he seem'd in justice skill'd,
When he his master's chair had fill'd :
Now umpire chosen for division,
Baith sware to stand by his decision.

Demure he looks ; the cheese he pales ;
He prives, it's good ; ca's for the scales ;
His knife whops throw't, in twa it fell ;
He puts ilk haff in either shell.
Said he, " We'll truly weigh the case,
And strictest justice shall have place."
Then lifting up the scales, he fand
The tane bang up, the other stand ;
Syne out he took the heaviest haff,
And ate a knoost o't quickly aff ;
And try'd it syne :—it now prov'd light.
" Friend Cats," said he, " we'll do ye right."
Then to the ither haff he fell,
And laid till't teughly tooth and nail ;
Till weigh'd again, it lightest prov'd.
The judge, wha this sweet process lov'd,
Still weigh'd the case, and still ate on,
Till clients baith were weary grown ;
And tenting how the matter went,
Cry'd, " Come, come, Sir, we're baith content."—
" Ye fools !" quoth he, " and justice too
Man be content as well as you."
Thus grumbled they, thus he went on,
Till baith the haves were near-hand done.
Poor Pousies now the daffin saw,
Of gawn for nignyes to the law ;
And bill'd the judge, that he wad please
To give them the remaining cheese.
To which his worship grave reply'd ;
" The dues of court man first be paid.—
Now, justice pleas'd, what's to the fore
Will but right scrimply clear your score ;
That's our decreet :—gae hame and sleep,
And thank us ye're win aff sae cheap."

CXXXVII.

FABLE XII.

THE CAMELEON.

Twa travellers, as they were walking,
'Bout the Cameleon fell a talking;
Sic think it shaws them mettled men,
To say I've seen, and ought to ken.
Says ane, " It's a strange beast indeed!
Four-footed, with a fish's head;
A little bowk, with a lang tail,
And moves far slawer than a snail;
Of colour like a blawart blue—"
Reply'd his nibour, " That's no true;
For well I wat his colour's green,
If ane may true his ain twa een;
For I in sun-shine saw him fair,
When he was dining on the air."—
" Excuse me," says the ither blade,
" I saw him better in the shade,
And he is blue."—" He's green, I'm sure."—
" Ye lied."—" And ye're the son of a whore."
Frae words there had been cuff and kick,
Had not a third come in the nick,
Wha tenting them in this rough mood,
Cry'd, " Gentlemen, what, are ye wood?
What's ye'r quarrel, an't may be speer'd?"—
" Truth," says the tane; " Sir, ye shall hear't:
The Cameleon, I say he's blue;
He threaps, he's green: now what say you?"—
" Ne'er fash ye'rsells about the matter,"
Says the sagacious arbitrator,
" He's black; sae nane of you are right;
I view'd him well with candle-light;
And have it in my pocket here,
Row'd in my napkin hale and feer."—

" Fy !" said ae cangler, " what d'ye mean?
I'll lay my lugs on 't that he's green."
Said th' ither, " Were I gawn to death,
I'd swear he's blue, with my last breath."—
" He's black," the judge maintain'd ay stout;
And to convince them, whop'd him out:
But to surprise to ane and a',
The animal was white as snaw.
And thus reprov'd them: " Shallow boys!
Away, away, make nae mair noise!
Ye're a' three wrang, and a' three right;
But learn to own your nibours' sight
As good as yours; your judgment speak,
But never be sae daftly weak,
T' imagine ithers will by force
Submit their sentiments to yours;
As things in various lights ye see,
They'll ilka ane resemble me."

CXXXVIII.

FABLE XIII.

THE TWA LIZARDS.

BENEATH a tree, ae shining day,
On a burn bank twa Lizards lay,
Beeking themsells now in the beams,
Then drinking of the cauller streams.
" Waes me !" says ane of them to th' ither,
" How mean and silly live we, brither !
Beneath the moon is ought sae poor,
Regarded less, or mair obscure?
We breathe indeed, and that's just a';
But, forc'd by destiny's hard law,
On earth like worms to creep and sprawl,—
Curst fate to ane that has a saul !

s 2

Forby, gin we may trow report,
In Nilus giant Lizards sport,
Ca'd crocodiles : ah ! had I been
Of sic a size, upon the green,
Then might I had my skair of fame,
Honour, respect, and a great name ;
And men with gaping jaws have shor'd,
Syne like a pagod been ador'd."

" Ah, friend !" replies the ither Lizard,
" What makes this grumbling in thy gizzard ?
What cause have ye to be uneasy ?
Cannot the sweets of freedom please ye ?
We, free frae trouble, toil, or care,
Enjoy the sun, the earth, and air,
The crystal spring, and greenwood shaw,
And beildy holes when tempests blaw.
Why should we fret, look blae or wan,
Tho' we're contemn'd by paughty man ?
If sae, let's in return be wise,
And that proud animal despise."

" O fy !" returns th' ambitious beast,
" How weak a fire now warms thy breast !
It breaks my heart to live sae mean ;
I'd like t' attract the gazer's een,
And be admir'd.   What stately horns
The deer's majestic brow adorns !
He claims our wonder and our dread,
Where'er he heaves his haughty head.
What envy a' my spirit fires,
When he in clearest pools admires
His various beauties with delyte ;
I'm like to drown myself with spite."

Thus he held forth ; when straight a pack
Of hounds, and hunters at their back,
Ran down a deer before their face,
Breathless and wearied with the chace :

The dogs upon the victim seize,
And beugles sound his obsequies.
But neither men nor dogs took tent
Of our wee Lizards on the bent;
While hungry Bawty, Buff, and Tray,
Devour'd the paunches of the prey.

Soon as the bloody deed was past,
The Lizard wise the proud addrest:
" Dear cousin, now pray let me hear
How wad ye like to be a deer?"

" Ohon!" quoth he, convinc'd and wae,
" Wha wad have thought it anes a-day?
Well, be a private life my fate,
I'll never envy mair the great!
That we are little fowk, that's true;
But sae's our cares and dangers too."

CXXXIX.

FABLE XIV.

MERCURY IN QUEST OF PEACE.

THE gods coost out, as story gaes,
Some being friends, some being faes,
To men in a besieged city:
Thus some frae spite, and some frae pity,
Stood to their point with canker'd strictness,
And leftna ither in dog's likeness.
Juno ca'd Venus whore and bawd,—
Venus ca'd Juno scaulding Jad;
E'en cripple Vulcan blew the low;
Apollo ran to bend his bow;
Dis shook his fork, Pallas her shield;
Neptune his grape began to wield.

" What plague !" cries Jupiter, " hey hoy !
    Man this town prove anither Troy ?
    What, will you ever be at odds,
    Till mankind think us foolish gods ?
    Hey ! mistress Peace, make haste, appear !"
    But madam was nae there to hear.
" Come, Hermes, wing thy heels and head,
    And find her out with a' thy speed !
    Trowth, this is bonny wark indeed !"

    Hermes obeys, and staptna short,
    But flies directly to the court ;
    For sure (thought he) she will be found
    On that fair complimenting ground,
    Where praises and embraces ran,
    Like current coin, 'tween man and man.
    But soon, alake ! he was beguil'd ;
    And fand that courtiers only smil'd,
    And with a formal flatt'ry treat ye,
    That they mair sickerly might cheat ye.
    Peace was na there, nor e'er could dwell
    Where hidden envy makes a hell.

    Neist to the ha', where justice stands
    With sword and balance in her hands,
    He flew ; no that he thought to find her
    Between the accuser and defender ;
    But sure he thought to find the wench
    Amang the fowk that fill the bench,
    Sae muckle gravity and grace
    Appear'd in ilka judge's face :
    Even here he was deceived again,
    For ilka judge stack to his ain
    Interpretation of the law,
    And vex'd themsells with had and draw.

    Frae thence he flew straight to the kirk :
    In this he prov'd as daft a stirk,

To look for Peace, where never three
In ev'ry point could e'er agree :
Ane his ain gait explain'd a text
Quite contrair to his neighbour next,
And teughly toolied day and night
To gar believers trow them right.

Then sair he sigh'd :—" Where can she be ?—
Well thought—the University :
Science is ane, these man agree."
There did he bend his strides right clever,
But is as far mistane as ever ;
For here Contention and Ill-nature
Had runkled ilka learned feature ;
Ae party stood for ancient rules,
Anither ca'd the ancients fools ;
Here ane wad set his shanks aspar,
And reese the man that sang Troy war ;
Anither ca's him Robin Kar.

Well, she's no here !—Away he flies
To seek her amangst families :
Tout ! what should she do there, I wonder ?
Dwells she with matrimonial thunder,
Where mates, some greedy, some deep drinkers,
Contend with thriftless mates or jinkers ?
This says 'tis black ; and that wi' spite,
Stifly maintains and threaps 'tis white.

Weary'd at last, quoth he, " Let's see
How branches with their stocks agree."
But here he fand still his mistake :
Some parents cruel were, some weak ;
While bairns ungratefu' did behave,
And wish'd their parents in the grave.

" Has Jove then sent me 'mang thir fowk,"
Cry'd Hermes, " here to hunt the gowk ?
Well I have made a waly round,
To seek what is not to be found."

Just on the wing—towards a burn,
A wee piece aff, his looks did turn ;
There mistress Peace he chanc'd to see
Sitting beneath a willow-tree.
" And have I found ye at the last ? "
He cry'd aloud, and held her fast.
" Here I reside," quoth she, and smil'd,
" With an auld hermit in this wild."—
" Well, Madam," said he, " I perceive
That ane may long your presence crave,
And miss ye still ; but this seems plain,
To have ye, ane man be alane."

<hr>

CXL.

FABLE XV.

THE SPRING AND THE SYKE.

FED by a living Spring, a rill
Flow'd easily a-down a hill ;
A thousand flowers upon its bank
Flourish'd fu' fair, and grew right rank.
Near to its course a Syke did lye,
Whilk was in summer aften dry,
And ne'er recover'd life again,
But after soaking showers of rain ;
Then wad he swell, look big and sprush,
And o'er his margin proudly gush.
Ae day, after great waughts of wet,
He with the crystal current met,
And ran him down with unco' din.
Said he, " How poorly does thou rin !
See with what state I dash the brae,
Whilst thou canst hardly make thy way."

The Spring, with a superior air,
Said, " Sir, your brag gives me nae care,
For soon 's ye want your foreign aid,
Your paughty cracks will soon be laid :
Frae my ain head I have supply,
But you must borrow, else rin dry."

FABLE XVI.

THE PHŒNIX AND THE OWL.

Phœnix the first, th' Arabian lord,
   And chief of all the feather'd kind,
A hundred ages had ador'd
   The sun with sanctity of mind.

Yet, mortal, ye man yield to fate;
   He heard the summons with a smile,
And, unalarm'd, without regret,
   He form'd himsell a fun'ral pile.

A Howlet, bird of mean degree,
   Poor, dosen'd, lame, and doited auld,
Lay lurking in a neighb'ring tree,
   Cursing the sun loot him be cauld.

Said Phœnix, " Brother, why so griev'd,
   To ban the Being gives thee breath?
Learn to die better than thou'st liv'd;
   Believe me, there's nae ill in death."

" Believe ye that?" the Owl reply'd :
   " Preach as ye will, death is an ill:
When young I ilka pleasure try'd,
   But now I die against my will.

" For you, a species by yoursell,
   Near eildins with the sun your god,

Nae ferly 'tis to hear you tell
 Ye're tir'd, and inclin'd to nod.

" It should be sae; for had I been
 As lang upon the warld as ye,
Nae tears should e'er drap frae my een,
 For tinsel of my hollow tree."

" And what," return'd th' Arabian sage,
 " Have ye t' observe ye have not seen?
Ae day's the picture of an age,
 'Tis ay the same thing o'er again.

" Come, let us baith together die:
 Bow to the sun that gave thee life,
Repent thou frae his beams did flee,
 And end thy poortith, pain, and strife.

" Thou wha in darkness took delight,
 Frae pangs of guilt could'st ne'er be free:
What won thou by thy shunning light?—
 But time flies on, I haste to die."

" Ye'r servant, Sir," reply'd the Owl,
 " I likena in the dark to lowp:
The byword ca's that chiel a fool,
 That slips a certainty for hope."

Then straight the zealous feather'd king
 To's aromatic nest retir'd,
Collected sun-beams with his wing,
 And in a spicy flame expir'd.

Meantime there blew a westlin gale,
 Which to the Howlet bore a coal;
The saint departed on his pile,
 But the blasphemer in his hole:

He died for ever.—Fair and bright
 The Phœnix frae his ashes sprang.
Thus wicked men sink down to night,
 While just men join the glorious thrang.

CXLII.

FABLE XVII.

THE BOY AND THE PIG.

Deep in a narrow craiged Pig
Lay mony a dainty nut and fig.
A greedy Callan, half a sot,
Shot his wee nive into the pot,
And thought to bring as mony out
As a' his fangs could gang about;
But the strait neck o't wadna suffer
The hand of this young foolish truffer,
Sae struted, to return again,
Which gae the gowkie nae sma' pain.
He gowls to be sae disappointed,
And drugs till he has maist disjointed
His shekelbane.—Anither lad
Stood by, wha some mair judgment had;
Said, "Billy, dinna grip at a',
And you with ease a part may draw."
This same advice to men I'd lend;
Ne'er for o'er much at anes contend,
But take the canniest gate to ease,
And pike out joys by twas and threes.

CXLIII.

FABLE XVIII.

THE MAN WITH THE TWA WIVES.

In ancient tales there is a story,
Of ane had twa Wives, whig and tory.
The Carlie's head was now attir'd
With hair, in equal mixture lyart.

T 2

His Wives (faith ane might well suffic'd)
Alternately was ay ill pleas'd :
They being reverse to ane another
In age and faith, made a curs'd pother
Whilk of the twa should bear the bell,
And make their man maist like themsell.
Auld Meg the tory took great care
To weed out ilka sable hair,
Plucking out all that look'd like youth,
Frae crown of head to weeks of mouth;
Saying, that baith in head and face,
Antiquity was mark of grace.
But Bess the whig, a raving rump,
Took figmalaries, and wald jump,
With sword and pistol by her side,
And cock a-stride a rowing ride
On the hag-ridden sumph, and grapple
Him hard and fast about the thrapple;
And with her furious fingers whirle
Frae youthfu' black ilk silver curle.
Thus was he serv'd between the twa,
Till no ae hair he had ava.

MORAL.

THE moral of this fable's easy,
But I sall speak it out to please ye.
'Tis an auld saying and a trow,
" Between twa stools the arse fa's throw."
Thus Britain's morals are much plucked,
While by two opposites instructed ;
Who still contending, have the trick
The strongest truths to contradict;
Tho' orthodox, they'll error make it,
If party opposite has spake it.
Thus are we keytch'd between the twa,
Like to turn deists ane and a'.

CXLIV.

FABLE XIX.

THE FABLE OF THE CONDEMNED ASS.

A DREADFUL plague, the like was sindle seen,
Cast mony a beast wame upwards on the green :
By thousands down to Acheron they sank,
To dander ages on the dowie bank,
Because they lay unburied on the sward
The sick survivors couldna give them eard.
The wowf and tod with sighing spent the day,
Their sickly stamacks scunner'd at the prey ;
Fowls droop the wing, the bull neglects his love ;
Scarce crawl the sheep, and weakly horses move :
The bauldest brutes that haunt Numidian glens,
Ly panting out their lives in dreary dens.
Thick lay the dead, and thick the pain'd and weak,
The prospect gart the awfu' Lion quake.

He ca's a council.—" Ah ! my friends," said he,
" 'Tis for some horrid faut sae mony die ;
Sae heaven permits.—Then let us a' confess,
With open breast, our crimes baith mair and less,
That the revengefu' gods may be appeas'd,
When the maist guilty wight is sacrific'd.
Fa't on the feyest : I shall first begin,
And awn whate'er my conscience ca's a sin.
The sheep and deer I've worried, now, alace !
Crying for vengeance, glowr me i' the face ;
Forby their herd, poor man ! to croun my treat,
Limb after limb, with bloody jaws I ate :
Ah, glutton me ! what murders have I done !—
Now say about, confess ilk ane as soon
And frank as I."—" Sire," says the pawky Tod,
" Your tenderness bespeaks you haf a god !

Worthy to be the monarch of the grove,
Worthy your friends' and a' your subjects' love.
Your scruples are too nice : what's harts or sheep?
An idiot crowd, which for your board ye keep ;
And where's the sin for ane to take his ain ?
Faith 'tis their honour when by you they're slain.
Neist, what's their herd ?—a man, our deadly fae !
Wha o'er us beasts pretends a fancy'd sway,
And ne'er makes banes o't, when 'tis in his power,
With guns and bows our nation to devour."
He said ; and round the courtiers all and each
Applauded Lawrie for his winsome speech.

The tyger, bair, and ev'ry powerfu' fur,
Down to the wilcat and the snarling cur,
Confest their crimes :—but wha durst ca' them crimes,
Except themsells?

The Ass, dull thing ! neist in his turn confest,
That being with hunger very sair opprest,
In o'er a dike he shot his head ae day,
And rugg'd three mouthfu's aff a ruck of hay :
" But speering leave," said he, " some wicked de'il
Did tempt me frae the parish priest to steal."
He said ; and all at anes the powerfu' croud,
With open throats, cry'd hastily and loud,
" This gypsie Ass deserves ten deaths to die,
Whase horrid guilt brings on our misery !"
A gaping wowf, in office, straight demands
To have him burnt, or tear him where he stands :
Hanging, he said, was an o'er easy death ;
He should in tortures yield his latest breath.
What, break a bishop's yard ! ah crying guilt !
Which nought can expiate till his blood be spilt.
The Lion signs his sentence, " hang and draw :"
Sae poor lang lugs man pay the kane for a'.

Hence we may ken, how power has eith the knack
To whiten red, and gar the blew seem black :
They'll start at winlestraes, yet never crook,
When Interest bids, to lowp out o'er a stowk.

———————

CXLV.

FABLE XX.

THE GODS OF EGYPT.

LANGSYNE in Egypt beasts were gods ;
  Sae mony, that the men turn'd beasts ;
Vermin and brutes but house or hald,
  Had offerings, temples, and their priests.

Ae day a Rattan, white as milk,
  At a cat's shrine was sacrific'd,
And pompous on the altar bled :
  The victim much god Badrans pleas'd.

The neist day was god Rattan's tour ;
  And that he might propitious smile,
A Cat is to his temple brought,
  Priests singing round him a' the while.

Odes, anthems, hymns, in verse and prose,
  With instruments of solemn sound,
Praying the lang-tail'd deity
  To bless their faulds and furrow'd ground.

" O ! plague us not with cats," they cry'd,
  " For this we cut ane's throat to thee."
" A bonny god indeed !" quoth Puss ;
  " Can ye believe sae great a lie ?

" What am I then that eat your god ?
   And yesterday to me ye bow'd ;
This day I'm to that vermin offer'd :
   God save us ! ye're a senseless crowd."

The close reflection gart them glowr,
   And shook their thoughts haf out of joint ;
But rather than be fash'd with thought,
   They gart the ax decide the point.

Thus we're Egyptians ane and a' ;
   Our passions gods, that gar us swither ;
Which, just as the occasion serves,
   We sacrifice to ane anither.

CXLVI.

FABLE XXI.

THE SPECTACLES.

AE day when Jove, the high director,
Was merry o'er a bowl of nectar,
Resolv'd a present to bestow
On the inhabitants below.
Momus, wha likes his joke and wine,
Was sent frae heaven with the propine.
Fast thro' the æther fields he whirl'd
His rapid car, and reached the warld ;
Conven'd mankind, and tald them Jove
Had sent a token of his love ;
Considering that they were short-sighted,
That faut should presently be righted.
Syne loos'd his wallet frae the pillions,
And toss'd out spectacles by millions.

There were enow, and ilk ane chose
His pair and cock'd them on his nose ;
And thankfully their knees they bended
To heaven, that thus their sight had mended.
Straight Momus hameward took his flight,
Laughing fou' loud, as well he might.
For ye man ken, 'tis but o'er true,
The glasses were some red, some blue,
Some black, some white, some brown, some green,
Which made the same thing different seem.
Now all was wrong, and all was right,
For ilk believ'd his aided sight,
And did the joys of truth partake,
In the absurdest gross mistake.

CXLVII.

FABLE XXII.

THE FOX TURNED PREACHER.

A LEARNED Fox grown stiff with eild,
Unable now in open field,
By speed of foot and clever stends,
To seize and worry lambs and hens ;
But Lowry never wants a shift
To help him out at a dead lift.
He cleath'd himsell in reverend dress,
And turn'd a preacher, naething less !
Held forth wi' birr 'gainst wier unjust,
'Gainst theft and gormandizing lust.
Clear was his voice, his tone was sweet,
In zeal and mien he seem'd complete ;
Sae grave and humble was his air,
His character shin'd wide and fair.

'Tis said the Lion had a mind
To hear him ; but Mess Fox declin'd
That honour : reasons on his side
Said that might snare him into pride :
But sheep and powtry, geese and ducks,
Came to his meeting-hole in flocks ;
Of being his prey they had nae fear,
His text the contrary made clear.

" Curst be that animal voracious,"
Cry'd he, " sae cruel and ungracious,
That chuses flesh to be his food,
And takes delight in waughting blood !—
What, live by murder !—horrid deed !
While we have trees, and ilka mead,
Finely enrich'd with herbs and fruits,
To serve and please the nicest brutes.
We should respect, dearly belov'd,
Whate'er by breath of life is mov'd.
First, 'tis unjust ; and, secondly,
'Tis cruel, and a cruelty
By which we are expos'd (O sad !)
To eat perhaps our lucky dad :
For ken, my friend, the saul ne'er dies,
But frae the failing body flies ;
Leaves it to rot, and seeks anither ;
Thus young Miss Goose may be my mither ;
The bloody wowf, seeking his prey,
His father in a sheep may slay ;
And I, in worrying lambs or cocks,
Might choak my grandsire Doctor Fox.
Ah ! heaven protect me frae sic crimes !
I'd rather die a thousand times."

Thus our bob-tail'd Pythagoras preach'd,
And with loud cant his lungs out-stretch'd.

His sermon sounded o'er the dale,
While thus he moraliz'd with zeal.
His glass spun out, he ceast, admir'd
By all who joyfully retir'd.

But after a' the lave was gane,
Some geese, twa chickens, and a hen,
Thought fit to stay a little space,
To tawk about some kittle case.
The doctor hem'd, and in he drew them,
Then quiet and decently he slew them ;
On whom he fed the good auld way.
Those who wan aff, thrice happy they.

CXLVIII.

FABLE XXIII.

THE BEE AND THE FLY.

BEFORE her hive, a paughty Bee
Observ'd a humble midding flie,
And proudly speer'd, what brought her there,
And with what front she durst repair
Amang the regents of the air.
" It sets ye well," the Flie reply'd,
" To quarrel with sic saucy pride !
They're daft indeed has ought to do
With thrawn contentious fowk like you."—
" Why, scoundrel, you!" return'd the Bee,
" What nation is sae wise as we?
Best laws and policy is ours,
And our repast the fragrant flow'rs :
No sordid nasty trade we drive,
But with sweet honey fill the hive ;

Honey maist gratefu' to the taste,
On which the gods themselves may feast.
Out of my sight, vile wretch! whose tongue
Is daily slacking through the dung;
Vile spirits, filthily content
To feed on stinking excrement!"
The Flie replied in sober way,
" Faith, we man live as well's we may:
Glad poverty was ne'er a vice,
But sure ill-natur'd passion is.
Your honey's sweet; but then how tart
And bitter's your malicious heart!
In making laws you copy heaven,
But in your conduct how uneven!
To fash at ony time a fae,
Ye'll never stick ye'rsells to slae,
And skaith ye'rsell mair sickerly
Than e'er ye can your enemy.
At that rate, ane had better have
Less talents, if they can behave
Discreet, and less their passions' slave."

CXLIX.

FABLE XXIV.

THE HORSE'S COMPLAINT.

" Ah! what a wretch'd unlucky corse
Am I!" cries a poor hireling horse:
" Toil'd a' the day quite aff my feet,
With little time or ought to eat:
By break of day, up frae my bed
Of dirt I'm rais'd to draw the sled,
Or cart, as haps to my wanluck,
To ca' in coals, or out the muck;

Or drest in saddle, howse, and bridle,
To gallop with some gamphrel idle,
That for his hiring pint and shilling,
Obliges me, tho' maist unwilling,
With whip, and spur sunk in my side,
O'er heights and hows all day to ride;
While he neglects my hungry wame,
Till aft I fa' and make him lame;
Who curses me should ban himsell,
He starv'd me, I with faintness fell.

"How happy lives our baron's ape!
That's good for nought but girn and gape,
Or round about the lasses flee,
And lift their coats aboon their knee;
To frisk and jump frae stool to stool,
Turn up his bum, and play the fool;
Aft rives a mutch, or steals a spoon,
And burns the bairns' hose and shoon:
Yet while I'm starving in the stable,
This villain's cock'd upon the table,
There fed and rees'd by all around him,
By foolish chiels, the pox confound them!"

"My friend," says a dowse-headed ox,
"Our knight is e'en like other folks:
For 'tis not them who labour maist
That commonly are paid the best:
Then ne'er cast up what ye deserve,
Since better 'tis to please than serve."

CL.

TIT FOR TAT.

BE-SOUTH our channel, where 'tis common
To be priest-ridden, man and woman ;
A father anes, in grave procession,
Went to receive a wight's confession,
Whase sins, lang gather'd, now began
To burden sair his inner man.
But happy they that can with ease
Fling aff sic loads whene'er they please !
Lug out your sins, and eke your purses,
And soon your kind spiritual nurses
Will ease you of these heavy turses.

   Cries Hodge, and sighs, " Ah ! father ghostly,
I lang'd anes for some jewels costly,
And staw them frae a sneaking miser,
Wha was a wicked cheating squeezer,
And much had me and others wrang'd,
For which I aften wish'd him hang'd."—
The father says, " I own, my son,
To rob or pilfer is ill done ;
But I can eith forgive the faut,
Since it is only tit for tat."

   The sighing penitent gade furder,
And own'd his anes designing murder ;
That he had lent anes guts a skreed,
Wha had gi'en him a broken head.
Replies the priest, " My son, 'tis plain
That's only tit for tat again."

   But still the sinner sighs and sobs,
And cries, " Ah ! these are venial jobs,
To the black crime that yet behind
Lies like Auld Nick upon my mind :

I dare na name't; I'd lure be strung
Up by the neck, or by the tongue,
As speak it out to you : believe me,
The faut you never wad forgive me."
The haly man, with pious care,
Intreated, pray'd, and spake him fair ;
Conjur'd him, as he hop'd for heaven,
To tell his crime, and be forgiven.

    " Well then," says Hodge, " if it maun be,
Prepare to hear a tale frae me,
That when 'tis tald, I'm unko feard,
Ye'll wish it never had been heard :
Ah me ! your reverence's sister,
Ten times I carnally have—kist her."
" All's fair," returns the reverend brother,
" I've done the samen with your mother
Three times as aft ; and sae for that
We're on a level, tit for tat."

CLI.

THE PARROT.

An honest man had tint his wife,
And, wearied of a dowie life,
Thought a parroquet bade maist fair,
With tatling to divert his care :
For the good woman sair he griev'd ;
He 'ad needed nane if she had liv'd !

    Streight to a bird-man's shop he hies,
Who, stock'd with all that wing the skies,
And give delight with feathers fair,
Or please with a melodious air ;

Larks, gowdspinks, mavises, and linties,
Baith hame bred, and frae foreign countries ;
Of parrots he had curious choice,
Carefully bred to make a noise ;
The very warst had learn'd his tale,
To ask a cup of sack or ale ;
Cry westlin herrings, or fresh salmons,
White sand, or Norway nuts like almonds.
Delighted with their various claver,
While wealth made all his wits to waver,
" He cast his look beneath the board,
Where stood ane that spake ne'er a word :
" Pray what art thou stands speechless there ?"
Replied the bird, " I think the mair."
The buyer says, " Thy answer's wise,
And thee I'll have at any price.
What must you have ?"—" Five pounds."—" 'Tis thine
The money, and the bird is mine."

Now in his room this feather'd sage
Is hung up in a gilded cage,
The master's expectations fully
Possest to hear him tauk like Tully :
But a hale month is past and gane,
He never hears a rhyme but ane ;
Still in his lugs he hears it rair,
" The less I speak I think the mair."—
" Confound ye for a silly sot,
What a dull idiot have I got !
As dull mysell, on short acquaintance,
To judge of ane by a single sentence !"

CLII.

THE ECLIPSE.

Upon his gilded chariot, led by hours,
  With radiant glories darting through the air,
The Sun, high sprung in his diurnal course,
  Shed down a day serenely sweet and fair.
The earth mair beautiful and fertile grew ;
    The flow'ry fields in rich array,
    Smil'd lovely on the beamy day,
Delightful for the eye to view ;
    Ceres, with her golden hair,
    Displaying treasure ilka where,
While useful plenty made her stalks to bow.

A thousand little suns glanc'd on the wave ;
  Nature appear'd to claim the Sun's respect,
All did sae blyth and beauteously behave.
" Ah !" cry'd the moon, " too much for him ye deck ;
My aking een cannot this glory bear ;
    This Sun pretends nane in the sky
    Can shine but him, then where am I ?
Soon I the contrary shall clear :
    By ae bauld strake,
    With him I'll make
My equal empire in the heaven appear.

" 'Tis I that gives a lustre to the night,
  Then should not I my proper right display,
And now, even now dart down my silver light ?
  I give enough, this Sun gives too much day."
The project fram'd, pale Cynthia now to shaw
    Her shining power, right daftly run
    Directly 'tween the earth and Sun.

Unwise design ! the world then saw
　　Instead of light, the Moon
　　Brought darkness in at noon,
And without borrowing, had no light at a'.

Thus many empty and imprudent men,
　　Wha to their ain infirmities are blind,
Rax yont their reach, and this way let us ken
　　A jealous, weak, and insufficient mind.

CLIII.

THE MONK AND THE MILLER'S WIFE.

Now lend your lugs, ye benders fine,
Wha ken the benefit of wine ;
And you wha laughing scud brown ale,
Leave jinks a wee, and hear a tale.

　　An honest miller won'd in Fife,
That had a young and wanton wife,
Wha sometimes thol'd the parish priest
To mak' her man a twa-horn'd beast.
He paid right mony visits till her,
And to keep in with Hab the miller,
He endeavour'd aft to mak' him happy,
Where'er he ken'd the ale was nappy.
Sic condescension in a pastor,
Knit Halbert's love to him the faster ;
And by his converse, troth 'tis true,
Hab learn'd to preach when he was fou.
Thus all the three were wonder pleas'd,
The wife well serv'd, the man well eas'd.
This ground his corns, and that did cherish
Himself with dining round the parish.
Bess, the good wife, thought it nae skaith,
Since she was fit to serve them baith.

When equal is the night and day,
And Ceres gives the schools the play,
A youth sprung frae a gentle pater,
Bred at Saint Andrew's alma mater,
Ae day gawn hameward, it fell late,
And him benighted by the gate.
To lye without, pit-mirk, did shore him,
He couldna see his thumb before him;
But clack, clack, clack, he heard a mill,
Whilk led him by the lugs theretill.
To tak' the threed of tale alang,
This mill to Halbert did belang;
Not less this note your notice claims,
The scholar's name was Master James.

Now, smiling muse, the prelude past,
Smoothly relate a tale shall last
As lang as Alps and Grampian hills,
As lang as wind or water mills.

In enter'd James, Hab saw and ken'd him,
And offer'd kindly to befriend him
With sic good cheer as he could make,
Baith for his ain and father's sake.
The scholar thought himself right sped,
And gave him thanks in terms well bred.
Quoth Hab, " I canna leave my mill
As yet; but step ye west the kill
A bow-shot, and ye'll find my hame;
Gae warm ye, and crack with our dame,
Till I set aff the mill, syne we
Shall tak what Bessy has to gi'e."
James, in return, what's handsome said,
O'er lang to tell, and aff he gade.
Out of the house some light did shine,
Which led him till't as with a line:
" Arriv'd, he knock'd, for doors were steekit;
Straight throw a window Bessy keekit,

v 2

And cries, " Wha's that gi'es fowk a fright
At sic untimous time of night ?"
James, with good humour, maist discreetly,
Tald her his circumstance completely.
" I dinna ken ye," quoth the wife,
" And up and down the thieves are rife ;
Within my lane, I'm but a woman,
Sae I'll unbar my door to nae man :
But since 'tis very like, my dow,
That all ye're telling may be true,
Hae, there's a key, gang in your way
At the neist door, there's braw ait strae ;
Streek down upon't, my lad, and learn
They're no ill lodg'd that get a barn."
Thus, after meikle clitter clatter,
James fand he couldna mend the matter ;
And since it might na better be,
With resignation took the key ;
Unlockt the barn, clam up the mow,
Where was an opening near the how,
Through whilk he saw a glent of light,
That gave diversion to his sight :
By this he quickly could discern,
A thin wa' sep'rate house and barn ;
And throw this rive was in the wa',
All done within the house he saw :
He saw what ought not to be seen,
And scarce gave credit to his een,
The parish priest, of reverend fame,
In active courtship with the dame !
To lengthen out description here
Would but offend the modest ear,
And beet the lewder youthfu' flame
That we by satire strive to tame.
Suppose the wicked action o'er,
And James continuing still to glowr ;
Wha saw the wife as fast as able

Spread a clean servite on the table,
And syne, frae the ha' ingle, bring ben
A piping het young roasted hen,
And twa good bottles stout and clear,
Ane of strong ale, and ane of beer.

But, wicked luck ! just as the priest
Shot in his fork in chucky's breast,
Th' unwelcome miller ga'e a roar,
Cry'd, " Bessy, haste ye ope the door."
With that the haly letcher fled,
And darn'd himsell behind a bed ;
While Bessy huddl'd a' things by,
That nought the cuckold might espy ;
Syne loot him in ; but, out of tune,
Speer'd why he left the mill sae soon ?
" I come," said he, " as manners claims,
To crack and wait on Master James,
Whilk I should do tho' ne'er sae bissy ;
I sent him here, good wife, where is he ? "—
" Ye sent him here ! " quoth Bessy, grumbling ;
" Ken'd I this James ? A chiel came rumbling,
But how was I assur'd, when dark,
That he had been nae thievish spark,
Or some rude wencher gotten a dose,
That a good wife could ill oppose ? "—
" And what came of him ? speak nae langer ; "
Cries Halbert, in a Highland anger.
" I sent him to the barn," quoth she ;
" Gae quickly bring him in," quoth he.

James was brought in ; the wife was bawked ;
The priest stood close ; the miller cracked :
Then ask'd his sunkan gloomy spouse,
What supper she had in the house,
That might be suitable to gi'e
Ane of their lodger's qualitie ?

Quoth she, " Ye may well ken, goodman,
Your feast comes frae the pottage-pan ;
The stov'd or roasted we afford
Are aft great strangers on our board."—
" Pottage," quoth Hab, " ye senseless tawpie !
Think ye this youth's a gilly-gawpy ;
And that his gentle stamock's master
To worry up a pint of plaister
Like our mill-knaves that lift the lading,
Whase kytes can streek out like raw plaiding ?
Swith, roast a hen, or fry some chickens,
And send for ale frae Maggy Picken's."—
" Hout I," quoth she, " ye may well ken,
'Tis ill brought but that's no there ben ;
When but last owk, nae farder gane,
The laird got a' to pay his kain."

   Then James, wha had as good a guess
Of what was in the house as Bess,
With pawky smile, this plea to end,
To please himsell, and ease his friend,
First opened, with a slee oration,
His wond'rous skill in conjuration :
Said he, " By this fell art I'm able
To whop aff any great man's table
Whate'er I like to make a meal of,
Either in part, or yet the hail of ;
And, if ye please, I'll shaw my art."
Cries Halbert, " Faith, with all my heart."
Bess sain'd herself, cry'd, " Lord, be here ! "
And near-hand fell a-swoon for fear.
James leugh, and bade her naithing dread ;
Syne to his conjuring went with speed :
And first he draws a circle round,
Then utters mony a magic sound
Of words, part Latin, Greek, and Dutch,
Enow to fright a very witch.

That done, he says, " Now, now, 'tis come,
And in the boal beside the lum :
Now set the board, good wife, gae ben,
Bring frae yon boal a roasted hen."
She wadna gang, but Haby ventur'd ;
As soon as he the aimbrie enter'd,
It smell'd sae well he short time sought it,
And, wond'ring, 'tween his hands he brought it.
He view'd it round, and thrice he smell'd it,
Syne with a gentle touch he felt it.
Thus ilka sense he did conveen,
Lest glamour had beguil'd his een :
They all in ane united body,
Declar'd it a fine fat how towdy.
" Nae mair about it," quoth the miller,
" The fowl looks well, and we'll fa' till her."
" Sae be 't," says James ; and in a doup
They snapt her up baith stoup and roup.

   " Neist, O !" cries Halbert, "could your skill
But help us to a waught of ale
I'd be oblig'd t' ye a' my life,
And offer to the deel my wife,
To see if he'll discreeter mak' her,
But that I'm fleed he winna tak' her."
Said James, "Ye offer very fair ;
The bargain's hadden, sae nae mair."

   Then thrice he shook a willow wand,
With kittle words thrice gave command ;
That done, with look baith learn'd and grave
Said—"Now ye'll get what ye wad have.
Twa bottles of as nappy liquor
As ever ream'd in horn and bicquer,
Behind the ark that hads your meal
Ye'll find twa standing corkit well."

He said, and fast the miller flew,
And frae their nest the bottles drew.
Then first the scholar's health he toasted,
Whase art had gart him feed on roasted ;
His father neist, and a' the rest
Of his good friends that wish'd him best,
Which were o'er langsome at the time
In a short tale to put in rhyme.

　　Thus, while the miller and the youth
Were blythly slocking of their drowth,
Bess fretting, scarcely held frae greeting,
The priest inclos'd stood vex'd and sweating.

　　" O wow !" said Hab, "if ane might speer,
Dear Master James, wha brought our cheer ?
Sic laits appear to us sae awfu',
We hardly think your learning lawfu'."

　　" To bring your doubts to a conclusion,"
Says James, "ken I'm a Rosicrucian,
Ane of the set that never carries
On traffic with black deels or fairies ;
There's mony a spirit that's no deel
That constantly around us wheel.
There was a sage call'd Albumazor,
Whase wit was gleg as ony razor;
Frae this great man we learn'd the skill
To bring these gentry to our will,
And they appear, when we've a mind,
In ony shape of human kind.
Now if you'll drap your foolish fear,
I'll gar my Pacolet appear."

　　Hab fidg'd and leugh, his elbuck clew,
Baith fear'd and fond a sp'rit to view ;
At last his courage wan the day,
He to the scholar's will gave way.

Bessy by this began to smell
A rat, but kept her mind to 'rsell.
She pray'd like howdy in her drink ;
But, meantime, tipt young James a wink.
James frae his e'e an answer sent,
Which made the wife right well content,
Then turn'd to Hab, and thus advis'd—
" Whate'er you see, be nought surpris'd.
But, for your saul, move not your tongue ;
And ready stand with a great rung,
Syne, as the sp'rit gangs marching out
Be sure to lend him a sound rout,—
I bidna this by way of mocking,
For nought delytes him mair than knocking."

Hab got a kent, stood by the hallan,
And straight the wild, mischievous callan,
Cries—" Rhadamanthus husky mingo,
Monk, horner, hipock, jinko, jingo,
Appear in likeness of a priest ;
No like a deel, in shape of beast,
With gaping shafts to fleg us a',—
Wauk forth, the door stands to the wa'."

Then, frae the hole where he was pent,
The priest approached, right well content.
With silent pace strade o'er the floor,
Till he was drawing near the door,
Then, to escape the cudgel, ran ;
But was not miss'd by the goodman,
Wha lent him on his neck a lounder
That gart him o'er the threshold founder.
Darkness soon hid him frae their sight,—
Ben flew the miller in a fright :
" I trow," quoth he, " I laid well on ;
But, wow ! he's like our ain Mess John."

CLIV.

THE DAFT BARGAIN.

At market anes, I watna how,
Twa herds between them coft a cow.
Driving her hame, the needfu' hacky,
But ceremony, chanc'd to k——y.
Quoth Rab (right ravingly) to Raff,—
" Gin ye'll eat that digested draff
Of Crummy, I shall quat my part."——
" A bargain be't with a' my heart,"
Raff soon reply'd, and lick'd his thumb
To gorgle't up without a gloom ;
Syne till't he fell, and seem'd right yap
His mealtith quickly up to gawp.
Haff-done, his heart began to scunner,
But lootna on till Rab strak under,
Wha, fearing skair of cow to tine,
At his daft bargain did repine.
" Well, well," quoth Raff, "tho' ye was rash,
I'll scorn to wrang ye, senseless hash !
Come, fa' to wark as I ha'e done,
And eat the ither haff as soon ;
Ye's save ye'r part."—"Content," quoth Rab ;
And slerg'd the rest o't in his gab.
Now what was tint, or what was won,
Is eithly seen,—my story 's done.
Yet, frae this tale, confed'rate states may learn
To save their cow, and yet no eat her sharn.

CLV.

THE TWA CUT-PURSES.

In borrows-town there was a fair,
And mony a landart coof was there ;
Baith lads and lasses busked brawly,
To glow'r at ilka bonny waly,
And lay out ony ora-bodles
On sma' gimcracks that pleas'd their noddles,—
Sic as a jocktaleg, or sheers,
Confeckit ginger, plumbs, or pears.

These gaping gowks twa rogues survey,
And on their cash this plot they lay :—
The tane, less like a knave than fool,
Unbidden, clam the high cookstool,
And pat his head and baith his hands
Through holes where the ill-doer stands.
Now a' the crowd with mouth and een
Cry'd out—"What does this ideot mean ?"
They glowr'd and leugh, and gather'd thick,
And never thought upon a trick,
Till he beneath had done his job
By tooming poutches of the mob ;
Wha now possest of routh of gear,
Scour'd aff as lang's the coast was clear.

But, wow ! the ferly quickly chang'd ;
When through their empty fobs they rang'd :
Some girn'd, and some look'd blae wi' grief ;
While some cry'd out—"Fy ! had the thief."
But ne'er a thief or thief was there,
Or could be found in a' the fair.
The jip, wha stood aboon them a',
His innocence began to shaw ;

Said he—"My friends, I'm very sorry
To hear your melancholy story;
But sure where'er your tinsel be,
Ye canna lay the wyte on me."

CLVI.

THE LURE.

THE sun just o'er the hills was peeping,
The hynds arising, gentry sleeping,
The dogs were barking, cocks were crawing,
Night-drinking sots counting their lawin;
Clean were the roads, and clear the day
When forth a falconer took his way,
Nane with him but his she knight-errant,
That acts in air the bloody tyrant;
While with quick wing, fierce beak, and claws,
She breaks divine and human laws;
Ne'er pleas'd but with the hearts and livers
Of peartricks, teals, moor-powts, and plivers:
Yet is she much esteem'd and dandl'd,
Clean lodg'd, well fed, and saftly handl'd.
Reason for this need be nae wonder,
Her parasites share in the plunder.
Thus sneaking rooks about a court,
That make oppression but their sport,
Will praise a paughty bloody king,
And hire mean hackney poets to sing
His glories; while the deel be licket
He e'er attempt but what he sticket.

So, Sir, as I was gawn to say,
This falconer had tane his way

O'er Calder-moor ; and gawn the moss up,
He there forgather'd with a gossip :
And wha was't, trow ye, but the deel
That had disguis'd himsell sae weel
In human shape, sae snug and wylie,
Jude took him for a burlie bailie :
His cloven cloots were hid with shoon,
A bonnet coor'd his horns aboon :
Nor spat he fire, or brimstone rifted,
Nor awsome glowr'd ; but cawmly lifted
His een and voice, and thus began :
" Good morning t' ye, honest man ;
Ye're early out ; how far gae ye
This gate ?—I'm blyth of company.
What fowl is that, may ane demand,
That stands sae trigly on your hand ?"—
" Wow ! man," quoth Juden, "where won ye ?
The like was never speer'd at me !
Man, 'tis a hawk, and e'en as good
As ever flew or wore a hood."—
" Friend, I'm a stranger," quoth auld Symmie,
" I hope ye'll no be angry wi' me ;
The ignorant maun ay be speering
Questions, till they come to a clearing.
Then, tell me mair : What do ye wi't ?
Is't good to sing, or good to eat ?"
" For neither," answer'd simple Juden ;
" But helps to bring my lord his food in.
When fowls start up that I wad hae,
Straight frae my hand I let her gae ;
Her hood tane aff, she is not langsome
In taking captives, which I ransome
With a dow's wing, or chicken's leg."—
" Trowth," quoth the deel, "that's nice. I beg
Ye'll be sae kind as let me see
How this same bird of yours can flee."
" T' oblige ye, friend, I winna stand."

Syne loos'd the falcon frae his hand.
Unhooded, up she sprang with birr,
While baith stood staring after her.
" But how d'ye get her back?" said Nick.
" For that," quoth Jude, " I have a trick.
Ye see this Lure? It shall command
Her, upon sight, down to my hand."
Syne twirl'd it thrice, with—whieu, whieu, whieu,
And straight upon't the falcon flew.
" As I'm a sinner," cries the deel,
I like this pastime wonder weel;
And since ye've been sae kindly free
To let her at my bidding flee,
I'll entertain ye in my gate."
Meantime—it was the will of Fate—
A hooded friar (ane of that clan
Ye have descriv'd by Father Gawin,*
In " Master-Keys ") came up, good saul!
Him Satan cleek'd up by the spaul,
Whip'd aff his hood, and, without mair,
Ga'e him a toss up in the air.
High flew the son of Saint Loyola,
While startled Juden gave a hola!
Bombaz'd with wonder, still he stood,
The ferly had maist curdled his blood,
To see a monk mount like a facon!
He 'gan to doubt if he was wakin.
Thrice did he rub his een to clear,
And having master'd part o's fear,
" His presence be about us a'!"
He cries, " the like I never saw.

---

* The Reverend Anthony Gawin,—formerly a Spanish Roman Catholic priest, now an Irish Protestant minister,—who hath lately wrote three volumes on the tricks and whoredoms of the priests and nuns; which book he names " Master-Keys to Popery."

See, see! he like a lavrock tours ;
He'll reach the starns in twa 'r three hours !
Is't possible to bring him back ?"—
" For that," quoth Nick, " I have a knack :
To train my birds I want na Lures,
Can manage them as ye do yours :
And there's ane coming hie gate hither,
Shall soon bring down the haly brither."

This was a fresh young landart lass,
With cheeks like cherries, een like glass ;
Few coats she wore, and they were kilted,
And " John come kiss me now " she lilted,
As she skift o'er the benty knows,
Gawn to the bught to milk the ewes :
Her in his hand slee Belzie hint up,
As eith as ye wad do a pint-stoup,
Inverted, wav'd her round his head ;
Whieu, whieu, he whistled, and with speed,
Down, quick as shooting starns, the priest
Came souse upon the lass's breast.

The moral of this tale shews plainly,
That carnal minds attempt but vainly
Aboon this laigher warld to mount,
While slaves to Satan.

THE THREE BONNETS:

A TALE.

IN FOUR CANTOS.

1722.

THE PERSONS.

DUNIWHISTLE, father to Joukum, Bristle, and Bawsy.

JOUKUM, in love with Rosie.

BRISTLE, a man of resolution.

BAWSY, a weaker brother.

BARD, a narrator.

BEEF, porter to Rosie.

GHAIST, the ghost of Duniwhistle.

ROSIE, an heiress.

THE THREE BONNETS.

CANTO I.

BARD.

WHEN men o' mettle thought it nonsense
To heed that clepping thing ca'd conscience,
And by free thinking had the knack
O' jeering ilka word it spak',
And, as a learned author speaks,
Employ'd it like a pair o' breeks,
To hide their lewd and nasty sluices,
Whilk eith slipt down for baith these uses :
Then Duniwhistle, worn wi' years,
And gawn the gate o' his forbears,
Commanded his three sons to come,
And wait upon him in his room :
Bade Bristle steek the door ; an' syne
He thus began :—

DUNIWHISTLE.

      Dear bairns o' mine,
I quickly maun submit to fate,
And leave you three a good estate,
Which has been honourably won,
An' handed down frae sire to son,

But clag or claim, for ages past :
Now, that I mayna prove the last,
Here's three permission bonnets for ye,
Which your great gutchers wore before ye ;
An' if ye'd hae nae man betray ye,
Let naething ever wile them frae ye ;
But keep the bonnets on your heads,
An' hands frae signing foolish deeds,
An' ye shall never want sic things,
Shall gar ye be made o' by kings :
But if ye ever wi' them part,
Fu' sair ye'll for your folly smart :
Bare-headed then ye'll look like snools,
And dwindle down to silly tools.
Haud up your hands now, swear an' say,
As ye shall answer on a day,
Ye'll faithfully observe my will,
An' a' it's premises fulfil.

BRISTLE.

My worthy father, I shall strive
To keep your name an' fame alive,
An' never shaw a saul that's dastard,
To gar fowk tak' me for a bastard :
If e'er by me ye're disobey'd,
May witches nightly on me ride.

JOUKUM.

Whae'er shall dare, by force or guile,
This bonnet aff my head to wile,
For sic a bauld attempt shall rue,
And ken I was begot by you :
Else may I like a gipsy wander,
Or for my daily bread turn pander.

BAWSY.

May I be jyb'd by great an' sma',
And kytch'd like ony tennis-ba',
Be the disgrace o' a' my kin,
If e'er I wi' my bonnet twin.

BARD.

Now, soon as each had gi'en his aith,
The auld man yielded up his breath ;
Was row'd in linen white as snaw,
And to his fathers borne awa'.
But scarcely he in moss was rotten,
Before his test'ment was forgotten,
As ye shall hear frae future sonnet,
How Joukum sinder'd wi' his bonnet ;
And bought frae senseless billy Bawsy,
His, to propine a giglet lassie ;
While worthy Bristle, not sae donner'd,
Preserves his bonnet, and is honour'd.
Thus Caractacus did behave,
Tho' by the fate o' war a slave ;
His body only, for his mind
No Roman pow'r could break or bind :
Wi' bannet on he bauldly spak' ;
His greatness gart his fetters crack :
The victor did his friendship claim,
And sent him wi' new glories hame.

But leave we Briss an simile,
And to our tale wi' ardour flee.

Beyond the hills, where lang the billies
Had bred up queys, and kids, and fillies,
And foughten mony a bloody battle
Wi' thieves that came to lift their cattle ;

There liv'd a lass kept rary shows
And fiddlers ay about her house ;
Wha at her table fed and ranted,
Wi' the stout ale she never wanted :
She was a winsome wench and waly,
And could put on her claes fu' brawly ;
Rumble to ilka market-town,
And drink and fight like a dragoon :
Just sic like her wha far aff wander'd,
To get hersell weil Alexander'd.
Rosie had word o' meikle siller,
Whilk brought a hantle o' wooers till her.
Amang the rest, young master Jouk
She conquer'd ae day wi' a look.
Frae that time forth, he ne'er could stay
At hame to mind his corn or hay ;
But grew a beau, and did adorn
Himself wi' fifty bows o' corn,—
Forby what he took on to rig
Him out wi' linen, shoon, and wig,
Snuff-boxes, sword-knots, canes, and washes,
And sweeties, to bestow on lasses ;
Could newest aiths genteelly swear,
And had a course o' flaws perquire ;
He drank, and danc'd, and sigh'd to move
Fair Rosie to accept his love.
After dumb signs, he thus began,
And spak' his mind to 'er like a man.

JOUKUM.

O tak' me, Rosie, to your arms,
And let me revel o'er your charms.
If ye say Na, I needna care
For raips or tethers made o' hair,
Penknives or pools I winna need ;
That minute ye say Na, I'm deid.

O let me lie within your breast,
And at your dainty teazle feast ;
Weil do I like your goud to finger,
And fit to her your st—— singer,
While on this sun side o' the brae
Belangs to you, my limbs I'll lay.

ROSIE.

I own, sweet sir, ye woo me frankly,
But a' your courtship sars sae rankly
O' selfish interest, that I'm flead
My person least employs your head.

JOUKUM.

What a distinction's this your making,
When your poor lover's heart is breaking !
Wi' little logic, I can shew
That every thing you ha'e is you :
Besides the beauties o' your person,
These beds o' flowers you set your a— on,
Your claiths, your lands, and lying pelf,
Are every ane your very self,
And add fresh lustre to these graces
Wi' which adorn'd your saul and face is.

ROSIE.

Ye seem to ha'e a loving flame
For me, and hate your native hame,
That gars me ergh to trust you meikle,
For fear you should prove false and fickle.

JOUKUM.

In troth, my rugged billy Bristle
About his gentrie mak's sic fistle,
That if a body contradict him
He's ready wi' a durk to stick him ;

That wearies me o' hame, I vow,
And fain would live and die wi' you.

BARD.

Observing Jouk a wee tate tipsy,
Smirking reply'd the pawky gipsy.

ROSIE.

I wad be very wae to see
My lover tak' the pet, and die.
Wherefore, I am inclin'd to ease ye
And do what in me lies to please ye;
But first, ere we conclude the paction,
You must perform some gallant action,
To prove the truth o' what you've said,
Else, for you, I shall die a maid.

JOUKUM.

My dearest jewel, gi'e 't a name,
That I may win baith you and fame.
Shall I gae fight wi' forest bulls?
Or cleave down troops wi' thicker sculls?
Or shall I douk the deepest sea,
And coral pou for beads to thee?
Penty the pope upon the nose?
Or p— upon a hundred beaus?

ROSIE.

In troth, dear lad, I wad be laith
To risk your life, or do ye skaith.
Only employ your canny skill
To gain and rive your father's will,
Wi' the consent o' Briss and Bawsy,
And I shall in my bosom hawse ye,
Soon as the fatal bonnets three
Are ta'en frae them and gi'en to me.

JOUKUM.

Which to preserve I gied my aith.
But now the cause is life and death :
I must, or wi' the bonnet part,
Or twin wi' you and break my heart :
Sae tho' the aith we took was awfu',
To keep it now appears unlawfu'.
Then, love, I'll answer thy demands,
And flee to fetch them to your hands.

BARD.

The famous jilt o' Palestine
Thus drew the hoods o'er Samson's een,
And gart him tell where lay his strength,
O' which she twinn'd him at the length ;
Then gied him up in chains to rave,
And labour like a galley slave :
But, Rosie, mind, when growing hair
His loss of pith 'gan to repair,
He made of thousands an example,
By crushing them beneath their temple.

CANTO II.

BARD.

THE supper sowin-cogs and bannocks
Stood cooling on the sole o' winnocks,
And, cracking at the westlin gavels,
The wives sat beeking o' their navels,
When Jouk his brither Bristle found,
Fetching his ev'ning wauk around
A score of ploughmen o' his ain,
Wha blythly whistled on the plain.

Jouk three times congee'd, Bristle anes,
Then shook his hand, and thus begins :

BRISTLE.

Wow ! brither Jouk, where ha'e ye been ?
I scarce can trow my looking een,
Ye're grown sae braw : now weirds defend me !
Gin that I had nae maist miskend ye.
And where gat ye that braw blue stringing,
That's at your houghs and shuthers hinging ?
Ye look as sprush as ane that's wooing ;
I ferly, lad, what ye've been doing.

JOUKUM.

My very much respected brither,
Should we hide ought frae an anither,
And not, when warm'd wi' the same blood,
Consult ilk ane anither's good ?
And be it ken'd t' ye, my design
Will profit prove to me and mine.

BRISTLE.

And, brither, troth it much commends
Your virtue, thus to love your friends ;
It makes me blyth, for aft I said,
Ye were a clever mettled lad.

JOUKUM.

And sae, I hope, will ever prove,
Gif ye befriend me in my love :
For Rosie, bonny, rich, and gay,
And sweet as flow'rs in June or May,
Her gear I'll get, her sweets I'll rifle,
Gif ye'll but yield me up a trifle ;
Promise to do 't, and ye'se be free
Wi' ony thing pertains to me.

BRISTLE.

I lang to answer your demand,
And never shall for trifles stand.

JOUKUM.

Then she desires, as a propine,
These bonnets, Bawsy's, your's, and mine ;
And well I wat that's nae great matter,
Gif I sae easily can get her.

BRISTLE.

Ha, ha ! ye Judas, are ye there ?
The d— then nor she ne'er get mair.
Is that the trifle that ye spoke o' ?
Wha think ye, Sir, ye mak' a mock o' ?
Ye silly mansworn, scant o' grace !
Swith let me never see your face.
Seek my auld bonnet aff my head !
Faith, that's a bonny ane indeed !
Require a thing I'll part wi' never !
She's get as soon a lap o' my liver :
Vile whore and jade ! the woody hang her.

BARD.

Thus said, he said nae mair for anger,
But curs'd and ban'd, and was nae far
Frae treading Jouk among the glar.
While Jouk, wi' language glibe as oolie,
Right pawkily kept aff a toolie.
Weil masked wi' a wedder's skin,
Although he was a tod within,
He hum'd and ha'd, and wi' a cant
Held forth as he had been a saint,
And quoted texts to prove we'd better
Part wi' a sma' thing for a greater.

JOUKUM.

Ah ! brither, may the furies rack me
Gif I mean ill ! but ye mistak' me.
But gin your bonnet's sic a jewel,
Pray gie't or keep't, Sir, as you will ;
Since your auld-fashion'd fancy rather
Inclines till't than a hat and feather :
But I'll go try my brither Bawsy,
Poor man, he's nae sae daft and sawcy,
Wi' empty pride to crook his mou',
And hinder his ain gude, like you.
Gif he and I agree, ne'er doubt ye,
We'll mak' the bargain up without ye ;
Syne your braw bonnet and your noddle
Will hardly baith be worth a bodle.

BARD.

At this bauld Bristle's colour chang'd,
He swore on Rose to be reveng'd ;
For he began now to be flied
She'd wile the honours frae his head ;
Syne, wi' a stern and canker'd look,
He thus reprov'd his brither Jouk.

BRISTLE.

Thou vile disgrace o' our forbeirs !
Wha lang wi' valiant dint o' weirs,
Maintain'd their right 'gainst a' intrusions
O' our auld faes the Rosicrucians,
Dost thou design at last to catch
Us in a girn wi' this base match,
And for the hauding up thy pride,
Upo' thy brithers' riggins ride ?
I'll see you hang'd and her thegither
As high as Haman, in a tether,

Ere I wi' my ain bonnet quat
For ony borrow'd beaver hat,
Whilk I, as Rosie taks the fykes,
Man wear or no just as she likes.
Then let me hear nae mair about her,
For if ye dare again to mutter
Sic vile proposals in my hearing,
Ye needna trust to my forbearing ;
For soon my beard will tak' a low,
And I shall crack your crazy pow.

BARD.

  This said, brave Bristle said nae mair,
But cock'd his bonnet wi' an air,
Wheel'd round wi' gloomy brows and muddy,
And left his brither in a study.

CANTO III.

BARD.

Now Sol wi' his lang whip gae cracks
Upon his neighering coursers' backs,
To gar them tak' th' Olympian brae,
Wi' a cart lade o' bleezing day ;
The country hind ceases to snore,
Bangs frae his bed, unlocks the dore,
His bladder tooms, and gi'es a rift,
Then tentily surveys the lift ;
And weary o' his wife and flaes,
To their embrace prefers his claes.
Scarce had the lark forsook her nest,
Whan Jouk, wha had got little rest,
For thinking o' his plot and lassie,
Got up to gang and deal wi' Bawsy.

Awa fast o'er the bent he gaed,
And fand him dozing on his bed,
His blankets creishy, foul his sark,
His curtains trimm'd wi' spider's wark ;
Soot-draps hang frae his roof and kipples,
His floor was a' tobacco spittles :
Yet on the antlers o' a deer
Hang mony an auld claymore and spear,
Wi' coat o' iron an target trusty,
Inch thick o' dirt, and unco rusty :
Enough appear'd to shaw his billy,
That he was lazy, poor, and silly,
And wadna mak' so great a bustle
About his bonnet as did Bristle.
Jouk three times rugged at his shoulder,
Cried three times laigh, and three times louder :
At langrun Bawsy raik'd his een,
And cries, " What's that ? what d'ye mean ? "
Then looking up, he sees his brither.

BAWSY.

Good morrow, Jouk, what brings you hither ?
You're early up, as I'm a sinner
I seenly rise before my dinner.
Weil, what's ye'r news, and how gae's a' ?
Ye've been an unco time awa'.

JOUKUM.

Bawsy, I'm blyth to see you weil,
For me, thank God, I keep my heal :
Get up, get up, ye lazy mart,
I ha'e a secret to impart,
O' which when I gi'e you an inkling,
It will set baith your lugs a tinkling.

BARD.

Straight Bawsy rises, quickly dresses,
While haste his youky mind expresses :
Now rigg'd, and morning drink brought in,
Thus did slee gabbet Jouk begin.

JOUKUM.

My worthy brither, weil I wate
O'er feckless is your wee estate
For sic a meikle saul as yours,
That to things greater higher tow'rs ;
But ye lie loitering here at hame,
Neglectfu' baith o' wealth and fame,
Tho', as I said, ye ha'e a mind
That is for higher things design'd.

BAWSY.

That's very true, thanks to the skies,
But how to get them, there it lies.

JOUKUM.

I'll tell ye, Bawse, I've laid a plot
That only wants your casting vote,
And, if you'll gie 't, your bread is baken ;
But first accept o' this love-taiken :
Here tak' this gowd, and never want
Enough to gar you drink and rant ;
And this is but an arle-penny
To what I afterwards design ye ;
And in return, I'm sure that I
Shall naething seek that ye'll deny.

BAWSY.

And trouth now, Jouk, and neither will I,
Or after never ca' me billy ;

If I refuse, wae light upo' me.
This gowd, O wow! 'tis wonder bonny.

JOUKUM.

Ay, that it is; 'tis e'en the a'
That gars the plough o' living draw:
'Tis gowd gars sogers fight the fiercer;
Without it, preaching wad be scarcer;
'Tis gowd that maks some great men witty,
And puggy lasses fair and pretty;
Without it, ladies nice wad dwindle
Down to a wife that snooves a spindle.—
But to the point, and wave digression:
I mak' a free and plain confession
That I'm in love; and, as I said,
Demand frae you a little aid
To gain a bride, that eithly can
Mak' me fu' blest, and you a man:
Gi'e me your bonnet to present
My mistress wi', and your consent
To rive the daft auld-fashion'd deed
That bids ye wear it on your head.

BAWSY.

O gosh! O gosh! then, Jouk, ha'e at her;
If that be a', 'tis nae great matter.

JOUKUM.

These granted, she demands nae mair,
To let us in her riches skair;
Nor shall our herds, as heretofore,
Rin aff wi' ane anither's store,
Nor ding out ane anither's harns,
When they forgather 'mang the kairns;
But freely may drive up and down,
And sell in ilka market-town

Belangs to her, which soon ye'll see,
If ye be wise, belang to me :
And when that happy day shall come,
My honest Bawsy, there's my thumb
That, while I breathe, I'se ne'er beguile ye,
Ye'se baith get gowd, and be a bailly.

BAWSY.

Faith, Jouk, I see but little skaith
In breaking o' a senseless aith,
That is imposed by doited dads,
To please their whims, on thoughtless lads.
My bonnet ! welcome to my bonnet,
And meikle good may ye mak' on it.
Our father's will, I'se mak' nae din
Tho' Rosie should apply't behin'.
But say, does Billy Bristle ken
This, your design, to mak' us men ?

JOUKUM.

Ay, that he does ; but the stiff ass
Bears a hard hatred at the lass,
And rattles out a hantle stories
O' blood and dirt, and ancient glories ;
Meaning foul feuds that us'd to be
Between ours and her family :
Bans, like a blockhead, that he'll ne'er
Twin wi' his bonnet for a' her gear ;
But you and I conjoin'd can ding him,
And, by a vote, to reason bring him :
If we stand closs, 'tis unco eith
To rive the test'ment spite o's teeth,
And gar him ply, for a' his clavers,
To lift his bonnet to our beavers.

BAWSY.

Then let the doof delight in drudging ;
What cause ha'e we to tent his grudging,
Tho' Rosie's flocks feed on his fells,
If you and I be weil oursells ?

BARD.

Thus Jouk and Bawsy were agreed,
And Briss man yield, it was decreed.—
Thus far I've sung, in Highland strains,
O' Jouk's amours, and pawky pains,
To gain his ends wi' ilka brither,
Sae opposite to ane anither :
O' Bristle's hardy resolutions,
And hatred to the Rosicrucians ;
O' Bawsy put in slav'ry neck-fast,
Selling his bonnet for a breakfast.
What follows on't, o' gain or skaith,
I'se tell when we ha'e ta'en our breath.

CANTO IV.

BARD.

Now soon as e'er the will was torn,
Jouk, wi' twa bonnets, on the morn,
Frae Fairyland, fast bang'd away,
The prize at Rosie's feet to lay ;
Wha, sleely, when he did appear,
About his success 'gan to speer.

JOUKUM.

Here, bonny lass, your humble slave
Presents you wi' the things you crave,
The riven will and bonnets twa,
Which maks the third worth nought ava :

Our pow'r gi'en up, now I demand
Your promis'd love, and eke your hand.

BARD.

Rose smil'd to see the lad outwitted,
And bonnets to the flames committed.
Immediately an awfu' sound,
As ane wad thought, raise frae the ground ;
And syne appear'd a stalwart ghaist,
Whase stern'and angry looks amaist
Unhool'd their sauls :—shaking, they saw
Him frae the fire the bonnets draw :
Then came to Jouk, and wi' twa' rugs
Increas'd the length o' baith his lugs ;
And said—

GHAIST.

Be a' thy days an ass,
An hackney to this cunning lass ;
But, for these bonnets, I'll preserve them
For bairns unborn that will deserve them.

BARD.

Wi' that he vanish'd frae their een,
And left poor Jouk wi' breeks not clean :
He shakes, while Rosie rants and capers,
And ca's the vision nought but vapours ;
Rubs o'er his cheeks and gab wi' ream,
Till he believes 't to be a dream :
Syne to her closet leads the way,
To soup him up wi' usquebæ.

ROSIE.

Now, bonny lad, ye may be free
To handle ought pertains to me ;

z 2

And ere the sun, tho' he be dry,
Has driven down the westlin sky,
To drink his wamefu' o' the sea,
There's be but ane o' you and me.
In marriage ye sall ha'e my hand ;
But I maun ha'e the sole command
In Fairyland, to saw and plant,
And to send there for ought I want.

BARD.

Ay, ay, cries Jouk, a' in a fire,
And stiffening into strong desire.

JOUKUM.

Come, haste thee, let us sign and seal ;
And let my billies gang to the deil.

BARD.

Here, it wad mak' o'er lang a tale
To tell how meikle cakes and ale,
And beef, and broe, and gryce, and geese,
And pies a' rinning o'er wi' creesh,
Was serv'd upon the wedding-table,
To mak' the lads and lasses able
To do, ye ken, what we think shame
(Tho' ilk ane does't) to gi'e't a name.
But true it is they soon were buckled,
And soon she made poor Jouk a cuckold,
And play'd her bawdy sports before him
Wi' chiels that car'd na tippence for him ;
Beside, a Rosicrucian trick
She had o' dealing wi' Auld Nick ;
And whene'er Jouk began to grumble,
Auld Nick in the neist room wad rumble.
She drank, and fought, and spent her gear
Wi' dice, and selling o' the mear.

Thus living like a Belzie's get,
She ran hersell sae deep in debt,
By borrowing money at a' hands,
That yearly income o' her lands
Scarce paid the interest o' her bands.
Jouk, ay ca'd wise behind the hand,
The daffin o' his doings fand :
O'er late, he now began to see
The ruin o' his family :
But past relief lar'd in a midding,
He's now oblig'd to do her bidding.
Awa wi' strict command he's sent
To Fairyland to lift the rent,
And wi' him mony a caterpillar,
To rug frae Briss and Bawsy siller ;
For her braid table maun be serv'd,
Tho' Fairy fowk should a' be starv'd.
Jouk, thus surrounded wi' his guards,
Now plunders haystacks, barns, and yards ;
They drive the nowt frae Bristle's fauld,
While he can nought but ban and scald.

BRISTLE.

Vile slave to a hussy ill-begotten,
By mony dads, wi' claps half rotten !
Were't no for honour o' my mither,
I should na think ye were my brither.

JOUKUM.

Dear brother, why this rude reflection ?
Learn to be gratefu' for protection.
The Peterenians, bloody beasts !
That gar fowk lick the dowps o' priests,
Else on a brander, like a haddock,
Be broolied, sprowling like a paddock ;
These monsters, lang ere now, had come,
Wi' faggots, taz, and tuck o' drum,

And twin'd you o' your wealth and lives,
Syne, without speering, kiss'd your wives,
Had not the Rosicrucians stood
The bulwarks o' your rights and blood ;
And yet, forsooth, ye girn and grumble,
And, wi' a gab unthankfu', mumble
Out mony a black unworthy curse,
When Rosie bids ye draw your purse ;
When she's sae gen'rously content
With not aboon thirty per cent.

BRISTLE.

Damn you and her ! tho' now I'm blae,
I'm hopefu' yet to see the day,
I'll gar ye baith repent that e'er
Ye reav'd by force awa my gear,
Without or thanks, or making price,
Or ever speering my advice.

JOUKUM.

Peace, gowk ! we naething do at a'
But by the letter o' the law :
Then nae mair wi' your din torment us,
Growling like ane *non compos mentis*,
Else Rosie issue may a writ,
To tie you up baith hand and fit,
And dungeon ye but meat or drink,
Till ye be starv'd and die in stink.

BARD.

Thus Jouk and Bristle, when they met,
Wi' sic braw language ither tret.
Just fury glows in Bristle's veins,
And tho' his bonnet he retains,
Yet on his crest he mayna cock it,
But in a coffer close maun lock it.
Bareheaded thus he e'en knocks under,
And lets them drive awa the plunder.

Sae have I seen, beside a tow'r,
The king of brutes oblig'd to cour,
And on his royal paunches thole
A dwarf to prog him wi' a pole ;
While he wad show his fangs, and rage
Wi' bootless wrangling in his cage.—
Now follows that we tak' a peep
O' Bawsy, looking like a sheep,
By Bristle hated and despised,
By Jouk and Rosie little priz'd.
Soon as the horse had heard his brither
Joukum and Rose were prick'd thegither,
Awa he scours o'er height and how,
Fu' fidgin fain whate'er he dow,
Counting what things he now did mister,
That wad be gi'en him by his sister.
Like shallow bards, wha think they flee,
Because they live sax storeys high,
To some poor lifeless lucubration
Prefixes fleeching dedication,
And blythly dream they'll be restor'd
To alehouse credit by my Lord.
Thus Bawsy's mind in plenty row'd,
While he thought on his promis'd gowd
And bailieship, which he wi' fines
Wad mak like the West India mines ;
Arrives, wi' future greatness dizzy,
Ca's, where's Mess Jouk ?

BEEF.

Mess Jouk is bissy.

BAWSY.

My Lady Rose, is she at leisure ?

BEEF.

No, Sir, my Lady's at her pleasure.

BAWSY.

I wait for her or him, go shew.

BEEF.

And pray you, master, wha are you ?

BAWSY.

Upo' my saul, this porter's saucy ?
Sirrah, go tell my name is Bawsy,
Their brither wha made up the marriage.

BEEF.

And sae I thought by your daft carriage.
Between your houghs gae clap your gelding,
Swift hame and feast upon a spelding,
For there's nae room beneath this roof
To entertain a simple coof,
The like o' you, that nane can trust,
Wha to your ain ha'e been unjust.

BARD.

This said, he dadded to the yate,
And left poor Bawsy in a fret,
Wha loudly gowl'd, and made a din
That was o'erheard by a' within.
Quoth Rose to Jouk—"Come, let's away,
And see wha's yon mak's a' this fray."
Awa' they went, and saw the creature
Sair runkling ilka silly feature
O' his dull phiz, wi' girns and glooms,
Stamping, and biting at his thumbs.
They tented him a little while,
Then came full on him wi' a smile,
Which soon gart him forget the torture
Was rais'd within him by the porter.

Sae will a sucking weanie yell,
But shake a rattle or a bell
It hauds its tongue ; let that alane,
It to its yamering fa's again ;
Lilt up a sang, and straight it's seen
To laugh wi' tears into its een.
Thus eithly anger'd, easily pleas'd,
Weak Bawsy lang they tantaliz'd
Wi' promises right wide extended
They ne'er perform'd, nor ne'er intended :
But now and then, when they did need him,
A supper and a pint they gie'd him :
That done, they ha'e nae mair to say
And scarcely ken him the neist day.
Poor fallow ! now this mony a year,
Wi' some faint hope, and rowth o' fear,
He has been wrestling wi' his fate,
A drudge to Joukum and his mate.
While Bristle saves his manly look,
Regardless baith o' Rose and Jouk,
Maintains right quietly 'yond the kairns,
His honour, conscience, wife, and bairns,
Jouk and his rumblegarie wife
Drive on a drunken gaming life,
'Cause, sober, they can get nae rest,
For Nick and Duniwhistle's ghaist,
Wha in the garrets aften tooly,
And shore them wi' a bloody gully.

Thus I ha'e sung, in hamelt rhyme,
A sang that scorns the teeth of time ;
Yet modestly I hide my name,
Admiring virtue mair than fame.
But tent ye wha despise instruction
And gi'es my wark a wrang construction,
Frae 'hind my curtain, mind I tell ye,
I'll shoot a satire through your belly :

But wha wi' havins jees his bonnet,
And says—"Thanks t'ye for your sonnet,"
He shanna want the praises due
To generosity.—Adieu.

THE EAGLE AND THE ROBIN REDBREAST.

THE Prince of all the fethert kind
That with spread wings outflees the wind,
And tours far out of human sicht
To view the schynand orb of licht :
This ryall bird, tho' braif and great,
And armit strang for stern debait,
Nae tyrant is, but condescends
Aftymes to treit inferiour friends.

Ane day, at his command did flock
To his hie palace, on a rock,
The courtiers of ilk various syze
That swiftly swim in christal skyis.
Thither the valiant Tersals doup,
And heir rapacious Corbies croup,
With greidy Gleds, and slie Gormahs,
And dinsome Pyis, and clatterin Daws;
Proud Pecocks, and a hundred mae,
Bruscht up thair pens that solemn day,
Bowd first submissive to my lord,
Then tuke thair places at his borde.

Mein tyme, quhile feisting on a fawn,
And drinking blude frae lammies drawn,
A tunefull Robin trig and zung
Hard by upon a bour-tree sung.

He sang the Eagle's ryall lyne,
His persing ee and richt divyne
To sway out owre the fetherit thrang,
Quha dreid his martial bill and fang ;
His flicht sublime, and eild renewit,
His mynd with clemencie endewit.
In safter notes, he sang his luve ;
Mair hie, his beiring bolts for Jove.

The monarch bird, with blythness, heard
The chaunting litil silvan bard,
Calit up a buzart, quha was then
His favourite and chamberlane.
" Swith to my treasury," quod he,
" And to zon canty Robin gie
As meikle of our currant geir
As may mentain him throw the zeir ;
We can weil spair't, and it's his due."
He bad, and furth the Judas flew
Straight to the bench quhair Robin sung,
And, with a wickit lieand tung,
Said—" Ah ! ze sing sae dull and ruch,
Ze haif deivt our lugs mair than enuch ;
His majestie hes a nyse eir,
And nae mair of zour stuff can beir ;
Poke up your pypes, be nae mair sene
At court ; I warn ze as a frein."

He spak, quhyle Robinis swelling breist,
And drouping wings, his greif exprest ;
The teirs ran happing doun his cheik,
Grit grew his hairt, he could nocht speik,
No for the tinsell of rewaird,
But that his notis met nae regaird.
Straicht to the schaw he spred his wing,
Resolvit again nae mair to sing,

A 3

Quhair princelie bountie is supprest
By sic with quhome they ar opprest,
Quha cannot beir, because they want it,
That ocht suld be to merit grantit.

THE CONCLUSION.

THE AUTHOR'S ADDRESS TO HIS BOOK, IN IMITATION OF HORACE.

DEAR, vent'rous book, e'en take thy will,
And scowp around the warld thy fill :
Wow ! ye're newfangle to be seen,
In gilded Turkey clad, and clean.
Daft, giddy thing ! to dare thy fate,
And spang o'er dykes that scar the blate ;
But mind, when anes ye're to the bent,
Altho' in vain, ye may repent.
Alake ! I'm fleed thou aften meet,
A gang that will thee sourly treat,
And ca' thee dull for a' thy pains,
When damps distress their drowzie brains.
I dinna doubt, whilst thou art new,
Thou 'lt favour find frae not a few ;
But when thou 'rt ruffled and forfairn,
Sair thumb'd by ilka coof or bairn,
Then, then by age ye may grow wise,
And ken things common gi'e nae price.
I'd fret, wae's me ! to see thee lye
Beneath the bottom of a pye ;
Or cow'd out page by page, to wrap
Up snuff, or sweeties, in a shap.

Awa, sic fears ! gae spread my fame,
And fix me an immortal name ;
Ages to come shall thee revive,
And gar thee with new honours live.
The future critics, I foresee,
Shall have their notes on notes on thee ;
The wits unborn shall beauties find
That never enter'd in my mind.

Now when thou tells how I was bred
But hough enough * to mean a trade,
To balance that, pray let them ken
My saul to higher pitch could sten :
And when ye shaw I'm scarce of gear,
Gar a' my virtues shine mair clear :
Tell, I the best and fairest please ;
A little man that lo'es my ease,
And never thole these passions lang
That rudely mint to do me wrang :

Gin ony want to ken my age,
See anno Dom. † on title page ;
This year, when springs, by care and skill,
The spacious leaden conduits ‡ fill,
And first flow'd up the Castle-hill ;
When South-Sea projects cease to thrive,
And only North-Sea seems alive,
Tell them your author's thirty-five.

---

* Very indifferently.

† The first edition of his poems was published in 1721.

‡ The new lead pipes for conveying water to Edinburgh, of four inches and a half diameter within, and six tenths of an inch in thickness ; all cast in a mould invented by the ingenious Mr. Harding of London.

A GLOSSARY;

OR,

AN EXPLANATION

OF THE

SCOTISH WORDS,

Which are used in the Poems of ALLAN RAMSAY; and which
are rarely found in modern English Writings.

CORRECTED AND AMENDED.

A GLOSSARY,

&c., &c., &c.

Some General Rules, showing wherein many Southern and Northern Words are originally the same,—having only one letter changed for another ; or sometimes one letter taken away or one added.

I. *In many words ending with an* L *after an* A *or* U, *the* L *is rarely sounded.*

SCOTISH.	ENGLISH.	SCOTISH.	ENGLISH.
A'	All	Sma	Small
Ba	Ball	Sta	Stall
Ca	Call	Wa	Wall
Fa	Fall	Fou *or* fu	Full
Ga	Gall	Pou *or* pu	Pull
Ha	Hall	Woo *or* oo	Wool

II. *The* L *changes to* A, W, *or* U, *after* O *or* A, *and is frequently sunk before another Consonant ; as—*

Bawm	Balm	Gowd	Gold
Bauk	Baulk	Haff	Half
Bouk	Bulk	Howms	Holms
Bow	Boll	How	Hole, *or* Hollow
Bowt	Bolt	Maut	Malt
Caff	Calf	Pow	Poll
Cow	Coll, *or* Clip	Row	Roll
Faut	Fault	Scawd	Scald
Fause	False	Stown	Stolen
Fawn	Fallen	Wawk	Walk
Fowk	Folk		

III. *An* O *before* LD, *changes to* A, *or* AU; *as,*

Auld	Old	Hald *or* had	Hold
Bauld	Bold	Sald	Sold
Cauld	Cold	Tald	Told
Fauld	Fold	Wad	Would

IV. The O, OE, or OW, is changed to A, AE, AW, or AI; as—

SCOTISH.	ENGLISH.	SCOTISH.	ENGLISH.
Ae *or* ane	One	Lang	Long
Aeten	Oaten	Mae	More
Aff	Off	Maist	Most
Aften	Often	Mair	More
Aik	Oak	Mane	Moan
Aith	Oath	Na	No
Ain *or* awn	Own	Nane	None
Alane	Alone	Naithing	Nothing
Amaist	Almost	Pape	Pope
Amang	Among	Rae	Roe
Airs	Oars	Raip	Rope
Aits	Oats	Raw	Row
Apen	Open	Saft	Soft
Awner	Owner	Saip	Soap
Bain	Bone	Sair	Sore
Bair	Boar	Sang	Song
Baith	Both	Slaw	Slow
Blaw	Blow	Snaw	Snow
Braid	Broad	Strake	Stroak
Claith	Cloth	Staw	Stole
Craw	Crow	Stane	Stone
Drap	Drop	Saul	Soul
Fae	Foe	Tae	Toe
Frae	Fro *or* from	Taiken	Token
Gae	Go	Tangs	Tongs
Gaits	Goats	Tap	Top
Grane	Groan	Thrang	Throng
Haly	Holy	Wae	Woe
Hale	Whole	Wame	Womb
Halesome	Wholesome	Wan	Won
Hame	Home	War	Worse
Hait *or* het	Hot	Wark	Work
Laith	Loath	Warld	World
Laid	Load	Wha	Who
Lain *or* len	Loan		

V. The O or U is frequently changed into I; as—

Anither	Another	Ither	Other
Bill	Bull	Mither	Mother
Birn	Burn	Nits	Nuts
Brither	Brother	Nise	Nose
Fit	Foot	Pit	Put
Fither	Fother	Rin	Run
Hinny	Honey	Sin	Sun

A

ABEET, albeit, although
Ablins, perhaps
Aboon, above
Aeten, oaten
Aik, oak
Aikerbread, the breadth of an acre
Air, long since. It, early. Air up, soon up in the morning.
Ambrie, cupboard.
Anew, enow.
Annual-rent, yearly interest of money.
Apen, open.
Arles, earnest of a bargain.
Ase, ashes.
Ase-midding, dunghill of ashes.
Asteer, stirring.
Atains, or Atanes, at once, at the same time.
Attour, out-over.
Auld-farren, knowing, shrewd
Auld Reeky, a cant name for Edinburgh ; old and smoky
Aurglebargin, or Eagglebargin, to contend and wrangle
Awsome, frightful, terrible
Aynd, the breath

B

Ba', ball
Back-sey, a sirloin
Badrans, a cat
Baid, staid, abode
Bairns, children
Balen, whalebone
To ban, to curse
Bang, is sometimes an action of haste, We say, "he, or it, came with a bang." A bang also means a great number : "of customers she had a bang"
Bangster, a blustering roaring person

BIR

Bannocks, a sort of unleavened bread, thicker than cakes, and round
Barken'd, when mire, blood, &c., hardens upon a thing like bark
Barlikhood, a fit of drunken angry passion
Barrow-trams, the staves of a hand-barrow
Batts, colick
Bauch, sorry, indifferent
Baul, or Bauld, bold
Bawbee, halfpenny
Bawk, a rafter, joist : likewise, the space between corn fields
Bawsy, bawsand-fac'd, is a cow, or horse, with a white face
Bedeen, immediately, in haste
Beft, beaten
Begoud, began
Begrutten, all in tears
Beik, to bask
Beild, or beil, a shelter
Bein, or been, wealthy, comfortable. A been house, a warm well-furnished one.
Beit, or beet, to help, repair
Bells, bubbles
Beltan, the 3d of May, or Rood-day
Belzie, Beelzebub
Bended, drunk hard
Benn, the inner room of a house
Bennison, blessing
Bensell, or bensail, force
Bent, the open field
Benty, overgrown with coarse grass
Beuk, baked
Bicker, a wooden dish
Bickering, fighting, running quickly. School-boys battling with stones
Bigg, build. Bigget, built. Biggings, buildings
Biggonet, a linen cap or coif
Billy, brother
Bink, a bench to sit on, either by the door, or near the fire
Byre, or byar, a cow house
Birks, birch-trees

BOU

Birle, to carouse. When common people join their halfpennies for purchasing liquor, they call it "birling a bawbee"

Birn, a burnt mark

Birns, the stalks of burnt heath

Birr, force, flying swiftly with a noise

Bisy, Busy

Bittle, or beetle, a wooden mall for beating hemp, or a fuller's club

Black-a-vic'd, of a black complexion

Blae, black and blue, the colour of the skin when bruised

Blaflum, beguile

Blate, bashful

Blatter, a rattling noise

Blawart, a blue flower that grows among corn

Bleech, to blanch or whiten

Bleer, to make the eye water

Bleeze, blaze

Blether, foolish discourse. Bletherer, a babbler. Stammering is called blethering.

Blin, cease. "Never blin," never have done

Blinkan, the flame rising and falling, as of a lamp when the oil is exhausted

Boak, or boke, retch

Boal, a little press or cupboard in the wall

To Boast, to threaten or scold at

Bodin, or bodden, provided or furnished

Bodle, one-sixth of a penny English

Bodword, an ominous message. Bodwords are now used to express ill-natured messages

Boglebo, hobgoblin or spectre

Bonny, beautiful

Bonnywalys, toys, gew-gaws

Boss, empty

Bouk, bulk

Bourd, jest or dally

Bouser, a rafter

Bouze, to drink

BUS

Bowt, to bolt

Brochen, water-gruel of oat-meal

Brae, the side of a hill, a steep bank

Braid, broad

Braird, the first sprouting of corns

Brander, a gridiron

Brands, calves of the legs

Brang, brought

Brankan, prancing, a capering

Branks, wherewith the rustics bridle their horses

Branny, brandy

Brattle, noise, as of horse feet

Brats, rags, aprons of coarse linen

Braw, brave; fine in apparel

Brecken, fern

Brent-brow, smooth high forehead

Brigs, bridges

Briss, to press

Brock, a badger

Broe, broth

Browden, fond

Browster, brewer. Browst, a brewing

Bruliment, or Brulziement, a broil

Bucky, the large sea snail: a term of reproach, when we express a cross-natured fellow by "thrawn bucky"

Buff, nonsense: as, "he blather'd buff"

Bught, the little fold where the ewes are inclosed at milking-time

Buller, to bubble: the motion of water at a spring head, or noise of a rising tide

Bumbazed, confused; made to stare and look like an ideot

Bumbee, an humble bee

Bumler, a bungler

To Bummil, to bungle

Bung, completely fuddled, as it were to the bung

Bunkers, a bench, or sort of long low chests that serve for seats

Burd-alane, solitary bird

Burn, a brook

Busk, to deck, dress

Bustine, fustian, cloth

But, often used for without; as, "but feed or favour"

Bykes, or bikes, nests or hives of bees

Bygane, bypast

Byword, a proverb

C

Cadge, carry. Cadger is a country carrier, &c.

Caff, a calf; chaff

Callan, boy

Camschough, or Campsho, stern, grim, of a distorted countenance

Cangle, to wrangle

Canker'd, angry, passionately snarling

Canna, cannot

Cant, to tell merry old tales

Cantraips, incantations

Canty, cheerful and merry

Capernoited, whimsical, ill-natured

Car, sledge

Carena, care not

Carle, a word for an old man

Carline, an old woman. Girecarline, a giant's wife

Carts, cards,

Cathel, cawdle, an hot-pot made of ale, sugar, and eggs

Cauldrife, spiritless; wanting cheerfulness in address

Cauler, cool or fresh

Cawk, chalk

Cawsy, causeway, street

Chafts, chops,

Chaping, an ale measure or stoup, somewhat less than an English quart

A-Char, or a-jar, aside. When anything is beat a little out of its position, or a door or window a little opened, we say, "they are a-char, or a-jar"

Charlewain, Charleswain; the constellation called the plow, or ursa major

Chancy, fortunate, good-natured

Chanler, a candlestick

Chanler-chafts, lantern-jaw'd

Chat, a cant name for the gallows

Chiel or chield, a general term like fellow; used sometimes with respect, as—"He's a very good chiel;" and, contemptuously, "That chiel"

Chirm, chirp and sing like a bird

Chitter, chatter

Chorking, the noise made by the feet when the shoes are full of water

Chucky, a hen

Clan, tribe, family

Clank, a sharp blow or stroke that makes a noise

Clashes, chat

Clatter, to chatter

Claught, took hold

Claver, to speak nonsense

Claw, scratch

Cleek, to catch as with a hook

Cleugh, a den betwixt rocks

Clink, coin, money

Clinty, hard, stony

Clock, a beetle

Cloited, the fall of any soft, moist thing

Closs, a court or square; and frequently a lane or alley

Clour, the little lump that rises on the head, occasioned by a blow or fall

Clute, or cloot, hoof of cows or sheep

Cockernony, the gathering of a woman's hair, when it is wrapt or snooded up with a band or snood

Cockstool, a pillory

Cod, a pillow

Coft, bought

CUT

Cog, a pretty large wooden dish the country people put their pottage in

Cogle, when a thing moves backwards and forwards inclining to fall

Coly, a shepherd's dog

Coodie, a small wooden vessel used by some for a chamber-pot

Coof, a stupid fellow

Coor, to cover, and recover

Cooser, a stoned horse

Coost, did cast. Coosten, thrown

Corby, a raven

Cosie, warm and comfortable

Cotter, a cottager

Couthy, affable

Cowp, to turn over; also, a fall

Cowp, to change or barter

Cowp, a company of people; as— "merry, senseless, corky cowp"

Crack, to chat

Craig, a rock; the neck

Craw, crow

Creel, basket

Creepy, a low stool

Crish, grease

Croil, a crooked dwarf

Croon or crune, to murmur or hum over a song; the lowing of bulls

Crouse, bold, pert, overbearing

Crove, a cottage

Crummy, a cow's name

Cryn, to shrink or become less by drying

Cudeigh, a bribe, present

Culzie, to entice or flatter

Cun, to taste, learn, know

Cunzie or coonie, coin

Curn, a small parcel

Cursche, a kerchief; a linen dress worn by our highland women

Cutled, used kind and gaining methods for obtaining love and friendship

Cutty, short

D

Dab, a proficient

Dad, to beat one thing against another: "He fell with a dad;" "He dadded his head against the wall," &c.

Daft, foolish; and, sometimes, wanton

Daffin, folly, waggery

Daintiths, delicacies, dainties

Dainty, is used as an epithet of a fine man or woman

Dander, to wander to and fro or saunter

Dang, did ding, beat, thrust, drive. Ding, dang, moving hastily one on the back of another

Darn, to hide

Dash, to put out of countenance

Dawty, a fondling, darling. To dawt, to cocker and caress with tenderness

Deave, to stun the ears with noise

Deel, the devil

Deel-be-likit, the devil-a-bit

Dees, dairy-maids

Deray, merriment, jollity, solemnity, tumult, disorder, noise

Dern, secret, hidden, lonely

Deval, to descend, fall, hurry

Dewgs, rags or shapings of cloth

Didle, to act or move like a dwarf

Dight, decked, made ready; also, to clean

To Ding, to drive down, to beat, to overcome

Dink, prim

Dinna, do not

Dirle, a smarting pain quickly over

Dit, to stop or close up a hole

Divot, thin turf

Dock, the backside

Docken, a dock, the herb

Doilt, confused and silly

Doited, dozed or crazy, as in old age

Doll, a large piece; dole or share

Donk, moist

DRO

Donsie, affectedly neat; sometimes, dull and dreary; clean, when applied to any little person

Doofart, a dull, heavy-headed fellow

Dool or drule, the goal which gamesters strive to gain first, as at football

Dool, pain, grief

Dorts, a proud pet

Dorty, proud; not to be spoken to; conceited; appearing as disobliged

Dosend, cold, impotent

Dought, could, availed

Doughty, strong, valiant, able

Douks, dives under water

Dour, dowr, hard, severe, fierce

Douse, solid, grave, prudent

Dow, to will, to incline, to thrive

Dow, dove

Dow'd, (liquor) that is dead, or has lost the spirits; or withered (plant)

Dowff, mournful, wanting vivacity

Dowie, siekly, melancholy, sad, doleful

Downa, dow not, i. e., though one has the power, he wants the heart to do it

Dowp, the arse, the small remains of a candle, the bottom of an egg-shell: "better half egg as toom dowp"

Drant, to speak slow, after a sighing manner

Dree, to suffer, endure

Dreery, wearisome, frightful

Dreigh, slow, keeping at distance: hence, an ill payer of his debts we call dreigh: tedious

Dribs, drops,

Dring, the noise of a kettle before it boils

Drizel, a little water in a rivulet, scarce appearing to run

Droning, sitting lazily, or moving heavily; speaking with groans

Drouked, drenched, all wet

FAE

Dubs, mire

Duds, rags. Duddy, ragged

Dung, driven down, overcome

Dunt, stroke or blow

Dunty, a doxy

Durk, a poinard or dagger

Dusht, driven down

Dwine, to pine away

Dynles, trembles, shakes

Dyvour, a bankrupt

E

To Eag, to egg, to incite, stir up

Eard, earth, the ground

Edge of a hill, is the side or top

Een, eyes

Eild, age

Eildeens, of the same age

Eith, easy. Either, easier

Elbuck, elbow

Elf-shot, bewitched, shot by fairies

Ell-wand, the ell measure

Elritch, wild, hideous, uninhabited except by imaginary ghosts

Elson, a shoemaker's awl

Endlang, along

Ergh, scrupulous, when one makes faint attempts to do a thing, without a steady resolution

Esthler, ashler, hewn stone

Ether, an adder

Ethercap, or Ettercap, a venomous spiteful creature

Etle, to aim, design

Even'd, compared

Evite, to shun

Eydent, diligent, laborious

F

Fa, a trap, such as is used for catching rats or mice

Facing-tools, drinking-pots

Fadge, a spungy sort of bread in shape of a roll

Fae, foe

Fail, thick turf, such as are used for building dykes for folds, inclosures, &c.

Fair-faw, when we wish well to one, that a good or fair fate may befall him

Fait, neat, in good order

Fand, found

Fang, the talons of a fowl. To Fang, to grip, or hold fast

Fash, to vex or trouble. Fasheous, troublesome

Faugh, a colour between white and red. Faugh riggs, fallow ground

Faught, a broil

Fause, false

Fawn, fallen

Feck, a part, quantity; as, maist feck, the greatest number; nae feck, very few

Feckfow, able, active

Feckless, feeble, little and weak

Feed, or fead, feud, hatred, quarrel

Feil, many, several

Fen, shift. Fending, living by industry. Make a fen, fall upon methods

Ferlie, wonder

Fernzier, the last or forerun year

File, to defile or dirty

Fireflaught, a flash of lightning

Fistle, to stir, a stir

Fit, the foot

Fitsted, the print of the foot

Fizzing, whizzing

Flaffing, moving up and down; raising wind by motion, as birds with their wings

Flags, flashes, as of wind and fire

Flane, an arrow

Flang, flung

Flaughter, to pare turf from the ground

Flaw, lie or fib

Fleetch, to coax or flatter

Fleg, fright

Flet, the preterite of flyte, did chide

Flegeeries, gewgaws

Flewet, a smart blow

Fley, or flie, to affright. Fleyt, afraid or terrified

Flinders, splinters

Flit, to remove

Flite, or flyte, to scold or chide. Flet, did scold

Flushes, floods

Fog, moss

Fon, fond

Foordays, the morning far advanced, fair day-light

Forby, besides

Forebears, forefathers, ancestors

Forfairn, abused, bespattered

Forfoughten, weary, faint and out of breath with fighting

Forgainst, opposite to

Forgether, to meet, encounter

Forleet, to forsake or forget

Forestam, the forehead

Fou, drunk

Fouth, abundance, plenty

Fow-weel, full well

Fozy, spungy, soft

Fraise, to make a noise. We use to say, "one makes a fraise," when they boast, wonder, and talk more of a matter than it is worthy of, or will bear

Fray, bustle, fighting

Freik, a fool, light impertinent fellow

Fremit, strange, not a-kin

Fristed, trusted

Frush, brittle, like bread baken with butter

Fuff, to blow. Fuffin, blowing

Furder, prosper

Furthy, forward

Fuish, brought

Fyk, to be restless, uneasy

Furlet, four pecks

G

Gab, the mouth. To Gab, to prate

Gabbing, prating pertly. To Gab again, when servants give saucy returns when reprimanded

Gabby, one of a ready and easy expression; the same with auld gabbet

Gadge, to dictate impertinently, talk idly with a stupid gravity

To Gae, to go

Gafaw, hearty loud laughter. To gawf, to laugh

Gaist, or ghaist, a ghost

Gait, a goat

Gams, gums,

Gantrees, a stand for ale-barrels

Gar, to cause, make, or force

Gare, greedy, rapacious, earnest to have a thing

Gash, solid, sagacious. One with a long out chin, we call gash-gabbet, or gash-beard

Gate, way

Gaunt, yawn

Gaw, to take the pet, to be galled

Gawd, or gad, a bar of iron, a ploughman's rod

Gawky, an idle, staring, idiotical person

Gawn, going

Gaws, galls

Gawsy, jolly, buxom

To geck, to mock, to toss the head with disdain

Geed, or gade, went

Genty, handsome, genteel

Get, a brat, a child, by way of contempt or derision

Gielainger, an ill debtor

Gif, if

Gift, a wicked imp, a term of reproach

Gillygacus, or gillygapus, a staring gaping fool, a gormandizer

Gilpy, a roguish boy

Gimmer, a young sheep-ewe

Gin, if

Gird, to strike, pierce

Girn, to grin, snarl; also a snare or trap, such as boys make of horse-hair to catch birds

Girth, a hoop

Glaiks, the reflection of the sun thrown from a mirror; an idle good-for-nothing fellow. Glaiked, foolish, wanton, light. To give the glaiks, to beguile one by giving him his labour for his pains

Glaister, to bawl or bark

Glamour, a fascinating spell in order to deceive the eyes

Glar, mire, oozy mud

Glee, to squint. Gleed, or gleid, squint-eyed

Gleg, sharp, quick, active

Glen, a narrow valley between mountains

Gloom, to scowl or frown

Glowming, or gloming, the twilight or evening gloom

Glowr, to stare

Glunch, to hang the brow and grumble

Goan, a wooden dish for meat

Goolie, a large knife

Gorlings, or gorblings, young unfledged birds

Gossie, gossip

Gowans, daisies

Gove, to look with a roving eye

Gowf, or golf, besides the known game, a racket or sound blow on the chop, we call "a gowf on the haffet"

Gowk, the cuckoo. In derision, we call a thoughtless fellow, and one who harps too long on one subject, a gowk

Gowl, a howling; to bellow and cry

Gousty, ghastly, large, waste, desolate, and frightful

Graith, furniture, harness, armour

To Grane, to groan

Granny, grandmother, any old woman

Grape, a trident fork; also, to grope

Gree, prize, victory

To Gree, to agree

Green, or grien, to long for

Greet, to weep. Grat, wept

Grieve, an overseer

Gross, gross, coarse

Grotts, milled oats

Grouf, to lie flat on the belly

Grounche, or Glunsh, to murmur, grudge

Grutten, wept

Gryse, a pig

Gully, a large knife. A kail-gully, a knife for cutting cabbages

Gumption, good sense

Gurly, rough, bitter, cold (weather)

Gusty, savoury

Gutcher, goodsire, grandfather

Gysened, when the wood of any vessel is shrunk with dryness

Gytlings, young children

H

Had, hold

Haffet, the cheek, side of the head

Hagabag, coarse table-linen

Haggis, a kind of pudding made of the lungs and liver of a sheep, and boiled in the big bag

Hags, hacks, peat-pits, or breaks in mossy ground; portions of copsewood regularly cut

Hain, to save, manage narrowly

Hait, or het, hot

Hale, whole

Halesome, wholesome

Hallen, a fence of turf, twigs, or stone, built at the side of a cottage door, to screen from the wind

Hame, home

Hameld, domestic

Hamely, friendly, frank, open, kind

To hanker, to doubt or waver

Hanty, convenient, handsome

Harle, drag

Harns, brains. Harn-pan, the scull

Harship, hairship, mischance

Hash, a sloven

Haveren, or havrel, an insignificant chatterer, a half-witted fellow

Haughs, valleys, or low grounds on the sides of the rivers

Havins, good breeding

Haviour, behaviour

To hause, to hug

Hauslock, the wool that grows on the sheep's neck

Hawky, a cow; a white-faced cow

Haws, or haus, the throat or gullet

Heal, or heel, health, or whole

Heartsome, blyth and happy

Hecht, to promise, promised

Heepy, a person hypochondriac

Hereyestreen, the night before yesternight

Heeze, to lift up a heavy thing a little. A heezy is a good lift

Heftit, accustomed to live in a place

Heght or Hecht, promised ; also, named

Hempy, a tricky wag, such for whom the hemp grows

Hereit, or herried, ruined in estate : when a bird's nest is robbed, it is said to be herried

Hesp, a hasp, a clasp or hook, bar or bolt : also, in yarn, a certain number of cuts

Heather-bells, the heath blossom

Heugh, a rock or steep hill ; also, a coal-pit

Hiddils, or Hidlings, lurking, hiding places. To do a thing in hidlings, i.e. privately

To Hing, to hang

Hips, the buttocks

Hirple, to move slowly and lamely

Hirsle, to move as with a rustling noise

Hirsle, or hirdsale, a flock of cattle

Ho, a single stocking

Hobbleshew, confused racket, noise

Hodden-grey, coarse grey cloth

Hog, a sheep of two years old

Hool, husk. Hooled, inclosed

Hooly, slow

Host, or whost, to cough

JIB

Hou, or hu, a cap or roof-tree
How, low ground, a hollow
How! ho!
Howdered, hidden
Howdy, a midwife
Howff, a haunt, or accustomed rendezvous
Howk, to dig
Howms, holms, plains on river sides
Howt! fy!
Howtowdy, a young hen
Hurdies, the buttocks
Hurkle, to crouch or bow together like a cat, hedge-hog, or hare
Hyt, mad

I & J

Jack, a Jacket
Jag, to prick as with a pin
Jaw, a wave or gush of water
Jawp, the dashing of water
Iceshogles, icicles
Jee, to incline on one side. To jee back and fore, is to move like a balk up and down, to this and the other side
Jelly, pretty
Jig, to crack, to make a noise like a cart-wheel
Jimp, slender
Jip, gypsie
Ilk, each. Ilka, every
Ingan, onion
Ingine, genius
Ingle, fire
Jo, sweetheart
Jocktaleg, a clasp-knife
Jouk, a low bow
Irie, fearful, terrified, as if afraid of some ghost or apparition: also, melancholy
I'se, I shall; as, I'll, for I will
Isles, embers
Junt, a large joint or piece of meat
Jute, sour or dead liquor
Jibe, to mock. Gibe, a taunt

K

Kaber, a rafter
Kale, or kail, colewort; and sometimes, broth
Kacky, to dung
Kain, a part of a farm-rent paid in fowls
Kame, comb
Kanny, or canny, fortunate: also, wary, one who manages his affairs discreetly; cautious
Kebuck, a cheese
Keckle, to cackle like a hen, to laugh, to be noisy
Kedgy, or cadgie, jovial
Keek, to peep
Keel, or keil, black or red chalk
Kelt, cloth with a freeze, commonly made of native black wool
Kemp, to strive who shall perform most of the same work in the same time
Ken, to know; used in England as a noun: a thing within ken, i.e. within view
Kent, a long staff, such as shepherds use for leaping over ditches
Kepp, to catch a thing that moves towards one
Kiest, did cast. *Vide* coost
Kilted, tucked up
Kimmer, or cummer, a female gossip
Kirn, a churn; to churn
Kirtle, an upper petticoat
Kitchen, sauces or liquids eat with solid food: "hunger is good kitchen"
Kittie, a frolicsome wench
Kittle, difficult, mysterious, knotty (writings)
Kittle, to tickle, ticklish
Knacky, witty, facetious
Knoit, to beat or strike sharply
Knoosed, buffeted and bruised
Knoost, or knuist, a large lump
Know, a hillock

LAW

Knublock, a knob

Kow, goblin, or any person one stands in awe to disoblige, and fears

Ky, kine or cows

Kyth, to appear: "he'll kyth in his ain colours"

Kyte, the belly

L

Ladren, a rogue, rascal, thief

Laggert, bespattered, covered with clay

Laigh, low

Laith, loth

Laits, manners

Lak, or lack, undervalue, contemn; as, "he that lacks my mare, will buy my mare"

Landart, the country, or belonging to it; rustic

Lane, alone

Lang, long

Langour, languishing, melancholy. To hold one out of langour, i.e. divert him

Lang-nebit, long-nosed

Lang-syne, long ago: sometimes used as a substantive noun, auld lang-syne, old times by-past

Lankale, coleworts uncut

Lap, leaped

Lappered, cruddled or clotted

Lare, bog

Lare, a place for laying, or that has been lain in

Latter-meet, victuals brought from the master's to the servants' table

Lave, the rest or remainder

Lawin, a tavern reckoning

Lawland, low country

Lavrock, the lark

Lawty, or lawtith, justice, fidelity, honesty

LOO

Leal, true, upright, honest, faithful to trust, loyal: "a leal heart never lied"

Leam, flame

Lear, learning; to learn

Lee, untilled ground; also an open grassy plain

Leet, a chosen number, from which one or more is to be elected

Leglen, a milking-pail with one lug or handle

Leman, a kept miss

Lends, buttocks, loins

Leugh, laughed

Lew-warm, lukewarm

Libbet, gelded

Lick, to whip or beat: a wag or cheat we call a great lick

Lied, ye lied, ye tell a lie

Lift, the sky or firmament

Liggs, lies

Lilts, the holes of a wind instrument of music; hence, "lilt up a spring:"—"lilt it out," take off your drink merrily

Limmer, a whore

Limp, to halt

Lin, a cataract

Ling, quick career in a straight line: to gallop

Lingle, cord, shoemakers' thread

Linkan, walking speedily

Lintwhite, a linnet

Lire, breasts; also, the most muscular parts: sometimes the air or complexion of the face

Lirk, a wrinkle or fold

Lisk, the groin

Lith, a joint

Loan, or Loaning, a passage for the cattle to go to pasture left untilled; a little common, where the maids often assembled to milk the ewes

Loch, lake

Loe, to love

Loof, the hollow of the hand

Looms, tools, instruments in general, vessels

MEI

Loot, did let

Low, flame. Lowing, flaming

Lown, calm: keep lown, be secret

Loun, rogue, whore, villan

Lounder, a sound blow

Lout, to bow down, making courtesy ; to stoop

Luck, to enclose, shut up, fasten ; hence, lucken handed, close fisted ; lucken gowans, booths, &c.

Lucky, grandmother, or goody

Lug, ear, handle of a pot or vessel

Luggie, a dish of wood with a handle

Lum, the chimney

Lurdane, a blockhead

Lure, rather

Lyart, hoary or grey-haired

M

Magil, to mangle

Maiden, an engine used for beheading

Maik, or make, to match, equal

Maikless, matchless

Mailen, a farm

Makly, seemly, well-proportioned

Maksna, 'tis no matter

Malison, a curse, malediction

Mangit, galled or bruised by toil or stripes

Mank, a want

Mant, to stammer in speech

March, or merch, a landmark, border of lands

Marsh, the marrow

Marrow, mate, fellow, equal, comrade

Mask, to mash (brewing). Masking-loom, mash-vat

Mavis, a thrush

Maun, must. Mauna, must not, may not

Mawt, malt

Meikle, much, big, great, large

Meith, limit, mark, sign

NIE

Mends, satisfaction, revenge, retaliation : to make amends, to make a grateful return

Mense, discretion, sobriety, good breeding. Mensfou, mannerly

Menzie, a company of men, army, assembly, one's followers

Messen, a littledog, lap-dog

Midding, dunghill

Midges, gnats, little flies

Mim, affectedly modest

Mint, aim, endeavour

Mirk, dark

Miscaw, to give names

Misken, to neglect or not take notice of one ; also, let alone

Mislushious, malicious, rough

Mislers, necessities, wants

Mither, mother

Mony, many

Mools, the earth of the grave

Mou, mouth

Moup, to eat, generally used of children, or of old people, who have but few teeth, and make their lips move fast, though they eat but slow

Mow, a pile or bing, as of fuel, hay, sheaves of corn, &c.

Murgeon'd, made a mock of

Muckle, see meikle

Murgullied, mismanaged, abused

Mutch, a coif

Mutchkin, an English pint

N

Nacky, or knacky, clever, active in small affairs

Neese, nose

Nevel, a sound blow with the neive or fist

Newfangle, fond of a new thing

Nick, to bite or cheat. Nicked, cheated. Also, a cant word to drink heartily ; as, "he nicks fine"

Niest, next

PAU

Niffer, to exchange or barter

Niffnafan, trifling

Nignays, trifles

Nips, bits

Nither, to straiten. Nithered, hungered or half - starved in maintenance

Neive, the fist

Nock, notch or nick of an arrow or spindle

Noit, see Knoit

Nowt, cows, kine

Nowther, neither

Nuckle, new calved (cows)

O

Oe, a grandchild

O'er, or owre, too much; as, "a' o'ers is vice"

O'ercome, surplus

Ony, any

Or, sometimes used for ere, or before. Or day, *i.e.* before day-break

Ora, any thing over what is needful

Orp, to weep with a convulsive pant

Oughtlens, in the least, any thing

Owk, week

Owrlay, a cravat

Owsen, oxen

Owther, either

Oxter, the armpit

P

Paddock, a frog. Paddock-ride, the spawn of frogs

Paiks, chastisement. To paik, to beat or belabour one soundly

Pang, to squeeze, press, or pack one thing into another

Papery, popery

Pasement, livery-lace

Pat, did put

Paughty, proud, haughty

PRE

Pawky, witty or sly in word or action, without any harm or bad designs

Peer, a quay or wharf

Peets, turf for fire

Pegh, to pant

Pensy, finical, foppish, conceited

Perquire, by heart

Pet, a favourite, a fondling. To pettle, to dandle, feed, cherish, flatter. Hence, to take the pet, is to be peevish or sullen, as commonly pets are when in the least disobliged

Pibrouchs, such Highland tunes as are played on bag-pipes before the warriors when they go to battle

Pig, an earthen pitcher

Pike, to pick out or chuse

Pimpin, pimping, mean, scurvy

Pine, pain or pining

Pingle, to contend, strive, or work hard

Pirn, the spool or quill within the shuttle, which receives the yarn.

Pirny, (cloth or a web) of unequal threads or colours, stripped

Pit, to put

Pith, strength, might, force

Plack, two bodles, or the third of a penny English

Plenishing, household furniture

Pople, or paple, the bubbling, purling, or boiling up of water

Poortith, poverty

Pou, pull

Pouse, to push

Poutch, a pocket

Pow, the poll, the head

Powny, a little horse or galloway; also a turkey

Pratick, practice, art, stratagem

Priving pratick, trying ridiculous experiments

Prets, tricks, rogueries. We say, "he played me a pret," *i.e.* cheated: "the callan's fou of prets," *i.e.* has abundance of waggish tricks

REE

Prig, to cheapen, or importune for a lower price of goods one is buying

Prin, a pin

Prive, to prove or taste

Propine, gift or present

Prym, or prime, to fill or stuff

Puke, to pluck

Pullieshees, pulleys

Putt a stane, throw a big stone

Q

Quaff, or queff, or quegh, a flat wooden drinking-cup formed of staves

Quat, to quit

Quey, a young cow

R

Rackless, careless: one who does things without regarding whether they be good or bad, we call him rackless handed

Rae, a roe

Raffan, merry, roving, hearty

Raird, a loud sound

Rair, roar

Rak, or rook, a mist or fog

Rape, a rope

Rashes, rushes

Rave, did rive or tear

Raught, reached

Rax, to stretch.   Raxed, stretched

Rax, andirons

Ream, cream : whence reaming as reaming liquor

Redd, to rid, unravel ; to separate folks that are fighting. It also signifies clearing of any passage. "I am redd," I am apprehensive

Rede, counsel, advice; as, "I wad na rede you to do that"

Reek, reach ; also, smoke

Reese, or ruse, to commend, extol

Reest, to rust, or dry in the smoke

SAR

Reft, bereft, robbed, forced, or carried away

Reif, rapine, robbery

Reik, or rink, a course or race

Rever, a robber or pirate

Rewth, pity

Rice, or rise, bulrushes, bramble branches, or twigs of trees

Rierd, a roar

Rife, or ryfe, plenty

Rift, to belch

Rigging, the back or rig-back, the top or ridge of a house

Rigs of corn, ridges

Ripples, a weakness in the back and reins

Rock, a distaff

Roove, to rivet

Rottan, a rat

Roundel, a witty, and often satiric kind of rhyme

Rowan, rolling

Rowt, to roar, especially the lowing of bulls and cows

Rowth, plenty

Ruck, a rick or stack of hay or corn

Rude, the red taint of the complexion

Ruefu', doleful

Rug, to pull, take away by force

Rumple, the rump

Rungs, small boughs of trees lopped off

Runkle, a wrinkle ; to ruffle

Rype, to search

S

Saebiens, seeing it is, since

Saikless, guiltless, free

Sained, blessed

Sair or sare, sore

Sairy, forlorn and pitiable

Sall, shall ; like soud for should

Sand-blind, purblind, short-sighted

Sape or saip, soap

Sar, savour or smell

Sark, a shirt

Saugh, a willow or fallow-tree

Saul, soul

Saw, an old saying or proverbial expression

Sawt, salt

Scad, scald

Scar, the bare places on the sides of hills washed down with rains

Scart, to scratch

Scauld, scold

Scawp, a bare, dry piece of stony ground

Scon, bread the country people bake over the fire, thinner and broader than a bannock

Scowp, to leap or move hastily from one place to another

Scowth, room, freedom

Scrimp, narrow, straitened, little

Scroggs, shrubs, thorns, briars. Scroggy, thorny

Scuds, ale; a late name given it by the benders or drinkers

Sculdudry, lewdness

Scunner, to loath

Sell, self

Seuch, furrow, ditch

Sey, to try

Shan, pitiful, silly, poor

Sharn, cow's dung

Shaw, a wood or forest

To Shaw, to shew

Shawl, shallow

Shawps, empty husks

Sheen, shining

Shellycoat, a goblin

Shiel, a shepherd's cot

Shill, shrill, having a sharp sound

Shire, clear, thin. We call thin cloth or clear liquor, shire; also, a clever wag, a shire lick

Shog, to wake, shake, or jog backwards and forwards

Shool, shovel

Shoon, shoes

Shore, to threaten

Shotle, a drawer

Sib, a-kin

Sic, such

Sicker, firm, secure

Sike, a rill or rivulet, commonly dry in summer

Siller, silver

Sindle or sinle, seldom

Sinsyne, since that time; lang sinsyne, long ago

Skail, to spill, to disperse; hence we say, "The kirk is skailing," for, the congregation is separating

Skair, share

Skaith, hurt, damage, loss

Skeigh, skittish

Skelf, shelf

Skelp, to run; used when one runs barefoot; also, a small splinter of wood; likewise, to flog the buttocks

Skiff, to move smoothly away

Skink, a kind of strong broth made of cows' hams or knuckles; also, to fill drink in a cup

Skirl, to shriek or cry with a shrill voice

Sklate, slate. Skailie is the fine blue slate

Skowrie, ragged, nasty, idle

Skreed, a rent, a hearty drinking bout

To Skreigh, to shriek

Skybald, a tatterdemalion

Skyt, to fly out hastily

Slade or Slaid, did slide, moved, or made a thing move easily

Slap or Slak, a gap or narrow pass between two hills; also, a breach in a wall

Slee, sly

Slerg, to bedaub or plaister

Slid, smooth, cunning, slippery; as—"He's a slid loun." Slidry, slippery

Slippery, sleepy

Slonk, a mire, ditch, or slough; to wade through a mire

Slote, a bar or bolt for a door

Slough, husk or coat

SPA

Smaik, a silly, little, pitiful fellow; the same with Smatchet

Smirky, smiling

Smittle, infectious or catching

Smoor, to smother

Snack, nimble, ready, clever

Sned, to cut

Sneg, to cut ; as—" Sneg'd off at the web end "

Snell, sharp, smarting, bitter, firm

Snib, to snub, check, or reprove ; to correct

Snifter, to snuff or breathe through the nose a little stopped

Snishing or Sneishing, snuff

Snod, metaphorically used for neat, handsome, tight

Snood, the band for tying up a woman's hair

Snool, to dispirit by chiding, hard labour, and the like ; also, a pitiful, grovelling slave

Snoove, to whirl round

Snotter, snot

Snurl, to ruffle or wrinkle

Sonsy, happy, fortunate, lucky ; sometimes used for large and lusty

Sore, sorrel, reddish-coloured

Sorn, to spunge or hang on others for maintenance

Soss, the noise that a thing makes when it falls to the ground

Soud, should

Sough, the sound of wind amongst trees, or of one sleeping

Souming, swimming

Soup, a sup

Souter, a shoemaker

Sowens, flummery, or oatmeal soured amongst water for some time, then boiled to a consistency, and eaten with milk or butter

Sowf, to conn over a tune on an instrument

Spae, to foretell or divine. Spaemen, prophets, augurs

Spain, to wean from the breast

STO

Spait, a torrent, flood, or inundation

Spang, a jump ; to leap or jump

Spaul, shoulder, arm

Speel, to climb

Speer, to ask, inquire

Spelder, to split, stretch, spread out, draw asunder

Spence, the place of the house where provisions are kept

Spill, to spoil, abuse

Spoolie, or spulzie, spoil, booty, plunder

Spraings, stripes of different colours

Spring, a tune on a musical instrument

Sprush, spruce

Spruttled, speckled, spotted

Spung, the fob

Spunk, tinder

Stalwart, strong and valiant

Stane, stone

Stang, did sting, to sting; also a sting or pole

Stank, a pool of standing water

Stark, strong, robust

Starns, the stars. Starn, a small moiety: we say, " ne'er a starn"

Staw, stole

Stey, steep ; as, " set a stout heart to a stey brae"

Steek, to shut, close

Stegh, to cram

Stend, or sten, to move with a hasty long pace

Stent, to stretch or extend, to limit or stint

Sting, a pole, a cudgel

Stirk, a steer or bullock

Stock-and-horn, a shepherd's pipe, made by inserting a reed pierced like a flute into a cow's horn ; the mouth-piece is like that of a hautboy

Stoit or Stot, to rebound or reflect

Stoken, to slake the thirst

Stoor, rough, hoarse

Stou, to cut or crop. A stou, a large cut or piece

SYN

Stound, a smarting pain or stitch

Stoup, a pot of tin of a certain measure. Milk stoup, a wooden milk-pail

Stour, dust agitated by winds, men, or horse feet. To stour, to run quickly

Stowth, stealth

Straitis, probably a kind of narrow kersey cloth, called Straits. See Bailey and Miege

Strand, a gutter

Strapan, clever, tall, handsome

Streek, to stretch

Striddle, to stride, applied commonly to one that is little

Strinkle, to sprinkle or strew

Stroot or Strute, stuffed full, drunk

Strunt, a pet: "To take the strunt," to be petted or out of humour

Studdy, an anvil, or smith's stithy

Sturdy, giddy headed; also, strong

Sture or Stoor, stiff, strong, hoarse

Sturt, trouble, disturbance, vexation

Stym, a blink, or a little sight of a thing

Suddle, to sully or defile

Sumph, blockhead

Sunkan, splenetic

Sunkots, something

Swak, to throw, cast with force

Swankies, clever young fellows

Swarf, to swoon away

Swash, swollen with drink

Swatch, a pattern

Swats, small ale

Swecht, burden, weight, force

Sweer, lazy, slow, loth

Sweeties, confections

Swelt, suffocated, chocked to death

Swith, begone quickly

Swither, to be doubtful whether to do this or that

Sybou, a small onion

Syke, a rill which is sometimes dry

Syne, afterwards, then

T

Tack, a lease

Tackel, an arrow

Taid, a toad

Taken, token

Tane, taken

Tane and tither, the one and t'other

Tangle, sea-weed

Tangs, the tongs

Tap, a head. Such a quantity of lint as spinsters put upon the distaff is called a lint-tap.

Tape, to use any thing sparingly

Tappit-hen, the Scots quart-stoup

Tarrow, to refuse what we love, from a cross humour

Tartan, cross-striped stuff of various colours, checkered; the Highland plaids

Tass, a little dram-cup

Tate, a small lock of hair, or any little quantity of wool, cotton, &c.

Tawpy, a foolish wench

Taz, a whip or scourge

Ted, to scatter, spread

Tee, a little earth on which those who play at the gowf set their balls before they strike them off

Teen or Tynd, anger, rage, sorrow

Teet, to peep out

Tensome, the number of ten

Tent, attention. Tenty, cautious

Thack, thatch

Thae, those

Tharmes, small tripes, catgut

Theek, to thatch

Thieveless, sleeveless, wanting propriety

Thig, to beg or borrow

Thir, these

Thole, to endure, suffer

Thow, thaw

Thowless, unactive, silly, lazy, heavy

Thrawart, froward, cross, crabbed

Thrawin, stern and cross-grained

Thrawn-gabbit, wry-mouthed

TWI

Threep or Threap, to aver, allege, urge, and affirm boldly

Thrimal or Thrummil, to press or squeeze through with difficulty

Thud, a blast, blow, storm, or the violent sound of these: "Cry'd heh at ilka thud," *i. e.*, gave a groan at every blow

Tid, tide or time, proper time; as— "He took the tid"

Tift, good order, health

Till, to. Till 't, to it

Tine, to lose. Tint, lost

Tinsel, loss

Tip or Tippony, ale sold for two-pence the Scots pint

Tippanizing, drinking twopenny ale

Tirle or Tirr, to uncover a house

Titty, sister

Tocher, portion, dowry

Tod, a fox

Tooly, to fight; a fight or quarrel

Toom, empty, applied to a barrel, purse, house, &c.; also, to empty

Tosh, tight, neat

Tosie, warm, pleasant, half fuddled

To the fore, in being, alive, un-consumed

Touse, or Tousle, to rumple, teaze

Tout, the sound of a horn or trumpet

Tow, a rope

Towmond, a year or twelvemonth

Tree, a cask of liquor, a nine-gallon tree

Trewes, hose and breeches all of a piece

Trig, neat, handsome

Troke, exchange

True, to trow, trust, believe

Truf, steal

Truncher, trencher, platter

Tryst, appointment

Turs, turfs, truss

Twin, to part with, or separate from

Twitch, touch

Twinters, sheep of two years old

WEA

Tydie, plump, fat, lucky

Tynd. *Vide* Teen

Tyst, to entice, stir up, allure

U & V

Ugg, to detest, hate, nauseate

Ugsome, hateful, nauseous

Virle, a ferrule

Vissy, to view with care

Umwhile, or umquhile, the late or deceased; some time ago; of old

Uneith, not easy

Ungeard, naked, not clad, un-harnessed

Unko, or unco, uncouth, strange

Unlusom, unlovely

Unsonsy, unlucky, ugly

Vougy, elevated, proud

Uundocht, or wandought, a silly weak person

W

Wad, or wed, pledge, wager, pawn; also, would

Wae, sorrowful

Waefu', woeful

Waff, wandering by itself

Wak, moist, wet

Wale, to pick and chuse

Wolop, to move swiftly with much agitation

Wally, chosen, beautiful, large

Wame, womb, the belly

Wandought, want of dought, im-potent

Wangrace, wickedness, want of grace

Wanter, a man who wants a wife

War, worse

Warld, world

Warlock, wizard

Wat, or wit, to know

Waught, a large draught

Wean, or wee ane, a child

WOO

Wee, little

Ween, thought, imagined, supposed

Weer, to stop or oppose

Weir, war

Weird, fate or destiny

Weit, rain

Wersh, insipid, wallowish, wanting salt

Whauk, whip, beat, flog

Whid, to fly quickly

Whilk, which

Whilly, to cheat. Whillywha, a cheat

Whindging, whining

Whins, furze

Whisht, hush, hold your peace

Whisk, to pull out hastily

Whittle, a knife

Whop, whip

Whomilt, turned upside down

Wight, stout, clever, active; also, a man or person

Willie-wands, willow-wands

Wiltu, wilt thou

Wimpling, a turning backward and forward, winding like the meanders of a river

Win, or won, to reside, dwell

Winna, will not

Winnocks, windows

Winsom, gaining, desirable, agreeable, complete, large

Wirrykow, a scarecrow or hobgoblin

Wisent, parched, dried, withered

Wistle, or whistle, to exchange money

Withershins, motion against the sun

Woo, wool

YUL

Wood, mad

Woody, the gallows: for a withy was formerly used as a rope for hanging criminals

Wordy, worthy

Wow, wonderful, strange

Wreaths of snow, when heaps of it are blown together by the wind

Wrush, washed

Wyliecoat, a jacket

Wysing, inclining. To wyse, to guide, to lead. Wysing-a-jee, guiding in a bending course

Wyson, the gullet

Wyte, to blame, blame

Y

Yamph, to bark, or make a noise like little dogs

Yap, hungry, having a longing desire for anything ready

Yealtou, yea wilt thou

Yed, to contend, wrangle

Yeld, barren, as a cow that gives no milk

Yerk, to do anything with celerity

Yesk, the hickup

Yett, gate

Yestreen, yesternight

Youdith, youthfulness

Youl, to yell

Yowden, wearied

Yowky, itchy

Youff, a swinging blow. To youff, to bark

Yuke, the itch

Yule, Christmas

APPENDIX.

APPENDIX.

SOME FEW OF THE CONTENTS

[OF THE "EVERGREEN."*]

HEIR mighty James the First, the best of kings,
Imploys the merry muse, and smyling sings.
Grave Balantyne, in verse divinely wyse,
Makis Vertew triumph owre fals fleechand Vyse.

And heir Dunbar does with unbound ingyne,
In satyre, joke, and in the serious schyne.
He to best poets skairslie zields in ocht ;
In language he may fail, but not in thocht.

Blyth Kennedie, contesting for the bays,
Attackis his freind Dunbar in comick layis,
And seims the fittest hand (of ony then)
Against sae fell a fae to draw his pen.

Heir Lethington the statisman courts the Nine,
Draps politicks a quhyle, and turns divyne ;
Sings the Creation, and fair Eden tint,
And promise made to man, man durst not hint.

To rouse couragious fyre behald the field,
Quhair Hardyknute, with lanss, bow, sword and scheild,
With his braif sonis, dantit the king of Norss,
And cleithed the plain with mony a saules cors.

---

* From a copy printed as a broadside, without date.

At Harlaw and Redsquire, the sons may leir,
How thair forbeirs were unacquaint with feir.

Quhen frae the dumps ze wald zour mind discharge,
Then tak the air in smiling Semplis berge :
Or heir him jyb the carlis did Grissy blame,
Quhen eild and spyte takis place of zouthheids flame.

Licht skirtit lasses, and the girnand wyfe,
Fleming and Scot haif painted to the lyfe.
Scot, sweit tungd Scot, quha sings the welcum hame
To Mary, our maist bony soverane dame ;
How lyflie he and amorous Stuart sing !
Quhen lufe and bewtie bid them spred the wing.

To mend zour morals, with delyt attend,
Quhyle Henryson dois guidness recommend ;
Quhyle truth throw his transport fablis schynes,
And all the mynd to what is just inclynes.

Amangst the starnis of ane immortal bleis,
Montgomery's quatorsimes sall evir pleis ;
His eisy sangs, his Cherry and the Slae,
Sall be esteimd quhyle sichs saft lufe betray.

Lindsay the lyon, hardly here is sene,
But in the third apartment of the Grene,*
He sall appeir as on the verdant stage ;
He towind the vyces of a corrupt aige.

Thair warkis I've publisht, neat, correct, and fair,
Frae antique manuscriptis, with utmost cair.
Thus to their fame, a monument we raise,
Quhilk sall endure quhyle tymis telled out be days.

---

* Ramsay intended to publish two additional volumes of the " Evergreen."

AN EPISTLE TO JAMES OSWALD, ON HIS LEAVING EDINBURGH.*

DEAR Oswald, could my verse as sweetly flow
As notes thou softly touchest with the bow,
When all the circling fair attentive hing
On ilk vibration of thy trembling string,
I'd sing how thou wouldst melt our souls away
By solemn notes, or cheer us wi' the gay,
In verse as lasting as thy tunes shall be,
As soft as thy new polish'd ' Danton me.'
   But wha can sing that feels wi' sae great pain
The loss for which Edina sighs in vain ?
Our concert now nae mair the ladies mind ;
They've a' forgot the gait to Niddery's wynd.
Nae mair the ' Braes of Ballandine' can charm,
Nae mair can ' Fortha's Bank ' our bosom warm,
Nae mair the ' Northern Lass ' attention draw,
Nor ' Pinky-house' gi' place to ' Alloa.'
   O Jamie ! when may we expect again
To hear from thee, the soft, the melting strain,
And, what's the loveliest, think it hard to guess,
' Miss S—t' or thy ' Lass of Inverness ? '
When shall we sigh at thy soft ' Cypress-grove,'
So well adapted to the tale of love ?
When wilt thou teach our soft Æidian fair
To languish at a false Sicilian air ;
Or when some tender tune compose again,
And cheat the town wi' David Rizo's name ?
Alas ! no more shall thy gay tunes delight,
No more thy notes sadness or joy excite,—
No more thy solemn bass's awful sound,
Shall from the chapel's vaulted roof rebound.
London, alas ! which aye has been our bane,
To which our very loss is certain gain,

---

* Attributed to Ramsay by Mr. David King. From the " Scots Magazine " of October, 1741.

Where our daft lords and lairds spend a' their rents,
In following ilka fashion she invents,
Which laws we like not aft on us entails,
And where we're forc'd to bring our last appeals.
Still envious of the little we had left,
Of Jamie Oswald last our town bereft.
'Tis hard indeed—but may you now repent
The day that to that spacious town you went.
If they thy value know as well as we,
Perhaps our vanish'd gold may flow to thee.
If so, be wise ; and when ye're well to fend,
Return again and here your siller spend.
Mean-while, to keep our heavy hearts aboon,
O publish a' your works, and send them soon.
We'll a' subscribe, as we did for the past,
And play while bows may wag or strings can last.
Farewell—perhaps, if you oblige us soon,
I'll sing again to a new fav'rite tune.

THE WYFE OF AUCHTERMUCHTY.*

In Auchtermuchty dwelt a man,
   An husband, as I heard it tawld,
Quha weil coud tipple out a can,
   And nowther luvit hungir nor cauld,
Till anes it fell upon a day,
   He yokit his plewch upon the plain ;
(But schort the storm wald let him stay,
   Sair blew the day with wind and rain.)

He lowsd the plewch at the lands end,
   And draife his owsen hame at ene ;
Quhen he came in he blinkit ben,
   And saw his wyfe baith dry and clene,

---

* From the " Evergreen." vol. i. p. 137.

(Set beikand by a fyre full bauld,
    Suppand fat sowp, as I heard say :)
The man being weary, wet, and cauld,
    Betwein thir twa it was nae play.

Quod he, quhair is my horses corn,
    My owsen has nae hay nor strae,
Dame, ye maun to the plewch the morn,
    I sall be hussy gif I may.
(This seid-time it proves cauld and bad,
    And ye sit warm, nae troubles se ;
The morn ye sall gae with the lad,
    And syne yeil ken what drinkers drie.)

Gudeman, quod scho, content am I,
    To tak the plewch my day about,
Sae ye rule weil the kaves and ky,
    And all the house baith in and out :
(And now sen ye haif made the law,
    Then gyde all richt and do not break ;
They sicker raid that neir did faw,
    Therefore let naithing be neglect.)

But sen ye will hussyskep ken,
    First ye maun sift and syne sall kned ;
And ay as ye gang butt and ben,
    Luke that the bairns dryt not the bed :
And lay a saft wysp to the kiln,
    We haif a dear farm on our heid ;
And ay as ye gane forth and in,
    Keip weil the gaislings frae the gled.

The wyfe was up richt late at ene,
    I pray luck gife her ill to fair,
Scho kirn'd the kirn, and skumt it clene,
    Left the gudeman but bledoch bair :
Then in the morning up scho gat ;
    And on hir heart laid her disjune,

And pat as mekle in her lap,
  As micht haif serd them baith at nune.

Says, Jok, be thou maister of wark,
  And thou sall had, and I sal ka,
Ise promise thee a gude new sark,
  Either of round claith or of sma.
Scho lowst the ousen aught or nyne,
  And hynt a gad-staff in her hand :
Up the gudeman raise aftir syne,
  And saw the wyfe had done command.

He draif the gaislings forth to feid,
  Thair was but sevensum of them aw,
And by thair comes the greidy gled,
  And lickt up five, left him but twa :
Then out he ran in all his mane,
  How sune he heard the gaislings cry ;
But than or he came in again,
  The kaves brak louse and suckt the ky

The kaves and ky met in the loan,
  The man ran with a rung to red,
Than by came an illwilly roan,
  And brodit his buttoks till they bled :
Syne up he tuke a rok of tow,
  And he sat down to sey the spinning ;
He loutit doun our neir the low,
  Quod he this wark has ill beginning.

(The leam up throu the lum did flow,
  The sute tuke fyre it flyed him than,
Sum lumps did fall and burn his pow ;
  I wat he was a dirty man ;
Yit he gat water in a pan,
  Quherwith he slokend out the fyre :
To soup the house he syne began,
  To had all richt was his desyre.)

Hynd to the kirn then did he stoure,
  And jumblit at it till he swat,
Quhen he had *rumblit* a full lang hour,
  The sorrow crap of butter he gat ;
Albeit nae butter he could get,
  Yit he was cummert with the kirn,
And syne he het the milk sae het,
  That ill a spark of it wad yirn.

Then ben thair cam a greidy sow,
  I trow he cund hir litle thank :
For in scho shot hir mekle mow,
  And ay scho winkit, and aye scho drank.
(He tuke the kirnstaff be the shank,)
  And thocht to reik the sow a rout,
(The twa left gaislings gat a clank,)
  That straik dang baith thair harns out.

Then he bure kendling to the kill,
  But scho start all up in a low,
Quhat eir he heard, what eir he saw,
  That day he had nae will to wow.
Then he gied to take up the bairns,
  Thocht to have fund them fair and clene ;
The first that he gat in his arms,
  Was a' bedirtin to the ene.

(The first it smelt sae sappylie,
  To touch the lave he did not grein :)
The deil cut aff their hands, quoth he,
  That cramd your kytes sae strute yestrein.
He traild the foul sheits down the gate,
  Thocht to haif wush them on a stane,
The burn was risen grit of spait,
  Away frae him the sheits has tane.

Then up he gat on a know heid,
  On hir to cry, on hir to schout :

b

Scho hard him, and scho hard him not,
    But stoutly steird the stots about.
Scho draif the day unto the nicht,
    Scho lowst the plewch, and syne came hame ;
Scho fand all wrang that sould been richt,
    I trow the man thocht mekle schame.

Quoth he, my office I forsake,
    For all the hale days of my lyfe ;
For I wald put a house to wraik,
    Had I been twenty days gudewyfe.
Quoth scho, weil *mot* ye bruke your place,
    For truely I sall neir *accept it ;*
Quoth he, feynd fa the lyars face,
    But yit ye may be blyth to get it.

Then up scho gat a mekle rung ;
    And the gudeman made to the dore,
Quoth he, dame, I sall hald my tung,
    For and we fecht I'll get the war :
Quoth he, when I forsuke my plewch,
    I trow I but forsuke my skill :
Then I will to my plewch again ;
    For I and this house will nevir do weil.

TO DOCTOR BOSWELL,*

WITH THE TWO VOLS. OF MY POEMS.

These are the flowings from my Quill,
    when in my youthful days
I scamper'd o'er the Muses' Hill,
    and panted after praise.

----

* " I think your readers may be interested in the verses which I enclose, written by Allan Ramsay, in a copy of his poems presented to my ancestor, Dr. John Boswell, uncle of Johnson's biographer."—From a Letter, by Mr. R. B. Boswell, to the Editor of *Notes and Queries.*

Ambitious to appear in print,
   my Labour was delyte,
Regardless of the envious Squint,
   or growling Critick's Spite.

While those of the best Taste and Sence
   indulg'd my native fire,
It bleezed by their benevolence,
   and heaved my genius higher.

Dear Doctor Boswell, such were they,
   resembled much by you,
Whose favours were the genial ray
   by which to fame I grew.

From my first setting out in Rhime,
   near fourty years have wheeld,
Like Israel's Sons, so long a Time
   through fancy's wiles I've reeld.

May powers propitious by me stand,
   since it is all my claim,
As they enjoyed their promised land,
   may I my promised fame.

While Blythness then on health attends,
   and love on Beauty's young,
My merry Tales shall have their friends,
   and Sonnets shall be sung.

        Sir, your humble Servant,

           ALLAN RAMSAY.

From my Bower on the Castle
Bank of Edinburgh, March the 10th, 1747.

THE THIMBLE.*

What god shall I invoke to raise my song ?
What goddess I of the celestial throng ?
Shall bright Apollo lend to me his aid ?
Shall chaste Lucina bring my muse to bed ?
Oh ! rather, greatest beauty of the sky,
I write for Lydia ; hear your vot'ry's cry !
You gave your charms to her—what can you then deny ?
  All o'er this globe, where Phœbus darts his rays,
What strange variety accosts our eyes !
We see how nations variously incline,
How different studies favour different men.
Some love to chase the fox throughout the day,
Others to dance the winter night away ;
Unlike to these, some love the trumpet's sound,
And cries of men, when gasping on the ground ;
To some, of fancy warm, it gives delight,
Instructed by the muses, verse to write
Of bards, some generals in fight rehearse ;
Others with groves and fountains crowd their verse,
Greater than theirs has fallen to my share—
A theme sublimer far demands my care ;
I sing the Thimble—armour of the fair.
  Hail ! heaven-invented engine ! gift divine !
You keep the tend'rest fingers free from pain.
Sing, lofty Muse, from whence the thimble sprung—
The thimble—safeguard of the fair and young.
  In ancient times, ere mortals learnt the trade,
Bright Venus for herself her mantles made.
As busied once in Crypian grove she sat,
Her turtles fondly sleeping at her feet,
With hands alone to sew the goddess tried,
Her wand'ring thoughts were otherwise employ'd ;

---

* From Chambers's Edition.

When lo ! her needle—strange effect of spite—
Wounded that skin it could not see so bright :
She starts—she raves—she trembles with the smart ;
The point that prick'd her skin went to her heart.
Sharp pain would not allow her long to stop ;
" My doves," she cried, " haste to Olympus' top ! "
The tim'rous beauty gets into her car—
Her pinion'd bearers swiftly cut the air.
As quick as thought they reach'd the sacred ground,
Where mighty Jove with Juno sat enthron'd.
" What ails my child ? " to her then cried the god ;
" Why thus in tears ? What makes you look so odd ?
Would you a favour beg ? " A while she stood,
Her ivory finger stain'd with purple blood ;
Then thus :—" Oh ! father of the gods," she pray'd,
" Grant I may be invulnerable made ! "
With look sedate, returned the awful sire—
" Daughter, you do not know what you desire ;
Would you to Pluto's gloomy regions run ?
Would you be dipt in Styx, like Thetis' son ?
Could you unfrighted view hell's dismal shore ?
What shall I say then ? Go, and stitch no more."
  Ashamed—unsatisfied—away she hies
To try her fate again beneath the skies.
" Shall I," she said, " While goddesses well drest,
Outshine each other at a birth-day feast—
Shall I in simple nakedness be brought,
Or clothed in rags ? Intolerable thought !
No ! rather may the blood my cheeks forsake,
And a new passage through my fingers take ! "
  In fertile Sicily, well known to fame,
A mountain stands, and Ætna is its name.
Tremendous earthquakes rend the flinty rock,
And vomit forth continual fire and smoke :
Here Vulcan forges thunderbolts for Jove—
Here frames sharp arrows for the god of love ;

His Cyclops with their hammers strike around—
The hollow caverns echo back the sound.

Here Venus brought her pigeons and her coach—
The one-eyed workmen ceased at her approach ;
When Vulcan thus :—My charmer ! why so pale ?
You seem prepared to tell some dismal tale.
Does fierce Tydides still his rage pursue ?
Or has your son his arrows tried on you ?"
" Ah no !" " What makes you bleed then ? answer quick."
" Oh no ! my lord, my husband ! Know, a prick
Of needle's point has made me wondrous sick."
" Fear not, my spouse !" said Vulcan, " ne'er again,
Never shall any needle give you pain."
With that the charming goddess he embraced,
Then in a shell of brass her finger cased.
" This little engine shall in future days,"
Continued he, " receive the poets' praise,
And give a fruitful snbject for their lays ;
This shall the lovely Lydia's finger grace—
Lydia, the fairest of the human race !"
He spoke—then, with a smile, the Queen of Love
Return'd him thanks, and back to Cyprus drove.

When Venus Lydia with beauty blest,
She granted her the thimble with the rest ;
Yet cannot brass or steel remain for aye—
All earthly things are subject to decay.
Of Babel's tow'r, so lofty and so proud,
No stone remains to tell us where it stood ;
The great, the wise, the valiant, and the just,
Cæsar and Cato, are return'd to dust ;
Devouring time to all destruction brings,
Alike the fate of thimbles—and of kings.
Then grieve not, Lydia ! cease your anxious care,
Nor murmur lest your favourite thimble wear.
All other thimbles shall wear out ere long,
All other thimbles, be they e'er so strong,
Whilst yours shall live for ever—in my song.